Urban Gardening as Politics

While most of the existing literature on community gardens and urban agriculture share a tendency towards either an advocacy view or a rather dismissive approach on the grounds of the co-optation of food growing, self-help, and voluntarism to the neoliberal agenda, this collection investigates and reflects on the complex and sometimes contradictory nature of these initiatives. It questions to what extent they address social inequality and injustice and interrogates them as forms of political agency that contest, transform, and re-signify "the urban".

Claims for land access, the right to food, the social benefits of city greening/ community conviviality, and insurgent forms of planning are multiplying within policy, advocacy, and academic literature; and are becoming increasingly manifested through the practice of urban gardening. These claims are symptomatic of the way issues of social reproduction intersect with the environment, as well as the fact that urban planning and the production of space remains a crucial point of an ever-evolving debate on equity and justice in the city. Amid a mushrooming of positive literature, this book explores the initiatives of urban gardening critically rather than apologetically. The contributors acknowledge that these initiatives are happening within neoliberal environments, which promote – among other things – urban competition, the dismantling of the welfare state, the erasure of public space, and ongoing austerity. These initiatives, thus, can either be manifestation of new forms of solidarity, political agency, and citizenship or new tools for enclosure, inequality, and exclusion. In designing this book, the progressive stance of these initiatives has therefore been taken as a research question, rather than as an assumption.

The result is a collection of chapters that explore potentials and limitations of political gardening as a practice to envision and implement a more sustainable and just city.

Chiara Tornaghi is Research Fellow in Urban Food Sovereignty and Resilience at the Centre for Agroecology, Water and Resilience (CAWR), Coventry University, UK, and Chair of the AESOP Sustainable Food Planning group.

Chiara Certomà is Marie Skłodowska-Curie fellow at the Centre for Sustainable Development (CDO), Ghent University and affiliate Researcher at the Sant'Anna School of Advanced Studies, Pisa.

Routledge Equity, Justice and the Sustainable City series

Series editors: Julian Agyeman, Zarina Patel,
AbdouMaliq Simone and Stephen Zavestoski

This series positions equity and justice as central elements of the transition toward sustainable cities. The series introduces critical perspectives and new approaches to the practice and theory of urban planning and policy that ask how the world's cities can become "greener" while becoming more fair, equitable and just.

Routledge Equity, Justice and the Sustainable City series addresses sustainable city trends in the global North and South and investigates them for their potential to ensure a transition to urban sustainability that is equitable and just for all. These trends include municipal climate action plans; resource scarcity as tipping points into a vortex of urban dysfunction; inclusive urbanization; "complete streets" as a tool for realizing more "livable cities"; the use of information and analytics toward the creation of "smart cities".

The series welcomes submissions for high-level cutting-edge research books that push thinking about sustainability, cities, justice and equity in new directions by challenging current conceptualizations and developing new ones. The series offers theoretical, methodological and empirical advances that can be used by professionals and as supplementary reading in courses in urban geography, urban sociology, urban policy, environment and sustainability, development studies, planning and a wide range of academic disciplines.

Housing Sustainability in Low Carbon Cities
Ralph Horne

Just Green Enough
Urban Development and Environmental Gentrification
Edited by Winifred Curran and Trina Hamilton

Design for Social Diversity, 2nd edition
Emily Talen and Sungduck Lee

Urban Gardening as Politics
Edited by Chiara Tornaghi and Chiara Certomà

For more information about this series, please visit: www.routledge.com/Routledge-Equity,-Justice-and-the-Sustainable-City-series/book-series/REJSCS

Urban Gardening as Politics

Edited by Chiara Tornaghi
and Chiara Certomà

Routledge
Taylor & Francis Group

LONDON AND NEW YORK

First published 2019
byRoutledge
2 Park Square, Milton Park, Abingdon, Oxon OX14 4RN

and by Routledge
711 Third Avenue, New York, NY 10017

Routledge is an imprint of the Taylor & Francis Group, an informa business

First issued in paperback 2021

British Library Cataloguing-in-Publication Data
A catalogue record for this book is available from the British Library

Library of Congress Cataloging-in-Publication Data
A catalog record for this book has been requested

ISBN: 978-0-415-79380-3 (hbk)
ISBN: 978-0-367-50039-9 (pbk)
ISBN: 978-1-315-21088-9 (ebk)

Typeset in Goudy
by Apex CoVantage, LLC

Contents

List of figures   vii
List of tables   viii
List of contributors   ix
Acknowledgements   xiii

1 **Politics and the contested terrain of urban gardening
   in the neoliberal city**   1
   CHIARA CERTOMÀ AND CHIARA TORNAGHI

2 **Everyday (in)justices and ordinary environmentalisms:
   community gardening in disadvantaged urban
   neighbourhoods**   12
   PAUL MILBOURNE

3 **A practice-based approach to political gardening:
   materiality, performativity, and post-environmentalism**   32
   CHIARA CERTOMÀ

4 **Cultivating food as a right to the city**   46
   MARK PURCELL AND SHANNON K. TYMAN

5 **Public-access community gardens: a new form of urban
   commons? Imagining new socio-ecological futures in
   an urban gardening project in Cologne, Germany**   66
   ALEXANDER FOLLMANN AND VALÉRIE VIEHOFF

6 **Challenging property relations and access to land for
   urban food production**   89
   GERDA R. WEKERLE AND MICHAEL CLASSENS

7 UK allotments and urban food initiatives: (limited?)
   potential for reducing inequalities   108
   WENDY M. MILLER

8 Contesting the politics of place: urban gardening in
   Dublin and Belfast   132
   MARY P. CORCORAN AND PATRICIA HEALY KETTLE

9 Exploring guerrilla gardening: gauging public views
   on the grassroots activity   148
   MICHAEL HARDMAN, PETER J. LARKHAM, AND DAVID ADAMS

10 The making of a strategizing platform: from politicizing
    the food movement in urban contexts to political
    urban agroecology   167
    BARBARA VAN DYCK, CHIARA TORNAGHI, SEVERIN HALDER,
    ELLA VON DER HAIDE, AND EMMA SAUNDERS

11 Contesting neoliberal urbanism in Glasgow's community
    gardens: the practice of DIY citizenship   186
    JOHN CROSSAN, ANDREW CUMBERS, ROBERT MCMASTER,
    AND DEIRDRE SHAW

12 Political gardening, equity, and justice: a research agenda   209
    CHIARA TORNAGHI AND CHIARA CERTOMÀ

    Index   216

Figures

3.1 The allotments in the *Parco delle Energie*, Rome; on the backdrop
a view of the densely populated Pigneto district in Rome   37
3.2 One of the flower beds realized by the guerrilla group *Giardinieri
Sovversivi Romani* on a former dumping area in Centocelle
district, Rome   38
5.1 The location of *Kölner NeuLand* in Cologne   72
5.2 The site of the urban gardening project *Kölner NeuLand*   74
6.1 Anan Lololi, Executive Director, African Food Basket in suburban
backyard garden   98
7.1 The capital-assets framework used in this research   114
9.1 The three guerrilla gardening sites, from left to right: F Troop,
the solo guerrilla, and the women's group   154
9.2 Hardman and F Troop in action   155

Tables

7.1 Different types of urban food activities, their land/space
    requirements, and key impacts   109
9.1 A basic overview of the data collected across the sites   158

Contributors

David Adams is Lecturer in Geography at the University of Birmingham, UK. Prior to this David was Senior Lecturer in Planning at Birmingham City University and a Planning Policy and Research Officer at Staffordshire County Council. David brings this experience to his academic post and teaches across both undergraduate and postgraduate courses. Contact: d.adams.4@bham.ac.uk

Chiara Certomà is Marie Skłodowska-Curie fellow at the Centre for Sustainable Development (CDO), Ghent University. Chiara's research focuses on innovative modes of geographical production, planning, and governance performed by heterogeneous, multi-layered, and multi-scalar networks. Contact: Chiara.Certoma@UGent.be

Michael Classens currently works in the public sector in Toronto, Ontario, Canada supporting Indigenous energy security. He has a PhD from the Faculty of Environmental Studies at York University, and was a SSHRC Postdoctoral Fellow in the Department of Geography at Western University. Contact: michael.classens@gmail.com

Mary P. Corcoran is Professor of Sociology at the National University of Ireland Maynooth. Her research interests lie primarily in the sociology of migration, urban transformation, and public culture, areas in which she has published widely. Contact: mary.corcoran@mu.ie

John Crossan is an independent researcher working across the fields of Human Geography and Education. His research interests centre upon the urban environment – its production, its use, and its potential. He has a PhD from the School of Geographical and Earth Sciences at the University of Glasgow and is currently training to be a secondary school teacher. Contact: www.johncrossan.co.uk

Andrew Cumbers is Professor in Regional Political Economy, University of Glasgow, Adam Smith Business School. He has a long track record of research into urban and regional development in old industrial cities and regions. He has carried out numerous funded research projects including two recent Joseph Rowntree Foundation projects on Globalization and Communities and

Declining Cities. His research has been published in international journals. Contact: Andrew.Cumbers@glasgow.gla.ac.uk

Alexander Follmann is a human geographer interested in human-environment interactions and urban environmental change. His past and current research focuses on (peri-)urban agriculture and urban rivers in Germany, India, and Kenya. He is currently a postdoctoral lecturer and researcher at the Institute of Geography and the Global South Studies Centre, University of Cologne, Germany. Contact: a.follmann@uni-koeln.de

Ella von der Haide is a gardener, activist, and documentary filmmaker of a series of five films on community gardens and their connection to social movements in Germany, South Africa, Argentina, and North America: "Another world is plantable!" (www.communitygarden.de). She also produces audiovisual research on queer-feminist ecologies in community gardens at the department of Open Space Planning, University Kassel, Germany. Contact: ella.von.der.haide@googlemail.com

Severin Halders´ activist geography is inspired by the everyday resistance of urban peasants in Rio, Bogotá, Maputo, and the *Allmende-Kontor* Network in Berlin. It is generated from within the popular education collective *orangotango*. His research aims towards the creation and critical reflection of solidarity relationships, horizontal knowledge exchange, and self-organized struggles. He holds a PhD and works at the Humboldt University of Berlin. Contact: severinhalder@gmail.com

Michael Hardman is Lecturer in Geography at the University of Salford, UK. His research interests are interdisciplinary but mainly concern the concept of Urban Agriculture, particularly the informal element of the practice. Mike is the only UK academic on the international Carrot City research group and has published widely on the topic of urban food growing. Contact: m.hardman@salford.ac.uk

Patricia Healy Kettle is an adjunct lecturer with the Dept. of Sociology, at the National University of Ireland, Maynooth. Her research interests lie primarily in environmental sociology, the sociology of food/food production, civil society, post-conflict reconciliation, and sustainable development. Dr. Healy Kettle conducted the first extensive empirical investigation on UA on the Island of Ireland and has published widely. Contact: patricia.healykettle@mu.ie

Peter Larkham is Professor of Planning at Birmingham City University, UK. He has published over 65 refereed journal papers, presented numerous papers at conferences across the globe, and edited and written several books. Peter is also Director of Research Degrees for the Faculty of Computing, Engineering and the Built Environment. Contact: Peter.Larkham@bcu.ac.uk

Robert McMaster is Professor of Political Economy, University of Glasgow, Adam Smith Business School. He has worked on numerous projects aimed at promoting social health economics emphasizing the influence of the social dimension on health and well-being. Robert is a visiting scholar at University of Missouri, Kansas City and Marquette University, Milwaukee. Contact: Robert.McMaster@glasgow.gla.ac.uk

Paul Milbourne is Professor of Human Geography in the School of Geography and Planning at Cardiff University. His research interests lie in the field of social geography and, more specifically, the geographies of welfare, poverty, homelessness, and justice. He also has interests in environmental geography, particularly urban nature, and environmental and food injustices. Contact: Milbournep@cardiff.ac.uk

Wendy M. Miller is a postdoctoral researcher in sustainability education at the University of Plymouth. She has been an amateur food grower as an allotment tenant for over 20 years in London and in Plymouth, and now on her Devon smallholding, and helped to draft the Plymouth Food Charter (www. foodplymouth.org). Contact: wendy.miller@plymouth.ac.uk

Mark Purcell is a professor in the Department of Urban Design & Planning at the University of Washington where he studies cities, political theory, and democracy. He is the author of *Recapturing Democracy* (2008), *The Down-Deep Delight of Democracy* (2013), and numerous articles in journals including *IJURR, Urban Geography, Antipode, Urban Studies*, and *Planning Theory*. His blog can be found at pathtothepossible.wordpress.com. Contact: mpurcell@uw.edu

Emma Saunders is a PhD student at Edinburgh University, UK. After two years of setting up a community gardening collective and working against the privatization of water in Paris, she shifted focus to study international labour organizing and become an active member of a Living Rent, Scotland's tenants' union. Contact: emmalo.saunders@gmail.com

Deirdre Shaw is Professor of Marketing and Consumer Research, University of Glasgow Adam Smith Business School. She has researched the area of consumption ethics throughout her career, publishing in international journals, including *Psychology and Marketing, Journal of Business Ethics, Marketing Theory, European Journal of Marketing, Business History*. With colleagues she has an ESRC seminar series 'Ethics in Consumption: Interdisciplinary Perspectives'. Contact: Deirdre.Shaw@glasgow.gla.ac.uk

Chiara Tornaghi is Research Fellow in Urban Food Sovereignty and Resilience at the Centre for Agroecology, Water and Resilience, Coventry University, UK, and Chair of the AESOP Sustainable Food Planning group. Her work focusses on urban political agroecology, food justice, and resourcefulness. She is co-founder of the International Forum for an Agroecological Urbanism. Contact: chiara.tornaghi@coventry.ac.uk

Shannon K. Tyman is currently completing her interdisciplinary PhD in the Built Environment at the University of Washington. She has a long history of participation in urban agriculture projects. Other than the urban food environment, her research interests include solidarity economies, post-industrial landscapes, and disability studies. Contact: shannon.tyman@gmail.com

Barbara Van Dyck works on science and society questions with a particular interest in political agroecology. Being trained, and critical towards her education as an engineer in the life sciences, she is particularly curious about the methods of questioning the world in ways which go beyond disciplinary and institutional boundaries. Contact: barbaravdyck@gmail.com

Valérie Viehoff is an urban geographer investigating the development of cities through an urban political ecology lens. Most recently her work has focused on 'austerity' and the potential role of (urban) commons in building better cities for the future. She is currently holding a scholarship by the Royal Geographical Society for completing a PGCE in Geography. Contact: v.viehoff@gmail.com

Gerda R. Wekerle is Professor Emerita and Senior Scholar, Faculty of Environmental Studies, York University, Toronto, Canada. She has published books on women and cities, safe cities, and anti-sprawl activism. She is a leader in Toronto-based urban agriculture initiatives and co-creator of a year-long exhibit at the Royal Ontario Museum on immigrants and their gardens. Contact: gwekerle@yorku.ca

Acknowledgements

(Editors) Chiara Tornaghi and Chiara Certomà would like to thank the series editors Stephen Zavestoski and Julian Agyeman for their suggestions and interest that provided the initial vision for this book. We would also like to thank handling editor Layla Walker for her patience during the making of this book. Chapter 1 and Chapter 12 contain some of the materials included in the editorial "Political gardening. Transforming cities and political agency" by Chiara Certomà & Chiara Tornaghi published in *Local Environment: The International Journal of Justice and Sustainability*, 20 (10), 2015.

2 Paul Milbourne

This chapter presents a revised and updated version of the paper "Everyday (in) justices and ordinary environmentalisms: community gardening in disadvantaged urban neighbourhoods" by Paul Milbourne published in *Local Environment: The International Journal of Justice and Sustainability*, 17 (9), 2012.

3 Chiara Certomà

This chapter includes part of the materials originally published in the paper "Critical Urban Gardening as a Post-Environmentalist Practice" by Chiara Certomà published in *Local Environment: The International Journal of Justice and Sustainability*, 16 (1), 2009.

4 Mark Purcell and Shannon K. Tyman

This chapter presents a revised and updated version of the paper "Cultivating food as a right to the city" by Mark Purcell & Shannon K. Tyman published in *Local Environment: The International Journal of Justice and Sustainability*, 20 (10), 2015.

5 Alexander Follmann and Valérie Viehoff

This chapter presents a revised and updated version of the paper "A green garden on red clay: creating a new urban common as a form of political gardening in

Cologne, Germany" by Alexander Follmann & Valérie Viehoff published in *Local Environment: The International Journal of Justice and Sustainability*, 20 (10), 2015.

6 Gerda R. Wekerle and Michael Classens

This chapter presents a revised and updated version of the paper "Food production in the city: (re)negotiating land, food and property" by Gerda R. Wekerle & Michael Classens published in *Local Environment: The International Journal of Justice and Sustainability*, 20 (10), 2015. The research underpinning this article was supported by a Social Science and Humanities (SSHRC) Research grant #435–2012–1717. The authors acknowledge the contribution of Don Leffers's research on property. Chiara Certomà and Chiara Tornaghi contributed to their understanding of the politics involved in gardening.

7 Wendy M. Miller

This chapter presents a revised and updated version of the paper "UK allotments and urban food initiatives: (limited?) potential for reducing inequalities" by Wendy M. Miller published in *Local Environment: The International Journal of Justice and Sustainability*, 20 (10), 2015. The author wishes to thank Professors Geoff Wilson and Richard Yarwood for their expert supervision during her PhD research, on which this paper is based. Thanks also to the University of Plymouth School of Geography for the studentship funding to make this research possible.

8 Mary P. Corcoran and Patricia Healy Kettle

This chapter presents a revised and updated version of the paper "Urban agriculture, civil interfaces and moving beyond difference: the experiences of plot holders in Dublin and Belfast" by Mary P. Corcoran & Patricia C. Kettle published in *Local Environment: The International Journal of Justice and Sustainability*, 20 (10), 2015. This chapter is based on original data collected by Dr. Patricia Healy Kettle, a recipient of an Irish Research Council Doctoral Research Award.

9 Michael Hardman, Peter J. Larkham, and David Adams

This chapter presents a revised and updated version of the paper "Exploring guerrilla gardening: gauging public views on the grassroots activity" by David Adams, Michael Hardman, & Peter Larkham published in *Local Environment: The International Journal of Justice and Sustainability*, 20 (10), 2015.

10 Barbara Van Dyck, Chiara Tornaghi, Severin Halder, Ella von der Haide, and Emma Saunders

This chapter is the English original of a contribution which was translated into German with the title "Der Aufbau einer Strategieplattform: vom Politisieren urbaner Ernährungsbewegungen zu urbaner politischer Agrarökologie" and published in the book by Kumnig, Sarah; Rosol, Marit; Exner, Andrea*s (Eds. 2017): *Umkämpftes Grün – Zwischen neoliberaler Stadtentwicklung und Stadtgestaltung von unten*. Bielefeld: transcript, pp. 81–108. This version, which the authors call "The Ramallah Letters", is previously unpublished. They wish to thank the two reviewers who provided comments to the contribution prepared for the transcript book.

11 John Crossan, Andrew Cumbers, Robert McMaster, and Deirdre Shaw

This chapter presents a revised and updated version of the paper "Contesting neoliberal urbanism in Glasgow's community gardens: the practice of DIY Citizenship" by John Crossan, Andrew Cumbers, Robert McMaster, & Deirdre Shaw, published in *Antipode: A Radical Journal of Geography*, 48 (4), 2016.

1 Politics and the contested terrain of urban gardening in the neoliberal city

Chiara Certomà and Chiara Tornaghi

1. Introduction

When in January 2012 we issued a call for papers for what would later become a special issue on "political gardening" for the journal *Local Environment: The International Journal of Justice and Sustainability*, we were not confident about whether such a juvenile research topic would have been effectively able to attract the broad interest of worldwide scholars. At the time very few contributions explicitly connecting grassroots gardening practices with political activism had been published (notably Crouch and Ward, 1997; McKay, 2011); and the very idea that cultivating plants in the city could have been understood as a political gesture was – for many scholars and even practitioners – still quite a bizarre one. However, urban harvesters, guerrilla gardeners, community growers, and landsharers were promoting a diversified set of projects that, while interstitial and very often considered residual, were nonetheless significantly challenging the mainstream place-making of cities in the Global North and the face of the neighbourhoods in which they were located. The enthusiasm of gardeners made it apparent that a garden was much more than a parcel of land where flowers and vegetables are grown, instead it could be seen as a project to address social, cultural, or economic uneasiness. The increasing number of everyday experiences of grassroots actors together with the contemporary proliferation of scientific contributions – exploring the scope, meaning, and potentiality of urban gardening for addressing both ecological, environmental, social, and economic functions – reassured us about the potential interest this idea might have attracted. We proposed, therefore, in our special issue (Certomà and Tornaghi, 2015) that a new topic of research was actually emerging in social studies under the label of "political gardening". Not surprisingly soon after we circulated the call for papers in 2011 further publications came out, explicitly pointing out the political aspects of gardening (i.e. Eizenberg, 2012a; Reynolds, 2015). These were soon followed by a large number of works that enriched the debate with new perspectives and deeper analyses, many of which are cited across this book, in particular in chapters 1 and 3.

The current interest in social science research for political gardening motivates the collection (in revised form) of the original papers published in our special issue of *Local Environment: The International Journal of Justice and Sustainability*, which is enriched with new contents and landmark contributions. The aim of this book is to offer the reader with an overview of the diverse claims proposed in the micro-politics of garden activism, ranging from DIY landscaping and engaged ecology, to "digging for anarchy" and counter-neoliberal development, food sovereignty and the reconstruction of the urban commons, community empowerment and the "right to the city". The social solidarities and divisions, empowerment and learning processes, conflicts and negotiations of which these projects are fraught, are discussed in this compelling collection of chapters unpacking the forms, functioning, and meanings of urban gardening in the context of the neoliberal transformation of cities in the Global North. We believe they can contribute to a critical discussion of the "politics of urban space" (Tornaghi, 2014), and enrich the emerging debate on radical, critical, and political gardening (see, for example, Certomà, 2015).

This introductory chapter is structured as follows: in the next section (n.2) we locate the analysis of political gardening within a discussion on "the post-political", while in the following section (n.3) we propose a transversal reading of the chapters and introduce the narrative of this collection. In doing so, we aim to signpost the main issues emerging from within contemporary initiatives of political gardening, and we then conclude with a synopsis of the 12 chapters of this book. This introductory chapter is complemented by the concluding one (Chapter 12), in which we reflect on some key lessons learnt in light of the most recent debates in post-political literature.

2. Gardening in a post-political age

It is now broadly acknowledged that in the post-political age (Mouffe, 2005; Swyngedouw, 2008; Heynen et al., 2006), instead of being the outcome of regional and supra-regional parliamentary activity, politics turned out to be the emerging effect of extra-parliamentary negotiations between composite networks of actors upon common interests (Sassen, 2007). In such a context, Swyngedouw suggests that the "rise of a neoliberal governmentality [. . .] has replaced debate, disagreement and dissensus with a series of technologies of governing that fuse around consensus, agreement, accountancy metrics and technocratic environmental management" (Swyngedouw, 2009, p. 604). The new regimes of policing as "governance-beyond-the-state" (Swyngedouw, 2008) accentuates the imperatives of a globally connected neoliberalized market economy and, contrary to the belief that "new forms of neoliberal urban governance widen participation and deepen 'democracy', [. . .] this post-political condition in fact annuls democracy, evacuates the political proper – i.e. the nurturing of disagreement through properly constructed material and symbolic spaces for dissensual public encounter and exchange – and ultimately perverts and undermines the very foundation of a democratic polis" (Swyngedouw, 2009, p. 53). Nevertheless, the prominence of economic actors and global political elites taking advantage of the outward delocalization of political agency and largely contributing to the emergence of a neoliberal governmentality, often comes together with an unprecedented dynamicity of the governance sphere allowing new actors to operate in an enlarged and fluid political arena – despite being only partially able to actually re-politicize it (Diaz-Parra et al., 2015). Swyngedouw himself recognizes the possibility for progressive, egalitarian, and inclusive urbanites in spaces where "alternative forms of living, working and expressing are experimented with, where new forms of social and political action are staged" (Swyngedouw, 2009, p. 59). He further recognizes that this space corresponds to Soja's *Thirdspace* (Soja, 1996), at once real and imagined; a space whose unregulated and disruptive character allows the emergence of non-planned and spontaneous urbanity (Groth and Corjin, 2005). It is here where discontents of the post-political assessed the emancipatory potential of anti-austerity protests (Wilson and Swyngedouw, 2014) and critically engaged with the contemporary de-politicization of public debate. This included attempts to re-signify political agency through innovative forms of agency (such as experiments with informal economies, artistic performances, deliberately open transformation of public space via informal planning processes, etc.) that entail direct negotiations with private actors, companies, and associations, without the mediation of national and local authorities whose exclusive authority over territory and people has progressively diminished. However, it needs to be acknowledged that in the city increasingly animated by new political subjects, the recent demise of urban insurrectionary and radical movements of social justice and equity (i.e. *Occupy, Podemos, Right to the city platforms*, etc.) and the even stronger bite of austerity politics, scholars' optimism about the actual possibilities of these new political subjects to bring about transformative social change is vanishing. Contradictions, co-optation, institutionalization, and domestication have been permeating, insinuating, and transforming many of these initiatives and movements.

It was precisely when the contradictions began to emerge that we were looking to build a debate on political gardening. The question we posed was not so much whether urban gardening was political or post-political as a whole, but rather how, in what conditions, with which visions, contradictions, strengths, and facing which challenges, it could become a tool for progressive and emancipatory political agency in the neoliberal city. We agree with Passidomo that "While community-scale interventions may not interrupt the 'annihilation of space' by globalized capital, they do offer 'political moments' which can secure durable changes with the potential to 'trickle up' spatial scales" (Passidomo, 2016, p. 274); and we wonder what is the role of urban gardening in the neoliberal planning and governance model, and how it can achieve justice in the socio-political constitution of contemporary urbanity.

We are intrigued by direct action and practice-based approaches in the negotiation of public issues via the (material) building up of alternative settings. Citizen-led and grassroots-led claims over public land, spontaneous appropriation and rehabilitation of marginal and neglected spaces at the city periphery, new bilateral agreements for sharing private land beyond that predicated by conventional property rights, community stewardship of urban greens and parks, were just a few of the arrangements through which gardening in both public and private spaces was taking place in various urban contexts across the Global North.

These practices are generated by a complex political universe of urban gardeners whose aims (taking power, contesting power, abolishing powers, etc.) and means (peaceful protest, direct action, guerrilla uprising, riots, cultural opposition, DIY practices, etc.) are definitely heterogeneous; and whose struggles are often the result of their participation in, and learning through, translocal networks.

While heterogeneous and fragmented, we look at urban gardening as a distinctive and interesting field of investigation where political activism and place-making from below finds a fertile ground for merging and mutually constituting each other. Urban gardeners, guerrilla gardeners, harvesters, producers, and sharers have been forcing us to reconsider how the politics of urban space is determined by new forms of agency that affects our traditional understanding of urbanity.

As much as we have learnt about the multiple ways in which piecemeal, interstitial, and hands-on practices of resistance have worked through the gardens, our research trajectory on political gardening and the urban cultivation of food, even in the wake of its mainstreaming, has also taught us to see its limits. It has pushed us to see its structural residual position, the constraints of the food-disabling city (Tornaghi, 2017), and the spaces of resistance from which alternative visions of the world are nurtured, and solidarities shaped (Cadieux, 2013). The space of the urban gardens is a conglomerate of contradictory stories, people, and visions. The emerging awareness of climate change, food crisis, and unsustainable urbanization has opened up a space where new capital fixes are taking place, new "ways to markets" are being funded by transnational funding agencies, and where public authorities seek help in managing vulnerable constituencies and building resilient communities. These contradictions render the sphere of urban gardens a problematic one. But even as new competition for spaces, funding, legitimacy, survival, and resistance emerge, they still maintain their intrinsically political, non-consensual nature.

3. The multiple political meanings of gardening

The mushrooming of urban gardening initiatives in the past five years has been matched by sustained academic interest. Literature on urban gardening and its sister urban agriculture have been fuelled by the "discovery" of food in the city – a kind of "Eureka!" moment in urban and geographical studies. Many of these studies had a predominantly functional perspective – how they can solve problems of neoliberal urbanization such as food poverty, social disgregation, ill health, and climate change. To a much lesser extent researchers have been questioning the multiple meanings, contradictory practices, or inspiring stories that emerge in the day-to-day working of the gardens: the self-help, voluntarist, ambivalent, or even co-opted practices. Their cognitive dissonance. Their frictions with issues of survivalism.

The chapters included in this book aim to investigate and reflect on the complex and sometimes contradictory nature of gardening initiatives, by questioning and interrogating them as forms of political agency that contest, transform, and re-signify the urban. As editors we are interested in understanding the potential of urban gardening practices as agents of counter-neoliberal transformation of the city. We haven't taken the progressive political stance as a starting point, but as a working question.

The authors included in this collection have used a plurality of theoretical toolkits in their investigations, which include: the Lefebvrian and the Post-Marxist reading of autogestion and the collective management of (public) space, fuelled by a political awakening and mediated via the "right to the city" discourse (see chapters 4 and 5); the Political Ecology approach to environmental injustices (Agyeman and Evans, 2004) generated by everyday practices (see Chapter 2); the political urban agroecology perspective and its focus on more-than-human multi-species solidarities, socio-ecological justice, and post-capitalist perspective (see Chapter 10); the community economies perspective of J.K. Gibson-Graham (2006) and how it is able to produce alternative processes of social reproduction in the capitalist society (see Chapter 6); the DIY-oriented citizenship theory in the interpretation of guerrilla gardening groups (see Chapter 9); or the material semiotic approach to Post-environmentalist theory which generates a new performative form of politics in the garden (see Chapter 3).

In light of this diversity the following chapters offer the reader a compass to navigate the multiple forms in which the political unfolds in the gardens; and how it deals with cogent issues, such as the struggle/s for land access, food governance and justice, equity and sustainability transition, and contrasting social inequalities mediated by the spatiality of community gardens.

As a form of political urban activism, urban gardening initiatives are often in contrast to the pervasive neoliberal planning of city life (Sbicca, 2016), which produces the erasure of public spaces and commons, the decrease of social cohesion and solidarity links, the privatization of leisure and free time activities and subjugation to exploitative food regimes. Not accidentally many urban gardening initiatives are described as forms of "contested spaces" or "right to space" (Schmelzkopf, 2002), "actually existing commons" (Eizenberg, 2012b), counteracting and resisting rigid social doctrines (McKay, 2011) or inventing new forms of quiet activism (Pottinger, 2017). Nevertheless, it is hard to find a common definition for the variegated panorama of gardening initiatives under the pressure of contrasting forces (Darly and McClintock, 2017). They can be co-opted by neoliberal institutions (Allen and Guthman, 2006; Pudup, 2008), increase the process of uneven capitalist development (McClintock, 2014, 2018), or reinforce racism, oppression, and exclusion mechanisms (Ramírez, 2015; Safransky, 2014). As a consequence, scholarly readings frequently offered a concurrent description of urban gardening as a neoliberal(ized) practice (Pudup, 2008) fueling gentrification processes and broadening the distance between subsistence gardening for the poor and leisure gardening for the wealthy (Quastel, 2009).

While acknowledging these trends and other forms of neoliberal enclosure brought forward through urban gardening (i.e. the dismantling of social services and the privatization of public land as in Tornaghi, 2014), it is nonetheless important to be wary of reading the interests of deprived people as only consumption-increasing strategies, while many gardeners often combine the two ideas of improving urban ecologies and having extra means for helping the needy

(Flachs, 2010). Urban gardens are frequently described as improving the environmental and social quality of city space through solidarity, socialization, and education activities; community building (Beckie and Bogdan, 2010); and tackling food insecurity (Emmet, 2011; Alkon and Agyeman, 2011).

By adopting a critical gaze, in the following chapters radical enthusiasm is tempered by careful consideration of the transformative, cohesive, or divisive effects of gardening on the new communities of practice that form in the gardens and around them. We are interested in exploring what ideas about the city and belonging these practices embody and bring forward; how they make use of biological material as a means of political expression; how networks, hierarchies, and alliances are forged and carried onward; what innovative relations of care, decision-making, and politics of place they build; and what weaknesses, contradictions, or emancipatory potentials they carry with them. Our aim is to populate the link between political gardening and the politics of space with a range of reflections that, seen in their complexity, constitute the basis for furthering urban politics from the ground up. Political gardening projects, in fact, advance a form of political commitment that materializes through the practical arrangements of material things and living beings in the city space; and gathers together heterogeneous actors working towards an ideal future city they want to build in common. As a matter of fact, the direct commitment in the material transformation of public space, and the often-implicit alliances forged with non-human agents (such as plants and animals) in reconceptualising and practically changing the "nature" of the urban space represents the most striking challenge to the conventional understanding of political processes (Certomà, 2011).

4. Synopsis

As the following chapters will show, political gardening tackles a number of striking issues in the production of new socio-ecological urban arrangements.

The contributions in this collection are largely based on empirical research and scholar activism around the forms, means, and practices of urban gardening in a number of cities in the Global North, including the UK, Canada, Germany, Italy, Belgium, France, Ireland, and the US.

We decided to open this collection (Chapter 2) by re-publishing in its original form, followed by a post-script, one of the first scholarly pieces that explicitly addressed the political meaning of the connection between gardening, equity, and justice: the work of Paul Milbourne published back in 2012. Here Milbourne explains that studies of poverty in disadvantaged urban neighbourhoods have pointed to the contribution of despoiled local environments to social exclusion. Work in urban political ecology has highlighted the socio-environmental hybridity of injustices in the city, bringing a political dimension to debates on urban sustainability, while research on environmental justice has directed critical attention towards the local and everyday (urban) contexts of socio-ecological forms of injustice. The chapter explores the everyday spaces and mundane forms of (in) justice through a case study of urban community gardening. Drawing on materials derived from the study of 18 community gardening projects in disadvantaged urban neighbourhoods in the UK, the chapter highlights how these projects are using ordinary forms of environmentalism to produce new socio-ecological spaces of justice within the city.

The link between environmentalism, as a form of political engagement, and urban gardening is at the core of the third chapter. Here Chiara Certomà investigates the meaning of politics in political gardening, and suggests that the material politics approach is the one that better suits the purpose. This chapter focuses on environmental relationships that represent the public issues around which social actors, including human and non-humans, can gather and activate their agency capability. From such a perspective, urban gardening clearly exemplifies how the mobilization of biological material and the subsequent modification of public space is a direct form of political expression. Moreover, in the broad panorama of different forms of political engagements, the inspirational values of gardeners recall the post-environmentalist one, and make it possible to re-politicize mainstream environmental politics by means of their everyday practices in the urban space. The theoretical analysis is complemented by reference to cases in Europe showing how political gardening is working towards a transformation of the forms and aims of space-based political agency.

The potential for urban agriculture to disclose the inner and hidden mechanisms of urban politics is investigated by Purcell and Tyman in Chapter 4. They claim that the radical potential of food cultivation resides in its being an immediate materialization of Lefebvre's "right to the city" and a powerful means to achieve the *autogestion* of biophysical systems. By investigating the *Green Thumb* gardening group's activity in New York and the creation of the South Los Angeles Community Garden in Los Angeles they unveil the radical political and ecological potential of urban food gardening struggle to generate a city where inhabitants produce and directly manage urban space in a radically democratized city beyond both capitalism and the state. A new Lefebvrian "contract of citizenship" signals the beginning of a struggle for a generalized political awakening among citizens against the alienation of people, and towards the reappropriation of food production and the collective production of urban space.

The same interest for linking urban gardening initiatives to tangible contestations of neoliberal processes in the city is addressed by Alexander Follmann and Valerie Viehoff (Chapter 5) who present a case study from Cologne and engage in an analysis of urban gardeners' motivations in managing urban space as a common. They examine the origins of the emergence and functioning of the community garden *NeuLand* by linking local problems – such as the trajectory of the regeneration of a former brownfield – to wider debates on alternative and more sustainable socio-ecological futures that challenge the neoliberalising trend of mainstream redevelopment within German cities. While they acknowledge that the cohort of community gardeners is more likely than traditional allotment holders to be aware of their potential in terms of political impact, they investigate whether this is true in their case study, putting into critical scrutiny the intentions and strategies of the *NeuLand* project. Moreover, the authors investigate whether the growing of food in common is intentionally designed to demonstrate that commons are a liveable alternative to neoliberal urbanism and a strategical (rather than incidental) path for citizens to gain their right to be involved in the shaping of the city.

In the sixth chapter Gerda Wekerle and Michael Classens document how urban residents assert their right to grow their own food and challenge naturalized notions of private property and ownership by temporarily soft squatting a private development site in Toronto; and by redesignating private suburban backyards for commercial community food production and for garden sharing among individuals. The authors articulate the idea that the increasing interest in the agrarian potential of urban private property is a manifestation of the evolutionary development of urban food activism, focussed around "a new ethic of care for the land and for others", counteracting regressive public land management and articulating alternative visions of sustainability and food security. Taking Gibson-Graham's political agenda forward (2006), Wekerle and Classes convincingly argue that engaging with private property for urban food production is "a profoundly political expression of challenging the neoliberal condition by 'starting where you are'" (p. XXX).

Drawing on a case study from Plymouth, South West England, in Chapter 7 Wendy Miller looks at a rather classic form of gardening in contemporary Europe, the allotment, stressing its role in enabling access to one of the key resources that enable food sovereignty: land. Miller explores the highly politicized debates around their inception, and analyses the narratives that are mirrored in present day debates on urban gardening. Building upon the benchmark of the UK allotment system, Miller examines the opposing positions of those claiming gardening practices are able to enhance cohesive neighbourhoods and food justice, and those who view them as exclusionary practices. She uses food cycles and the capital-assets framework to see more clearly the different impacts of the many kinds of food-related activities seen in (peri-)urban areas in Plymouth and to evaluate the potential for reducing the inequalities of different food ventures. Conclusively, using allotments as a comparator, the author suggests that the key contingent factor for reducing inequalities on any parameter is the allocation of urban land.

The eighth chapter still focuses on allotments but on the other side of the Irish Sea. Mary Corcoran and Patricia Healy Kettle critically interrogate the capacity of urban gardening to act as a "space of potential" or public sphere wherein social divisions derived from ethno-religious divides and social class distinctions can be challenged and transcended via conviviality and gardening practices in Belfast and Dublin. Challenging the contentious view of allotments as apolitical sites for petty and increasingly bourgeois gardeners, the authors direct our attention to one of the fundamental premises of allotments as a public space: the commitment to individual labour (cultivation and cooperation) rooted in a common cause. Their analysis contributes to the debate on the possibility of a shared politics of place, nurtured by new citizenry's solidarity, mutuality, and trust that unfold in and through the cultivation of allotments. Urban gardening is thus presented as a kind of social leveller and allotments are described as public spaces where differences are rendered less salient because, on the site, processes provide the basis for renewed social cohesion.

On the basis of their on-the-field analysis, Michael Hardman, Peter Larkham, and David Adams (Chapter 9) contest the widespread celebration of guerrilla gardening as a radical practice, and instead show that it can be largely harmonious with the pre-existent uses of a place. Their research focuses on the daily activity of three guerrilla gardening groups in the Midlands region of England, and the social reaction of local inhabitants not directly involved in the gardening practices. This is intended to contest the non-relational understanding of guerrilla gardening of many writers, which often lacks recognition of the perception of those who live or work in nearby areas. The authors argue that romanticized commentaries on guerrilla gardening are adopted/provided by the majority of academics; these however show only one side of reality. Despite the very mixed reactions from local dwellers and workers that were collected through their research, what clearly emerges from their analysis is that in all the investigated cases the guerrillas colonized land without the notification, consultation, or involvement of those who interacted with the area on a more frequent basis.

In Chapter 10, Barbara Van Dyck, Chiara Tornaghi, Severin Halder, Ella von der Haide, and Emma Saunders exchange letters of solidarity where they share their experience as scholar-activists in the urban food movement. Their letters enmesh the emotional and the analytical, and how they unfold through the different roles they play as activists and scholars. In acknowledging the co-optative, conflictual, and neoliberal processes in which they have found themselves during their trajectories, the authors start jotting plans for more fulfiling, strategizing, and ethical pathways, which leaves behind more narrowly defined gardening projects, and aims to build an urban political agroecology.

In Chapter 11, Crossan, Cumbers, McMaster, and Shaw reflect on the link between community gardening and neoliberal co-optation in a post-industrial city. In their chapter they point out that even where neoliberal practices are evidenced, such practices do not define or foreclose other socio-political subjectivities at work in the gardens. They contend that community gardens in Glasgow cultivate collective practices that offer a glimpse of what a progressively transformative polity can achieve. Enabled by an interlocking process of community and spatial production, this form of citizen participation encourages them to reconsider their relationships with one another, their environment, and what constitutes effective political practice. Inspired by a range of writings on citizenship formation they term this DIY Citizenship.

References

Agyeman, J., and Evans, B., 2004. "Just sustainability": The emerging discourse of environmental justice in Britain? *The Geographical Journal*, 170(2), 155–164.

Alkon, A., and Agyeman, J., 2011. *Cultivating Food Justice: Race, Class and Sustainability.* Cambridge, MA: MIT Press.

Allen, P., and Guthman, J., 2006. From "old school" to "farm-to-school": Neoliberalization from the ground up. *Agriculture and Human Values*, 23(4), 401–415.

Beckie, M., and Bogdan, E., 2010. Planting roots: Urban agriculture for senior immigrants. *Journal of Agriculture, Food Systems and Community Development*, 1(2), 77–89.

Cadieux, K.V., 2013. Other women's gardens: Radical homemaking and public performance of the politics of feeding. In A. Hayes-Conroy and J. Hayes-Conroy (eds.), *Doing Nutrition Differently*. Aldershot: Ashgate.

Certomà, C., 2011. Critical urban gardening as a post-environmentalist practice. *Local Environment*, 16(10), 977–987.

Certomà, C., 2015. Expanding the "dark side of planning": Governmentality and biopolitics in urban garden planning. *Planning Theory*, 14(1), 23–43.

Certomà, C., and Tornaghi, C., 2015. Political gardening: Transforming cities and political agency. *Local Environment*, 20(10), 1123–1131.

Crouch, D., and Ward, C., 1997. *The Allotment: Its Landscape and Culture*. Nottingham: Five Leaves.

Darly, S., and McClintock, N., 2017. Introduction to urban agriculture in the neoliberal city: Critical European perspectives. *ACME*, 16(2), 224–231.

Diaz-Parra, I., Roca, B., and Romano, S., 2015. Political activists' frames in times of post-politics: Evidence from Kirchnerism in Argentina and Podemos in Spain. *Contemporary Social Science*, 10(4), 386–400.

Eizenberg, E., 2012a. The changing meaning of community space: Two models of NGO management of community gardens in New York City. *International Journal of Urban and Regional Research*, 36(1), 106–120.

Eizenberg, E., 2012b. Actually existing commons: Three moments of space of community gardens in New York City. *Antipode*, 44(3), 764–782.

Emmet, R., 2011. Community gardens, ghetto pastoral, and environmental justice. *Interdisciplinary Studies in Literature and Environment*, 18(1), 67–86.

Flachs, A., 2010. Food for thought: The social impact of community gardens in the greater Cleveland area. *Electronic Green Journal*, 130, 1–9.

Gibson-Graham, J.K., 2006. *A Postcapitalist Politics*. Minneapolis, MN: University of Minnesota Press.

Groth, J., and Corjin, E., 2005. Reclaiming urbanity: Indeterminate spaces, informal actors and urban agenda setting. *Urban Studies*, 42(3), 503–526.

Heynen, N., Kaika, M., and Swyngedouw, E., 2006. *In the Nature of Cities: Urban Political Ecology and the Politics of Urban Metabolism*. London: Routledge.

McClintock, N., 2014. Radical, reformist, and garden-variety neoliberal: Coming to terms with urban agriculture's contradictions. *Local Environment*, 19(2), 147–171.

McClintock, N., 2018. Cultivating (a) sustainability capital: Urban agriculture, eco-gentrification, and the uneven valorization of social reproduction. *Annals of the American Association of Geographers*, 108(2), 279–590, doi.org/10.1080/24694452.2017.1365582

McKay, G., 2011. *Radical Gardening*. London: Frances Lincoln Limited.

Mouffe, C. 2005. *On The Political*. London: Routledge.

Passidomo, C., 2016. Community gardening and governance over urban nature in New Orleans's Lower Ninth Ward. *Urban Forestry & Urban Greening*, 19, 271–277.

Pottinger, L., 2017. Planting the seeds of a quiet activism. *Area*, 49(2), 215–222.

Pudup, M., 2008. It takes a garden: Cultivating citizen-subjects in organized garden projects. *Geoforum*, 39(3), 1228–1240.

Quastel, N., 2009. Political ecologies of gentrification. *Urban Geography*, 30(7), 694–725.

Ramírez, M.M., 2015. The elusive inclusive: Black food geographies and racialized food spaces. *Antipode*, 47(3), 748–769.

Reynolds, K., 2015. Disparity despite diversity: Social injustice in New York city's urban agriculture system. *Antipode*, 47(1), 240–259.

Safransky, S., 2014. Greening the urban frontier: Race, property, and resettlement in Detroit. *Geoforum*, 56, 237–248.

Sassen, S., 2007. *A Sociology of Globalization*. New York: W.W. Norton & Company.

Sbicca, J., 2016. These bars can't hold us back: Plowing incarcerated geographies with restorative food justice. *Antipode*, 48(5), 1359–1379.

Schmelzkopf, K., 2002. Incommensurability, land use, and the right to space: Community gardens in New York city. *Urban Geography*, 23(4), 323–343.

Soja, E., 1996. *Thirdspace*. Oxford: Blackwell.

Swyngedouw, E., 2008. Civil society, governmentality and the contradictions of governance-beyond-the-state. In J. Hillier, F. Moulaert and S. Vicari (eds.), *Social Innovation and Territorial Development*. Aldershot: Ashgate.

Swyngedouw, E., 2009. The zero-ground of politics: Musings on the post-political city. *NewGeographies*, 1, 52–61.

Tornaghi, C., 2014. Critical geography of urban agriculture. *Progress in Human Geography*, 38(4), 551–567.

Tornaghi, C., 2017. Urban agriculture in the food-disabling city: (Re)defining urban food justice, reimagining a politics of empowerment, in *Antipode. A Radical Journal of Geography*, 49(3), 781–801.

Wilson, J., and Swyngedouw, E., 2014. *The Post-Political and Its Discontents: Spaces of Depoliticisation, Spectres of Radical Politics*. Edinburgh, UK: Edinburgh University Press.

2 Everyday (in)justices and ordinary environmentalisms

Community gardening in disadvantaged urban neighbourhoods

Paul Milbourne

1. Introduction: local environments of (in)justice

> geographical and conceptual extensions of environmental justice must have as central an emphasis on the local contexts of justice – a focus somewhat lacking to date.
>
> (Hobson 2006, p. 671)

Recent years have witnessed increased interest from human geographers and other social scientists in the relationship between justice, place, and environment in the UK. Three interrelated bodies of literature can be pointed to as evidence of this increasing interest. Place-based studies of urban poverty have begun to take more seriously the role of the local environment in shaping people's experiences of poverty, with attention being paid to how the limited provision of green space connects with the neglect of existing environmental spaces to reduce quality of life and compound residents' feelings of disempowerment (see Burrows and Rhodes 1998; Lupton and Power 2002; Lucas et al. 2004; Milbourne 2010).

Another area of work has been urban political ecology, which has opened up some innovative ways of approaching injustices in the city. Criticising previous environmental studies for their neglect of "the urban" and attacking urban studies for their marginalization of the environment, urban political ecologists have argued that the city is the "place where socio-environmental problems are experienced most acutely" (Heynen et al. 2006, p. 2). Particular attention has been paid to the ways in which cities are produced through hybrid processes that bring together social and ecological processes. For Heynen et al. (2006), the urban political ecology approach provides a means of unravelling the complex connections between economic, socio-cultural, political, and environmental processes that produce injustices within the city, as well as enabling discussions about urban sustainability to be re-positioned within the political realm:

> Political ecology attempts to tease out who (or what) gains from and who pays for, who benefits from and who suffers (and in what ways) from particular processes of metabolic circulatory change.
>
> (p. 12)

Environmental justice provides the third strand of academic work that has drawn attention to the spatialities of justice and environment. While early studies in this area tended to highlight the increased presence of environmental hazards in socially disadvantaged spaces within UK cities (see Walker and Bickerstaff 2000; Friends of the Earth 2001), more recent work has indicated the inherently geographical nature of environmental injustices, pointing to the ways that particular injustices and campaigns for environmental justice are bound up with the socio-ecological specificities of regions and places (see Walker and Bulkeley 2006; Holifield et al. 2009). For Hobson (2006), though, recent research has focused too much on what might be termed spectacular conflicts surrounding environmental injustices:

> Less apparent are the struggles for environmental justice, manifest in the daily practices of individuals and organizations. Far from being too mundane to be politically significant, these practices can illuminate the spatially manifest power relations central to environmental justice claims, offering detailed insights into how particular injustices become apparent through the use and control of space.
>
> (p. 671)

Similarly, Whitehead (2009) stressed the significance of everyday spaces within discourses of environmental justice. Drawing on Lefebvre's (1991) writings on everyday life, he highlighted the complexity of relations between socio-ecological justices and everyday urban spaces, suggesting that an everyday perspective provides a "new way of beginning to imagine ordinary forms of [socio-ecological] justice and of contemplating frameworks of action to mitigate against banal forms of disadvantage" (p. 669). The significance of the everyday is also evident from other works on environmental justice. For example, Warpole (2000) extended Williams' (1958) account of the ordinariness of culture to the environmental arena, demonstrating the significance of ordinary forms of environmentalism within processes of place-making and local responses to socio-environmental problems in the city. Indeed, a recent study by Burningham and Thrush (2001) illustrates not only the mundane nature of people's environmental concerns in disadvantaged places but also the importance of ordinary projects of environmentalism in addressing injustices within their everyday spaces.

My intention within this paper is to explore these local, everyday, and ordinary forms of socio-environmental (in)justice through a study of community gardening projects in disadvantaged urban neighbourhoods. Developed largely as a response to social and environmental forms of injustice, community gardening provides some interesting insights into the everyday forms and spaces of (in)justice. While research on community gardening in the USA has pointed to its socio-ecological hybridity, I want to suggest that it has largely steered clear of urban political ecological and environmental justice themes. Furthermore, the dominant focus on US cities and "conventional" forms of community gardening within this body of work has provided particular perspectives on their socio-ecological re-makings of everyday urban space. In the next couple of sections of this paper, I provide a critical discussion of key themes emerging from the community gardening literature in the USA and then utilize empirical materials from a recent study of community gardening projects in disadvantaged neighbourhoods in UK cities to highlight the significance of ordinary and everyday forms of socio-environmental (in)justice within the urban landscape.

Community gardening in the (US) city: growing spaces of social and environmental justice . . . every time a garden is born, there is the hope that the world will be made better by it, an unselfconscious but radically utopian belief. Meaning resides in the power of the garden to express, clarify, and reconcile oppositions and transform them into inspirations (Francis and Hester 1990, p. 10).

The garden has long been recognized as a powerful spatial metaphor that has been used to represent particular sets of relations between nature, society, and culture and to express personal and political power. As well as reflecting existing nature – society relations and power structures, Francis and Hester (1990) suggested that the garden acts as a "laboratory" within which new ideas and geometries of power can be formulated. The garden is also a space that has particular significance within people's everyday lives, being both part of and shaped by ordinary human experience and bound up with a diverse range of cultural creativities, identity formations, and sensory experiences (see Bhatti and Church 2001; Bhatti et al. 2009). In addition, it is claimed that gardening provides opportunities to escape and resist broader social, economic, and political forces that are imposed on people's life worlds. As Hodgkinson (2005) argued, "in maintaining your own patch of earth, you escape the world of money, governments, supermarkets and the industrial processes of food production. . . . In this sense, then, digging is anarchy in action" (p. 67).

Although gardening has largely been associated with individual actions in private spaces, recent years have witnessed the increased significance of collective forms of gardening in urban public spaces (see Hou et al. 2009). Moving beyond the ornamental and regimented public gardening practices within conventional green spaces in the city, what has become known as community gardening has been associated with more ordinary, everyday, and mundane urban spaces, eclectic styles of landscape design and broader sets of socio-environmental goals. Defined as "an organized, grassroots initiative whereby a section of land is used to produce food or flowers or both in an urban environment for the personal use or collective benefit of its members" (Glover et al. 2005), community gardening has its origins in American cities in the late nineteenth century, where gardens began to be developed by low income groups to grow food for local consumption on land that was attached little market value (Schmeizkopf 1995). In more recent times, community gardening projects have expanded their operations to respond to poverty, environmental degradation, and the lack of safe green spaces in deprived urban places (Ferris et al. 2001). As such, it is claimed that the American community gardening movement now embraces a broad range of horticultural, environmental, social, and political concerns (Stocker and Barnett 1998), combining "the best of environmental ethics, social activism and personal expression" and involving "a faith that what they [the gardeners] do not only helps the individual but strengthens the community" (Lawson 2005, p. 301).

Recent studies of community gardening in the USA have pointed to its social and environmental impacts in disadvantaged urban neighbourhoods: providing food security, improving health, renewing people's senses of pride in their areas, and creating new forms of social interaction and public participation (see Severson 1990; Hynes 1996; Armstrong 2000; Glover et al. 2005; Lawson 2005). This ability to address such a broad range of urban concerns has led Hou et al. (2009) to claim that community gardening represents "not only a tangible resource for individuals and communities but also an organizing concept for new ideas about quality of life and urban sustainability" (p. 29; see also Stocker and Barnett 1998). Constructing community gardening in these terms begins to open up some potentially useful engagements with environmental justice and urban political ecology. It also creates potentially interesting synergies between community gardening and the idea of "just sustainabilities" (Agyeman 2002; Agyeman and Evans 2004), which involves a rebalancing of the environmental and social dimensions of sustainability, and more explicit engagements between the concepts of sustainability and social justice.

Community gardening projects largely occupy the mundane or everyday spaces that have been neglected or abandoned by the local state or private landlords – what Whitehead (2009), drawing on the work of Lefebvre, has referred to as "remaindered" spaces. However, the abandonment of these spaces does not mean that they represent empty spaces as they are often awarded a significant meaning by local residents – as sites of neglect, waste, crime, and anti-social behaviour and as powerful symbols of urban disadvantage. Community gardening projects have sought to alter the meanings of these spaces, with the physical transformation of land also producing new spaces of identity, sociality, and empowerment. In addition, it is claimed that community gardening activities are producing new hybrid or "third spaces" that intersect public and private worlds and which are "part of the public domain and are the sites of many functions conventionally equated with the private sphere" (Schmeizkopf 1995, p. 379).

These readings of community gardening as projects of resistance and place-making have been subject to recent criticism. In an important review of American community gardening scholarship, Pudup (2008) called for the (re-)positioning of community gardening within more critical theoretical literatures. She argued that while it is generally acknowledged that community gardening projects have largely developed in response to periodic crises of capitalism, such as recessions, highly uneven processes of development, and struggles over civil rights, they should be viewed less as acts of local resistance towards external processes of change and more as mechanisms that support "the existing social order by helping it accommodate crisis and change" (p. 1229). For Pudup (2008), then, it is important to recognize that "the nature of the crisis and/or emergency has helped shape the discursive goals governing organized garden projects during these different eras" (p. 1229). In a similar way to McCarthy's (2005) recasting of community forestry in the USA as a vehicle of neoliberalism, Pudup suggested that the recent proliferation of community garden projects in the USA represents a further example of "roll-out" neoliberalism (Peck and Tickell 2002), whereby "voluntary and third sector initiatives organized around the principles of self-improvement and moral responsibility stand in for state sponsored social policies and programmes premised on collective responses to social risk" (p. 1229).

In the UK, there has been little research on community gardening in the city. Indeed, it is possible to point to only a couple of publications on the subject: the first publication, based largely on a postal survey of community gardening projects, points to the environmental and social inter-relationships bound up with community gardening and their impacts in relation to urban sustainability (Holland 2004), and the second publication discusses the "ordinary" creativities associated with a community garden in a disadvantaged urban neighbourhood in northern England (Milbourne 2009). Beyond these publications, it is possible to identify work on related types of collective gardening in the UK, most notably Crouch and Ward's (1988) influential study of allotment gardening, which highlights the cooperative forms of organization and ownership, and strong reciprocal relations that exist between gardeners associated with this form of gardening (see also Crouch 1989). However, allotment gardening represents a more regimented, regulated, and individualized form of communal gardening, which means that many of the themes emerging from the US community gardening literature are less relevant to its aims and activities.[1]

Although there may be little research evidence on community gardening in the UK, there is little doubt that it has become much more significant in urban places during the last few years. There exist two organizations that represent community gardens in the UK: the Federation of City Farms and Community Gardens (FCFCG, which acts as an umbrella organization for community gardening projects) and the Royal Horticultural Society (RHS), which promotes local community gardening projects through its annual "Britain in Bloom" campaign.[2] Recent membership data obtained for each organization reveal impressive rates of growth across the last decade. Membership of the FCFCG increased by 72% between 2006 and 2011, with the organization having 583 member projects in January 2011. Between 2007 and 2008, the RHS reported a 25% increase in community gardening groups involved in its "Britain in Bloom" campaign and had 360 groups registered on its "neighbourhood awards" scheme in 2007, the vast majority of which were located in disadvantaged urban neighbourhoods.

In the next section of this paper, I draw on materials from recent and ongoing research on community gardening in the UK to explore the relations between community gardening projects and socio-environmental (in)justices. In doing this, I want to both connect with and problematize key social, environmental, and spatial themes on community gardening within the US literature. Before engaging with these themes, though, it is useful to provide details of my research on community gardening in Britain. During the last three years, I have been studying the environmental and social actions and impacts of community gardening projects in disadvantaged neighbourhoods in various cities in England and Wales. This has involved working with 18 projects located in nine cities – Manchester (two projects), Salford, London (four), Southampton, Bristol, Nottingham, Cardiff (three), Newport, and Birmingham (four). The case study projects were selected using materials provided by the RHS and FCFCG and web-based searches of community gardens to provide a mix of projects working in disadvantaged urban places in relation to scale, duration, and location. Scale was measured in terms of both the physical size of the garden spaces and the number of people employed by the projects. In terms of location, projects were selected to reflect different sizes of city – ranging from Newport in south Wales to London – and in different regions – south-east England (four projects), south-west England (two), the Midlands (five) and north-west England (three), and south Wales (four).

The study has utilized qualitative methods to examine the social and environmental dimensions of these projects based on three phases of fieldwork. First, in order to provide a broader perspective on the development of community gardening in the UK, interviews were undertaken with ten national environmental, gardening, and community gardening organizations, including the RHS, FCFCG, and Groundwork Trust. Second, 22 semi-structured interviews were conducted with co-ordinators of the case study projects, with additional material on the projects being assembled from walking tours of the gardens and project documents. Third, more detailed research was undertaken with three of the projects, which involved interviews and group discussions with 35 project participants, visual ethnography, and participant observation within the gardens and at project events.[3] Most of the fieldwork was conducted in the summer months of 2009 and 2010,[4] with longer term engagements taking place with a couple of the projects.

In this paper, I draw mainly on the material from the interviews with project co-ordinators. This material has been analysed using the conventional qualitative approach of sorting and coding. The interviews provided a degree of structure to this analysis, given that they focused on six themes: project aims, beginnings, main activities, governance structures, impacts, and futures. The next section of this paper is structured around three themes that emerge from the analysis. First, attention is paid to the early visions of the case study projects, highlighting how different projects have been influenced by local contexts and a mix of social and environmental concerns. Second, the mechanisms through which projects were established are explored. Third, spatialities and, more particularly, the complex local geographies bound up with these projects are examined.

2. Growing new spaces of justice in UK cities

From the visits to the projects, interviews with their co-ordinators, and analysis of project materials, it is clear that the case study projects are located in spaces characterized by a broad range of social, economic, and environmental problems. However, it was often their problematic social and economic local contexts that were discussed by projects as this extract from web-based material on the Salford project illustrates: Unemployment rates in the area are higher than in Salford and national averages, with particularly high rates of youth and long-term unemployment. The area also suffers from high crime rates, with burglary and juvenile nuisance identified as specific problems. With the addition of low incomes, poverty, and debt through negative equity, these issues compounded to create an area of isolation, fear, and deep-rooted social exclusion for many individuals.

Within the interviews, these socio-economic problematics tended to be referenced through personal anecdote, based on the project co-ordinators' intimate everyday knowledge of their local area. In some cases, technical knowledge of the area's problems was utilized, with one person referring to the area's position within the official index of multiple deprivation to claim that "this area is one of the most deprived areas in Southampton and in south-east England" (Southampton). Beyond these themes of social disadvantage, sets of socio-cultural issues were mentioned by some of the co-ordinators. In one of the Birmingham areas, for example, street prostitution had been a significant problem in the recent past, with local residents feeling that they had lost control of their area. In a couple of other areas, the socio-cultural impacts of recent demographic shifts were viewed as problematic. In particular, the in-movement of asylum seekers, refugees, and economic migrants from various countries was seen by co-ordinators as producing new forms of cultural segregation in the local area.

Some project managers did refer to local environmental problems, including the lack of green space, the neglect of existing local environments, and traffic pollution. In one of the Cardiff project areas, mention was made of the dumping of waste products by builders in the shared space between properties, while a recent consultation with local residents in another area had revealed that "they talked about rats and rubbish – you talk to people about anything in this area and at some point rats and rubbish will come out" (Birmingham 1).

It should be noted, though, that in most cases, reference to these environmental themes was preceded by more significant discussion of local socio-economic problems.

3. Visions

The initial aims of the case study projects reflect the specific mixes of social, economic, environmental, and cultural issues present in their neighbourhoods in the period immediately before they were established. The interviews with co-ordinators revealed five main goals associated with these projects. First, a group of projects had been set up to improve the visual aesthetics of local public spaces. The neglected state of green public spaces was viewed by these project co-ordinators as a powerful symbol of the decline of their neighbourhood, and environmental improvement was very much constructed as being connected to broader sets of social and cultural change. As one coordinator commented, "we are interested in greening the place not just for the sake of greening the place but because . . . if we can transform the environment . . . we [change] the way the community feels" (Birmingham 2). In some cases, the idea of collective gardening followed the physical cleansing of these spaces, often in collaboration with the local authority, with local people seeking to reclaim and maintain these areas as community green spaces through gardening. In other cases, the focus was on small pockets of unkempt public green space that were part of the street landscape but had been neglected by the local state. Initially, tactics of guerrilla gardening[5] were employed to transform these spaces and then agreements had been made with the local authority to allow them to be managed by the group.

Second, some projects had been established to create new forms of green space in their high-density neighbourhoods. As one project coordinator in London commented:

> The aims are to provide a peaceful and relaxing space where local residents can come and just you know spend some time in an environment that's quite different from the urban environment that they usually live in. It was also to provide growing space of people who don't have gardens or allotments.
>
> (London 3)

Similarly, in Manchester, the lack of local green space was identified as a prime mover behind one of the projects. As its coordinator stated, although "there were bits of scrub land and things like that . . . there was [sic] needles everywhere and . . . it wasn't an inclusive space" (Manchester 2). Another of the London projects had been initiated to create green spaces in a slightly different way by using its community garden as a demonstration space within which local residents living in tower blocks were taught how to green their outdoor balconies through the creative use of planted containers and window boxes.

Third, a group of projects had been developed in response to social problems in the area. Here, community gardening was being used to mobilize different local groups into taking back control of local space. Often, the gardening project was associated with other forms of community action. For example, in a couple of cases, the gating of backspaces between domestic properties had prompted residents to develop ways of utilizing these "new" spaces, one of which was through collective gardening activities. With one of the Birmingham projects, the gardening idea had followed a successful campaign to rid the neighbourhood of street prostitution, with a group of residents looking for ways of connecting with local youth groups as well as improving the physical state of the area:

> why we are interested in greening the place is not just for the sake of greening the place but because it makes it safer and [for] youngsters in difficulty, who are a main interest of ours . . . the place was untidy, litter-strewn, a mess, uncared for.
>
> (Birmingham 2)

Fourth, community gardening projects related to the changing demographics of some of these urban neighbourhoods and the perceived need to create new forms of cultural integration. A couple of projects had been set up to work with refugees and asylum seekers, but had expanded their activities to engage with other communities and to address local issues of racism. As the coordinator of one of these projects commented:

> when we started the project here it was all about working with refugees and asylum seekers
> ... but we have taken it further than that in that we try to integrate people into it, into a genuine community. I mean, for instance, there is quite an issue of racism here. We've had a BNP councilor for the past few years.
>
> (London 3)

Another project had focused on what it saw as the cultural isolation of Bangladeshi women, establishing a community garden to "encourage them to get out because a lot of Bangladeshi women don't tend to come out of their houses" (London 2), while a couple of projects had sought to create a space for cultural integration, using gardening to bring together different ethnic and cultural groups, and reduce existing cultural tensions. Related to this, the Southampton project was attempting to develop faith-based forms of integration, providing the only "secular cultural space" in the area, within which people from different faiths could work together and "where people aren't going to feel challenged".

Finally, three of the projects had been established to provide therapeutic forms of gardening, involving the collective nurturing of land, plants, and people. In each case, community gardening had drawn on the principles of permaculture, mimicking the relationships that exist within natural ecologies and seeking to create new systems of environmental sustainability. These principles of permaculture, though, extended beyond horticultural practice to embrace relationships between people and the environment. As the Southampton coordinator stated, "what we want is for every time someone comes in here that they are enriching this space as much as they are enriching themselves, and so they get something out of it and the garden gets something out of it, and in that way the people develop and grow". Similarly, the coordinator of one of the London projects discussed the inter-relations between people, land, and fairness within their community garden:

> permaculture has this set of ethics, these three core ethics which kind of sit at the centre of any design . . . earth care, people care and fair share, and they [are] always represented as three circles interlocking and it is that bit in the middle that represents the holism of the process. So obviously we do a lot on earth care, the environmental and physical side of the work, but that doesn't take precedence over the social care that we provide and the social atmosphere that we try to create.

Within these discussions of therapeutic gardening, co-ordinators made reference to their work with vulnerable groups, including asylum seekers who had been victims of torture and people with mental health problems, pointing to the ways that permacultural techniques were providing "psychotherapy in a gardening setting" (London 3).

4. Beginnings

Reflecting the relatively recent growth of the community gardening movement in the UK, most of the projects included within the research had been established during the last couple of decades – nine had been set up in the 2000s and seven in the 1990s and the other two commenced in the 1980s. The most common means through which projects had been initiated – accounting for seven cases – was the closure of an existing community resource, such as a school or community centre, by the local authority, which prompted local groups to campaign for the continued use of the building and/or its surrounding green space as a community resource. As one coordinator commented:

> this site was a school playground and the school closed, which is now a mosque at the far end of the garden. So the school closed and this site was just derelict and because it is such a densely populated area with very little green space, local people thought it would be a good idea to try and have some sort of community space . . . [Its success] is due to the tenacity and persistence of different people over the years in this area who . . . initially came in and started with sort of pick axes trying to break up the tarmac and just plant through in little tiny beds.
>
> (Southampton)

In other cases, the community gardening project was initiated by particular individuals, either members of the local community or those employed by a voluntary organization working in the area, who had an interest in gardening. In one project, a resident who had recently moved back to the area had been shocked by its state of decline and, prompted by a drugs-related murder, decided to take action. As a dedicated Christian who had some horticultural knowledge and was also trained as a chef, he set about developing an idea for a community garden and café that would combine the collective growing, cooking, and consumption of its food produce. For two other projects – Salford and Birmingham 1 – the arrival of a community worker with knowledge of successful community gardening projects in other areas had prompted the project idea. Through informal conversations at community events, the seeds of the community gardening projects were sown and residents engaged with these workers to develop their projects. Chance encounters with knowledgeable individuals were also mentioned by co-ordinators. For example, a man who had been doing voluntary work at a permaculture centre in Australia returned to London and while undertaking further voluntary work "happened upon this place and a woman was actually setting up the project just as I came along and you know she didn't have any experience of gardening or permaculture" (London 3).

Other projects were established as spin-offs from broader funded projects in their area. In Birmingham, a grant awarded to a local environmental organization was used to develop a community gardening project aimed at developing the skills base of Bangladeshi women in the area. The Bristol project was part of a broader sustainability project that had received Big Lottery funding, "which was looking at ways of making [place name] more sustainable . . . to encourage people to walk rather than drive", while projects in Salford and Cardiff were linked to a crime reduction programme that had gated some of the "backspaces" in these areas.

Reflecting these different origins, the projects have drawn on different forms and scales of funding. Some of the projects mentioned in the preceding paragraphs have received significant amounts of funding from broader state-led projects that has met some of the initial infrastructural costs associated with the establishment of their projects, such as the enclosing of spaces and hard landscaping. These and most of the other projects, though, were operating within rather restricted and complex funding contexts at the time of the interviewing, being largely reliant on the unpaid labour of volunteers and the over time of staff, and a mix of funding sources – including small grants from public sector organizations, charities, and businesses, and fund-raising activities. Indeed, what emerged strongly from the interviews was the significant amount of work undertaken by project co-ordinators in an effort to secure sufficient funding to maintain their projects, with many unable to discuss their financial situations beyond the next financial year. That said, three of the projects had expanded the scale of their activities over recent years and were now operating as social enterprises, providing horticultural services to their local authority and other local and regional organizations both on and off the community gardening site.

5. Spatialities

As is clear from the preceding sections, these projects are being played out within rather ordinary and mundane spaces, adding further empirical weight to arguments about the significance of "the everyday" within socio-environmental forms of (in)justice. It was the abandonment, despoilment, or absence of everyday green spaces, or the loss of control over people's street spaces that had prompted the formation of most of these projects. Working in and on these spaces had not only altered the physical and aesthetic natures of these spaces but also transformed everyday interactions within them, developing new hybrid or third spaces that combine the public and private realms and producing new meeting places for diverse groups of the local population. As one of the London project co-ordinators commented:

> The most obvious one [achievement] is transforming the derelict abandoned site into a thriving and productive space, that's one, the most obvious, the visual sort of achievement. The other one is to bring together a whole range of people of different backgrounds in a social setting that they enjoy and they get a therapeutic benefit from.
>
> (London 3)

The case study research also points to the complexities of these everyday spaces of community gardening. While several of the projects conform to conventional spatial understandings of the community garden as a single, bounded and green space that sits within the built environment of the city, they nevertheless represent rather complicated spaces. Some are open-access sites that permit entry to all groups at all times, while others have been forced to limit access due to vandalism or limited staff resources. Certain projects are associated with a single community space that is used by all members of the project, while others combine communal areas with individual plots. In most cases, the work of the group is confined to the spaces of the community garden, but some projects have extended their gardening into other spaces, either through out-reach work or through the physical expansion of the project space. Lastly, while all projects are providing communal spaces for local residents, it is clear that a small number also have broader spatial concerns, catering for special needs groups, such as people with mental health problems, living beyond the immediate vicinity of the garden, engaging with immigrant groups, including refugees and asylum seekers, and addressing global socio-ecological issues:

> So one of the things that we did want to do . . . was to have an international garden of peace somewhere. To have some kind of little monument that represents world peace, not in a hippy sort of way but in a general sense of people being together and you know . . . working together and one of the lovely things about this garden that needs to be considered is that we have plants from all over the world here.
>
> (Southampton)

The activities of certain projects are located in other types of everyday spaces. Some are focused on the public spaces of the street, reflecting concerns about social and environmental problems within these spaces, as well as the limited availability of green space within their areas. On those streets lacking front gardens, containers of flowering plants have been placed at the front of residential properties. In other cases, small front gardens are being used to improve the aesthetics of the street and to provide "some ownership of public space even though it's not technically public space" (Bristol), while one of the London projects has translated its work in the community garden to the balconies of flats in large tower blocks. As its organizer commented:

> It's a built up area you see and . . . most people round here don't have gardens so we try and encourage, try and show people how to grow stuff in small spaces if you see what I mean, like a window box; you can grow a lot in a window box.
>
> (London 2)

In other cases, gardening activities are dispersed across the neighbourhood, transforming small patches of neglected public green space adjoining streets and creating networks of community gardening micro-spaces. One project coordinator referred to these as "confused public spaces" – spaces that were originally built into the urban landscape to provide elements of nature, "but as time has gone on, the bit of the council or other public body which owns them . . . don't maintain them and they drag the area down and make it look drab. So a key bit of what we do is civilise confused public spaces" (Birmingham 2).

A couple of projects are operating in what might be termed "backspaces" – narrow alleyways running behind rows of terraced houses in their areas, which had become dumping grounds for rubbish, places where drugs and alcohol were consumed, and entry points for house burglars. Following the gating and cleansing of these spaces by the local authority, residents had initiated community forms of gardening as a means of creating green spaces in areas that lacked gardens to the fronts and rears of their properties. In this sense, the gating of these spaces has produced effects somewhat different from those frequently reported in the gated communities literature (see Le Goix and Webster 2008), creating new socio-ecological places that are providing residents with a richer diversity of plants and wildlife, as well as new places of sociality and conviviality. As one of the RHS representatives commented in relation to a recent visit to the Salford project:

> I couldn't believe it. I have never experienced such a community in [that] every single person had the same story and they are all out talking to each other and having cups of tea on their tables that they had put in their alleys, saying 'I used to come home and be scared and run to my house and go into it and stay there. Now we spend our weekends out here talking to our neighbours'. It's just incredible.

6. Community gardening and socio-environmental (in)justices

From their rather humble beginnings, the community gardening projects included in this study have proceeded to produce an impressive range of socio-environmental transformations of their neighbourhood spaces. It is also clear that co-ordinators of these projects tend to emphasize the social impacts of their work, with environmental actions often constructed as the medium through which social, cultural, and political forms of transformation had been achieved. As a representative of the FCFCG suggested:

> Our interest is in how city farms and community gardens can benefit people where they live and how they foster belonging and pride of place. . . . The primary driver is about community empowerment and individual capacity building through the mechanism of local land management for growing.

What is evident from this study are the ways these projects are producing new socio-ecological spaces within these places, with horticultural and environmental practices being translated into new forms of sociality, public participation, sustainability, and justice. As one coordinator commented, "the flowers are just a very small part of what we have done; the social aspects are more important" (Manchester 1). Clearly, the mix of social and environmental impacts varies from one project to another, reflecting the missions of individual projects and the particular socio-ecological problems associated with their neighbourhoods. Some projects are placing more emphasis on developing new sets of relations between people, plants, and environments, while others are utilizing environmental and horticultural actions to initiate broader forms of social change. What cuts across all these projects, though, is the desire to address existing injustices – social, environmental, or socio-environmental – through the practice of communal gardening.

It would also appear that these community gardening projects complicate conventional approaches to environmental justice in that while they seek to deliver justice through working with and on the environment, they do not necessarily require environmental injustices as a prerequisite for action. Rather, the types of community gardening highlighted in this paper are concerned with making and, in many cases, remaking urban space through socio-ecological actions. In this sense, they are striving to deliver social justice through the medium of environmentalism and not always addressing the social consequences of environmental bads (see also Church and Elster 2002). It is also the case that some of these projects are drawing on the "earth care, people care and fair share" principles of permaculture to develop alternative discourses of sustainable development and environmental justice. What this means is that we need to remain sensitive to a broader range of relationships between "environment", "sustainability", and "justice" within academic readings of just sustainabilities and environmental justice, including the different roles of the environment as cause, medium, and outcome of socio-environmental actions.

Turning to themes bound up with urban political ecology, it is clear that the projects included within this study are creating new sets of relations between space, nature, politics, society, and culture within the city, highlighting the importance of the local environment within people's everyday senses of urban injustice as well as the ways in which community gardening is remaking the physical, ecological, and social spaces of the city through localized environmental actions. Community gardening thus represents an extremely interesting case study of the political ecology of the city, demonstrating the ability of environmental projects to re-shape lived urban spaces in social and ecological terms. In this sense, community gardening projects would seem to possess the "power to produce urban environments in line with the aspirations, needs and desires of those inhabiting these spaces, the capacity to produce the physical and social environment in which one dwells" (Heynen et al. 2006, p. 16).

The types of injustices being addressed by these community gardening groups are not those that tend to dominate within the mainstream environmental justice literature. Their projects are dealing with smaller scale, localized, and everyday forms of injustice – the types of remaindered injustices to which Whitehead (2009) referred – or else are providing particular responses to larger scale injustices, which then become the springboards for wider actions. Supporting Hobson's (2006) argument about the significance of the local contexts of justice, the research has highlighted the deliberate strategy adopted by projects of dealing with local and everyday manifestations of injustice and justice, of recognising the importance of everyday space within the lives of people in disadvantaged urban neighbourhoods, and so of working to improve this space. The site of the community garden has thus come to represent the spatial manifestation of transitions from injustice to justice as well as the empowerment of local community.

These everyday spaces and ordinary environmental practices of community gardening are also characterized by geographical complexities that have not received much discussion within the mainstream community gardening and environmental justice literatures. Not only do they contain different types of spaces – collective and individual spaces within the bounded community garden, front gardens, balconies, patches, and backspaces – but also there are different scales of action and meaning being played out within them, with some projects addressing more distant injustices experienced by refugees and asylum seekers alongside those encountered by residents within their immediate neighbourhoods.

Finally, the origins and goals of the case study projects would appear to complicate Pudup's (2008) construction of community gardening as a mechanism that supports the state during periods of economic and fiscal crisis. This study has uncovered little evidence to suggest that the UK projects have been initiated in response to the withdrawal of the (local) state from key areas of welfare provision. The closure of community spaces or buildings was related more to the mundane issues of shifting demographics, school improvement programmes, and the underuse of existing community centres than to financial cuts. It is also clear that while some projects were reacting to the abandonment of particular spaces by the local state, others were working in partnership with or had enthusiastically taken over projects that had been initiated by the local authority. In these cases, the absence of the local state provided opportunities as well as constraints, allowing them to wrestle back control of local space and to produce more meaningful and democratic community spaces. Interviews with national environmental and gardening organizations also suggest that it is grassroots pressure from community gardening groups – channelled through these organizations – that has led to increased recognition by central government of community gardening in disadvantaged urban neighbourhoods. This is not to deny that community gardening may be part of the "roll-out" neoliberal policy agenda in the UK (and the USA), rather to suggest that further research is required before more meaningful assessments can be made of the political positionings of community gardening in each country.

7. Developing new agendas for community gardening research

Six years on from the publication of this article, there now exists a much more developed academic literature on urban community gardening. While early scholarship on the subject was largely atheoretical and uncritical in nature, more recent work has begun to engage with key debates within urban studies, including neoliberal urbanism, urban political ecology, and urban justice. Attention has also been given to the affective natures of collective growing in the city, particularly the ways in which people's engagements with soil and plants help to cultivate new forms of citizenship, identity, sociality, and care both within and beyond the spaces of the community garden. That said, more work is needed to position community gardening research within critical debates concerning cities, urban space, and nature. In this final section of the paper, three broad themes concerning future research on community gardening are discussed.

The first of these concerns the relationship between community gardens and neoliberalism. It is widely recognized that this relationship is complex, with community gardens representing hybrids in terms of neoliberalism (McClintock 2014), simultaneously resisting and reinforcing the imposition of neoliberal policy in particular cities (Barron 2016; Milbourne 2012). Pudup (2008) is correct when she states that community gardening represents a response to broader processes of change and periods of crisis. As neoliberalism develops new responses to tackle emerging crises, so the purposes and activities associated with community gardening will inevitably change. The continued shrinkage of the state and further reductions in the funding of public and welfare services in some countries will no doubt lead to new challenges for community gardening projects. However, the "new" politics of austerity may also create the conditions for community gardening to develop a new sense of purpose, legitimacy, and permanency within the city.

Second, it would be useful to pay further attention to the justice dimensions of community gardening in an effort to develop more meaningful linkages with and contributions to theories of social, environmental, and spatial justice. In particular, researchers could look to extend Lefebvre's (1996) ideas of the "right to the city" to urban environments and landscapes in order to ask important questions about who has the right to create, alter, and destroy urban natures. Such research could make interesting connections with a developing body of academic work on the "right to landscape" (see Egoz et al. 2011), which approaches landscape in more grounded and vernacular terms as a "place of a habitus, the rights to which devolve to those who use it in a way judged to be moral by the communities who share it" (Olwig 2011, p. 17). This focus on rights could also allow community gardening researchers to engage more critically with recent and ongoing discussions about the development of alternative and more just urban food systems.

A third theme worthy of additional scrutiny is the spatialities of community gardening. Given that community gardens combine ideas of "public", "private", and "community" in producing communitarian spaces that are neither fully open nor closed in terms of its access and membership, they have much to contribute to ongoing debates about the changing nature of public space and publics in the city. Similarly, the work of community gardeners in and on spaces that might be described as mundane raises interesting questions about the role of "the ordinary" and "the everyday" within city living and urban studies. Approaching the city as a "granite garden" (Whiston Spirn 1984), where community gardens combine with domestic gardens, allotments, public parks, and other forms of green space to create a more significant urban gardening landscape, may also provide an opportunity for researchers of community gardening to engage with broader debates on sustainable urbanism and liveable cities.

Beyond these three research themes, critical attention needs to be given to where and how community gardening is researched. In terms of the where, community gardening has been explored almost exclusively in the context of the reintroduction of agriculture to cities in the Global North. In many countries of the Global South, farming has never actually moved out of the city. Instead, agriculture in and around many cities in the developing world continues to produce significant amounts of locally sourced foodstuffs for the urban population. Urban agriculture in these countries, though, is often viewed as a legacy of the past rather than part of the future agri-food system. It is also the case that the rapid pace of urbanization has problematized the continued existence of urban agriculture through planning policies and the pollution of urban farmland and water sources. Given the dominance of community growing research in Global North countries and these contrasts between urban growing in the North and the South, it would be good to develop new research agendas focused on the challenges and opportunities of urban agriculture in developing countries.

Community gardening research in the Global North has also been concentrated on a relatively small number of countries. A recent survey of journal articles on community gardening published between 1985 and 2011 reveals that 57 % were based on projects in the US, with three other countries – Australia, Canada, and the UK – accounting for a further 31 % of published articles (Guitart et al. 2012). What follows from this narrow focus on a small number of countries is that the community gardening literature is bound up with particular assumptions about property rights, governance systems, economy, politics, and nature-society relations. While there are signs that work is beginning to be undertaken in other (European) countries, it is clear that further research is needed to make sense of how community growing projects are both shaped by and impacting on economic, political, social, and cultural processes and systems in a larger number of countries.

Turning to how community gardens are researched, almost all published studies have followed a qualitative case study approach in an effort to provide in-depth accounts of individual projects in particular cities. To explore the broader significance of community growing within and across cities will necessitate the employment of multi-layered and multi-method research approaches that incorporate various spatial scales and combine qualitative and quantitative techniques. Guitart et al. (2012) provide a broader critique of community gardening research, arguing that it has been dominated by social scientific framings. They call for more attention to be paid to the physical and natural science dimensions of community growing, including soil, nutrition, and biodiversity, as well as the scientific possibilities and limitations of community growing in different places. Connecting such approaches with a broader range of social scientific research techniques could develop some really innovative programmes of interdisciplinary research on community gardening, providing more sophisticated understandings of the co-production of nature, the role of "more-than-human" actors, and the interactions between humans and nature within community gardening.

Notes

1 It should be noted, though, that the distinction between allotment and community gardening is becoming less clear.
2 Environmental organizations, such as Groundwork Trust, are also working with local groups in disadvantaged urban neighbourhoods to create and improve public green spaces.
3 These methods included observations at project meetings and in the gardens, participant observation through volunteer gardening, and the use of digital still image and video cameras by the researchers and participants.
4 I am grateful to Wendy Ball and Richard Carter-White for their involvement in this fieldwork.
5 Guerrilla gardening represents a more immediate, individualized, and aesthetic form of public gardening that is largely concerned with "beautifying empty space" and pays little regard to the ownership of the land (Reynolds 2008; see also Tracey 2007).

References

Agyeman, J., 2002. Constructing environmental (in)justice: Transatlantic tales. *Environmental Politics*, 11 (3), 31–53.
Agyeman, J. and Evans, B., 2004. 'Just sustainability': The emerging discourse of environmental justice in Britain? *The Geographical Journal*, 170 (2), 155–164.
Armstrong, D., 2000. A survey of community gardens in upstate New York. *Health and Place*, 6 (4), 319–327.
Barron, J., 2016. Community gardening: Cultivating subjectivities, space, and justice. *Local Environment: The International Journal of Justice and Sustainability*, 1–17.
Bhatti, M. and Church, A., 2001. Cultivating natures: Homes and gardens in late modernity. *Sociology*, 35 (2), 365–383.
Bhatti, M., Church, A., Claremont, A., and Stenner, P., 2009. 'I love being in the garden': Enchanting encounters in everyday life. *Social and Cultural Geography*, 10 (1), 61–76.
Burningham, K. and Thrush, D., 2001. *'Rainforests are a long way from here': The environmental concerns of disadvantaged groups*. York: Joseph Rowntree Foundation.
Burrows, R. and Rhodes, D., 1998. *Unpopular places? Area disadvantage and the geography of misery*. Bristol: Policy Press.
Church, C. and Elster, J., 2002. *Thinking locally, acting nationally: Lessons for national policy from work on local sustainability*. York: Joseph Rowntree Foundation.
Crouch, D., 1989. Patterns of co-operation in the cultures of outdoor leisure: The case of the allotment. *Leisure Studies*, 8 (2), 189–199.
Crouch, D. and Ward, C., 1988. *The allotment: Its landscape and culture*. London: Faber and Faber.
Egoz, S., Makhzoumi, J., and Pungetti, G. (eds.), 2011. *The right to landscape: Contesting landscape and human rights*. Farnham: Ashgate.
Ferris, J., Norman, C., and Sempik, J., 2001. People, land and sustainability: Community gardens and the social dimension of sustainable development. *Social Policy and Administration*, 35 (5), 559–568.
Francis, M. and Hester, R.T., 1990. *The meaning of gardens*. Cambridge, MA: MIT Press.
Friends of the Earth, 2001. *Pollution and poverty: Breaking the link*. London: Friends of the Earth.
Glover, T., Shinew, K., and Parry, D., 2005. Association, sociability, and civic culture: The democratic effect of community gardening. *Leisure Sciences*, 27 (1), 75–92.

Guitart, D., Pickering, C., and Byrne, J., 2012. Past results and future directions in urban community gardens research. *Urban Forestry and Greening*, 11, 364–373.

Heynen, N., Kaika, M., and Swyngedouw, E., 2006. *In the nature of cities: Urban political ecology and the politics of urban metabolism*. London: Routledge.

Hobson, K., 2006. Enacting environmental justice in Singapore: Performative justice and the green volunteer network. *Geoforum*, 37, 671–681.

Hodgkinson, T., 2005. Digging for anarchy. In: T. Richardson and N. Kingsbury, eds. *Vista: The culture and politics of gardens*. London: Frances Lincoln, 66–73.

Holifield, R., Porter, M., and Walker, G., 2009. Spaces of environmental justice: Frameworks for critical engagement. *Antipode*, 41 (4), 591–612.

Holland, L., 2004. Diversity and connections in community gardens: A contribution to local sustain-ability. *Local Environment*, 9 (3), 285–305.

Hou, J., Johnson, J.M., and Lawson, L.J., 2009. *Greening cities, growing communities: Learning from Seattle's urban community gardens*. Seattle, WA: Washington University Press.

Hynes, H., 1996. *A patch of Eden: America's inner-city gardeners*. White River Junction, VT: Chelsea Green Publishing Company.

Lawson, J., 2005. *City bountiful: A century of community gardening in America*. Berkeley: University of California Press.

Lefebvre, H., 1991. *Critique of everyday life*. London: Verso.

Lefebvre, H., 1996. *Writings on cities*. Tr. E. Kofman and E. Lebas. Oxford: Blackwell.

Le Goix, R. and Webster, C., 2008. Gated communities. *Geography Compass*, 2 (4), 1189–1214.

Lucas, K., Fuller, S., Psaila, A., and Thrush, D., 2004. *Prioritising local environmental concerns: Where there's a will there's a way*. York: Joseph Rowntree Foundation.

Lupton, R. and Power, A., 2002. Social exclusion and neighbourhoods. In: J. Hills, J. Le Grand and D. Piachaud, eds. *Understanding social exclusion*. Oxford: Oxford University Press, 118–140.

McCarthy, J., 2005. Devolution in the woods: Community forestry as hybrid neoliberalism. *Environment and Planning A*, 37 (6), 995–1014.

McClintock, N., 2014. Radical, reformist, and garden-variety neoliberal: Coming to terms with urban agriculture's contradictions. *Local Environment: The International Journal of Justice and Sustainability*, 19 (2), 147–171.

Milbourne, P., 2009. Growing places: Community gardening, ordinary creativities and place-based regeneration in a northern English city. In: T. Edensor, D. Leslie, S. Millington and S. Rantisi, eds. *Spaces of vernacular creativity*. London: Routledge, 141–154.

Milbourne, P., 2010. Putting poverty and welfare in place. *Policy and Politics*, 38 (1), 153–169.

Milbourne, P., 2012. Everyday (in)justices and ordinary environmentalisms: Community gardening in disadvantaged urban neighbourhoods. *Local Environment: The International Journal of Justice and Sustainability*, 17 (9), 943–957.

Olwig, K., 2011. The right rights to the right landscape. In: S. Egoz, J. Makhzoumi and G. Pungetti, eds. *The right to landscape: Contesting landscape and human rights*. Farnham: Ashgate, 39–49.

Peck, A. and Tickell, A., 2002. Neoliberalizing space. *Antipode*, 34 (3), 380–404.

Pudup, M.B., 2008. It takes a garden: Cultivating citizen-subjects in organized garden projects. *Geoforum*, 39, 1228–1240.

Reynolds, R., 2008. *On guerrilla gardening: A handbook for gardening without boundaries*. London: Bloomsbury.

Schmeizkopf, K., 1995. Urban community gardens as contested space. *Geographical Review*, 85 (3), 364–381.

Severson, R., 1990. United we sprout: A Chicago community garden story. In: M. Francis and R.T. Hester, eds. *The meaning of gardens.* Cambridge, MA: MIT Press, 80–85.

Stocker, L. and Barnett, K., 1998. The significance and praxis of community-based sustainability projects. *Local Environment,* 3 (2), 179–191.

Tracey, D., 2007. *Guerrilla gardening: A manualfesto.* Gabriola Island, BC: New Society Publishers.

Walker, G. and Bickerstaff, K., 2000. Polluting the poor: An emerging environmental justice agenda for the UK. CUCR paper. London: Goldsmiths College, University of London.

Walker, G. and Bulkeley, H., 2006. Geographies of environmental justice. *Geoforum,* 37 (5), 655–659.

Warpole, K., 2000. *In our backyard: The social promise of environmentalism.* London: Groundwork and Green Alliance.

Whiston Spirn, A., 1984. *The granite garden: Urban nature and human design.* New York: Basic Books.

Whitehead, M., 2009. The wood for the trees: Ordinary environmental justice and the everyday right to urban nature. *International Journal of Urban and Regional Research,* 33 (3), 662–681.

Williams, R., 1958. Culture is ordinary. In: J. Higgine, ed. *The Raymond Williams reader.* Oxford: Blackwell, 10–24.

3 A practice-based approach to political gardening

Materiality, performativity, and post-environmentalism

Chiara Certomà

1. Political gardening: from recognition to exploration

The 2009 economic and financial crisis, together with tragically broadening socio-economic disparities in worldwide cities, have given rise to spontaneous, citizens-led initiatives in public space planning and management. These initiatives have transformed many derelict urban areas into "laboratories" for experimenting with socio-ecological alternatives, such as urban gardening (Evans and Karvonen, 2010; Corsin Jimenez, 2014). Even though such urban gardens seem to only alleviate trivial and inconsequential problems, they actually address and affect some of the most striking social, economic, and political issues of our time. Urban gardening has challenged certain contemporary political and economic models through, amongst others, the re-publicization of small parcels of land, the provision of fresh vegetables to the neighbourhood, the organization of leisure time, and the re-creation of proximity linkage.

Such a perspective clashes with the common perception of gardening as a neighbourhood-primping activity that can be run by citizens' associations and institutions inspired by whatever socio-political vision, or even none at all. This understanding of gardening as a one-size-fits-all initiative has been adopted by many environmentalist associations and administrations (Rosol, 2012). For instance, the *Nature en Ville* project of the Genève City Council (*Nature en Ville*, 2018) aims at re-naturalising the city by favouring the establishment of urban ecological networks through funding and supporting proposals from neighbourhood associations. The Genève project shows how city administrations, torn between implementing neoliberal policies and empowering citizens, often de-potentiate the subversive character of urban gardening and agriculture initiatives to present them as win-win projects (Ernwein, 2017). For some time now, the political relevance of gardening the city has been purposely ignored in order to obtain an as broad as possible consensus, leading in some cases to paradoxical situations. For example, the former right wing mayor of Rome established the *Mayor's garden* in the City Council courtyard in 2010, which attracted a wide range of contrasting comments in the media and from (mainly leftist) gardeners' communities in the city (Lanzi, 2013).

Despite significant differences and divergences in terms of visions and objectives, urban gardening is now broadly acknowledged to have the potentiality to become a political gesture (Reynolds, 2014; Kato et al., 2014), even if significant divergences in terms of visions and objectives characterize different gardening initiatives. This idea was introduced in a special issue of *Local Environment: The International Journal of Justice and Sustainability* (Certomà and Tornaghi, 2015), whose editorial (re-proposed in Chapter 1 of the present book) stated that "Political gardening projects [. . .] advance a form of political commitment that materialises through the practical arrangements of things and living beings in the city space; and gathers together heterogeneous actors working towards an ideal future city they want to build in common" (p. 1124). The present chapter builds upon the assumption that specific, yet widespread, forms of urban gardening can be regarded as a means for political engagement because they advance proposals on the meaning, organization, and management of the public space, by inspiring decisions that apply to society as a whole. These particular forms of gardening the city, labelled as political gardening, are the objects of investigation in the following pages.

Social science scholars have already described the wide variety of actors involved in political gardening, as well as its agency and effects on different aspects of public life (McClintock, 2014).[1] However, the ontology of political gardening has not yet been thoroughly addressed, that is to say, what is the meaning of *politics* in political gardening? What kind of politics do we refer to when talking about political gardening?

Starting with an overview of different conceptualizations of the political in urban gardening practices, this chapter examines how the engagement with the materiality of a garden space can represent a form of political commitment. Subsequently, the connection between post-environmentalist theory and political gardening is introduced to provide suggestions on how the garden can become a space of collective involvement where society–environment relationships assume new meanings.

2. What does *politics* mean in political gardening?

Politics is conventionally understood as the "governance of a country or area, especially the debate between parties having power" (OED, 2017); the effects of government exerted by deputed institutions; or even the set of principles and beliefs guiding a societal formation. While these definitions immediately resonate with our conception of traditional, parliamentary political activity, they can easily be reinterpreted as descriptions of the underlying objective of political gardening. In fact, political gardening entails the governance of an area (albeit a very limited one), subject to the power interplay of different actors advancing different visions, inspired by different values and aiming toward different goals. In addition, political gardening might be generated or confronted with multiple levels and procedures of government implemented by deputed institutions; and, most obviously, it proposes future scenarios as an alternative to the current settings. The most immediate consequence of this acknowledgement is that urban gardening is liberated from its hobbyist label as having limited significance and an even more limited impact, to be re-established as a form of societal engagement deserving serious political consideration.

Up until now, literature addressing the political aspects of urban gardening has generally presented two different, yet partially overlapping, narratives of the organization of urban space.

The first one frames urban gardening within contemporary urban neoliberal politics (Quastel, 2009; Barron, 2016; Perkins, 2010). In many circumstances urban gardening initiatives rather than work as disruptive practices against the dominant neoliberal city paradigm are proposed by city administrations themselves and prompt citizens to take responsibility for restoring and maintaining derelict areas of no interest for private investment, as it was the case in the *Kinderbaurnhof Mauerplatz Kreuzberg* garden, Berlin (Rosol, 2012). Together with community gardens, also the creation of allotments gardens may generate some ambiguity. Urban allotments stem from the UK tradition where individual parcels of land are allocated and can be legitimately fenced. However, in other European countries and the US, new allotments sometimes coincide with community gardens or complement them. This makes their status unclear, especially when gardeners turn them into fenced, quasi-private backyard-like gardens, and engage in few or no collective initiatives. Thus, these gardens can hardly be interpreted as revolutionary experiences, but rather as private appropriation of public space (Pudup, 2008; Weisman, 2009; Smith and Kurtz, 2003), thus generating new enclosures and gentrification phenomena (Tornaghi, 2014). For instance, the *Orti di Via della Consolata* in Rome were extensively funded by the city administration in 2010 as showcase initiatives for urban gardening and are now rapidly developing into quasi-private vegetable gardens.

The second dominant narrative has its roots in the "right to city" discourse (Schmelzkopf, 2002; Mitchell, 2003) and adopts an advocacy approach, praising citizens' collective reappropriation of urban space (Purcell, 2002, 2013; Staeheli et al., 2002). Political gardening is described as a progressive and access-widening activity, enhancing social life and cohesion, with the garden becoming a site for subversive events or a manifestation of critical engagement (McKay, 2011). This politically liberatory function of the garden, as a space falling outside of both institutional control and rigid social doctrines, has inspired the creation of many anarchist gardens. For instance, *'t Landhuis* in Ghent was created on a former private estate from an original squatting initiative of a radical, socio-ecological collective, who complemented the gardening project with an agenda of (counter) cultural events. The explicit aim was to oppose the administration's redevelopment plans, which might have led to gentrificiation of this peripheral area of the city (Certomà and Notteboom, 2017).

This second narrative takes a slightly different approach by interpreting political gardening as a practical realization of ecological citizenship (Dobson, 2003; Travaline and Hunold, 2010; Del Sesto, 2015). Citizens are invited to directly engage in the transformation of their living space through do-it-yourself initiatives, and to advance an affirmative kind of politics via participatory democracy processes (Parés et al., 2014; Davies, 2011), which have progressively evolved from participation-by-invitation to participation-by-mobilization mode (Bonet-Martí, 2014; Holston, 1998). Within this framework, many (engaged) scholars have extensively explored how the creation of allotments, community gardens, and street gardening performances affect public life and political decisions (at least) at a local level; as well as how these gardens became the loci for enhancing collective care of the *res publica* and fostering social cohesion (Colding et al., 2013).[2] However, in most of the analyses describing the meaning (Kurtz, 2001), the involved actors (Hardman and Larkham, 2014), the organizational structure (Clarke, 2010), and the governance processes (Ioannou et al., 2016) of political gardening, the question remains whether urban gardening is only a further expression of traditional bottom-up political processes, or is it actually advancing a different understanding of the *nature* of political agency?

3. Political gardening as a form of material politics

Gardening can be seen as not so much a continuation of (traditional) politics by other means, but rather a different form of politics performed *via* the mobilization of biological material and the activation of material semiotic networks in the space of the *polis*. There is of course a significant difference between debating a law in Parliament and planting tomatoes; nevertheless, the political nature of urban gardening clearly emerges when and if we understand politics as a matter of practices rather than discourses. To do so, material politics offers an appropriate standpoint (see Mol and Law, 2002; Barry, 2001). This approach surpasses the common object-avoiding tendency in political philosophy (Hinchliffe and Bingham, 2008) and suggests that a new understanding of politics can emerge from bringing to the fore the matter of concern, in other words, what is being discussed at public assemblies (Weibel and Latour, 2005). By focusing on the object of contention, material politics moulds the boundaries of ontological categories in which different actors are classified, and shows how they contribute in common to shaping the world they inhabit (Marres, 2012). These actors may form (temporary) political assemblies in order to tackle a common public issue, despite having different reasons and opinions. Notably, they may gather around urban planning and governance problems that are multi-layered, multi-scalar, and multi-causal, and that require general engagement because single individuals lack the capability to impact on them (Marres, 2005).

The case of the *Parco di via delle Palme* in Rome illustrates that vastly diverse social actors can come together around the common aim of restoring an abandoned public park, and, through daily negotiations, begin to reconsider and give a new shape to the materiality of their living space. In fact, the park's renovation and revitalization was realized with the joint effort of young squatters from the nearby social centre, primary school pupils and teachers, neighbourhood citizens' associations, local organizations for the disadvantaged, and a senior centre (Coordinamento Parco, 2013). As the park came back to life, a new bottom-up generated management plan granted adequate space for all the actors involved and succeeded in mitigating arising conflicts on a case-by-case basis (InfoBuild, 2013).

Together with suggesting that political agency is not confined to the sphere of discursive action but roots in the subject matter of daily practices, material politics also advances the challenging premise that heterogeneous social assemblies comprise both human and non-human actors (Whatmore, 2002). While networking is, in general, considered to be imperative in the formation and maintenance of a gardening project (Armstrong, 2000; Smith and Kurtz, 2003), for both communication and organization reasons (Nicholls, 2009; Ghose and Pettygrove, 2014), questioning who/what is involved in the networks might be equally relevant. Common practices mobilizing living beings and non-living things can reveal forgotten or ignored environmental relations. The association of human and non-human is crucial for the reconstitution of urban space and the emergence of new forms of political expression. "Actor-network theory" (the best known expression of material politics) explains that both humans and non-humans have sufficient coherence to generate effects, to alter the course of events, and to make a difference in the state of the world (Latour, 2004, 2005). Although non-humans cannot take part in traditional political debates, they are able to advance their preferences through material practices. For instance, a place is not only planned and managed by human actors, but can be *claimed* by the sea, *invaded* by birds, chemically *transformed* by resident plants, *flooded* by rain, *connected* by the worldwide web, and so on. Hinchliffe and Whatmore (2006) demonstrated this in their analysis of Birmingham's recombinant ecology that makes the city enjoyable for different kinds of beings. They suggested that spatial division between civic and wild, town and country, human and non-human is nonsense. Indeed, urban inhabitants were shown to be "complex assemblages, mutually affecting and affected by their field of becoming" (Hinchliffe and Whatmore, 2006, p. 128). This implies that the co-fabrication of reality is constrained, but not determined, by the traditional political processes, because cities are inhabited by humans and non-humans whose interaction determines the form and functioning of the urban space. For example, the history of the *Parco delle Energie* in Rome shows how unexpected (and unintentional) cooperation between heterogeneous actors can generate politically relevant initiatives. Originally intended to turn a former industrial brownfield land into an educational park, the plan for the area underwent long and complex negotiations between the city administration, a building company, citizens' and urban gardeners' associations. Most striking was the relationship which developed between, on the one hand, the citizens committed to the struggle for providing one of the most polluted and overpopulated districts of the city with a public green area and, on the other hand, a lake that literally arose due to excavation works by a company who got permission to build a shopping mall in the park. The lake became an "ally" of the civic movement and was named "the fighting lake" because, by its very presence, it was able to do what years of civic protest had not, namely halt any new building plans in the *Parco delle Energie*. The ruins of the former industrial plant and the unfinished structures already constructed by the building company were occupied by over 40 resident and migratory bird species, while the massive presence of water determined the resurgence of ecological networks with about 20 species of small mammals and fish travelling the subterraneous hydrological systems of the city (Passatore, 2014). Because of the re-naturalization of the area, urban gardeners already cultivating some parcels included in the park were able to prove the excellent quality of water, air, and soil for growing edible vegetables (Figure 3.1). Any previously submitted plan needed to be reviewed in consideration of the new (non-human) actors that had entered the sphere of political negotiation over the fate of this portion of public space; and a brand new project for an industrial-ecological reserve was proposed by neighbourhood organizations.

Within the material politics framework, politics is above all practiced in "form of life"; and calls for different ways of heterogeneous co-existence and material participation through the deployment of technologies of societal creation (Marres, 2012). Political gardening can be seen as a sort of "performative politics" because it changes the form and functioning of (part of) the city space just by working for these changes to happen. Such an understanding of performativity obviously reverses the one provided by the socio-linguistic tradition, which claims the right of language to be considered as fully belonging to the domain of acts (Austin, 1955; Searle, 1969; Butler, 1993). While these socio-linguistic studies explored the "power to produce the ontological effect of bringing something into being through the repetition of performative acts" (Rose-Redwood and Glass, 2014, p. 2) and thus affirmed that "to *say* something is to *do* something", the performativity of political gardening demonstrates that "to do something is to

Figure 3.1 The allotments in the *Parco delle Energie*, Rome; on the backdrop a view of the densely populated Pigneto district

Source: author

say something", more precisely, to say something politically relevant. In contrast to the performative pretence of discursive politics to change reality by the mere invocation of change, political gardening creates change by simply making it real.

4. Political gardening as post-environmentalism

As argued above, political gardening promotes political claims through action; but what are these claims about? The material character of political gardening implies a strong connection with environmental politics, as it places the materiality of the environmental conditions at the core of political agency. Gardeners are able to deal with socio-environmental issues (Allen, 1997) because their practical intervention on (public) space transforms the values, the attitudes, and the understanding of civic life in a direct and simple way. For instance, the *Giardinieri Sovversivi Romani*, one of the many guerrilla gardening groups worldwide, has been able to change the behaviour of the locals by continuously caring for a few large and derelict flower beds in Rome (Giardinieri Sovversivi Romani, 2018). In *Via delle Gardenie*, a trafficked street in the east of Rome, flower beds were used as dumping grounds for a long time; guerrilla gardeners transformed them into pleasant green spots hosting a variety of bushes and flowers (Figure 3.2),

Figure 3.2 One of the flower beds realized by the guerrilla group *Giardinieri Sovversivi Romani* on a former dumping area in Centocelle district, Rome

Source: author

with some benches nearby. Ever since, locals have been bringing in new plants and watering them before sitting down in the evening shadow. Such a simple and minimal act of care demonstrates the need for adequate political and administrative initiatives to alleviate the problems of overcrowded and grimy peripheries in the city, to stimulate ethnical integration (the neighbourhood is characterized by a high presence of first generation Southeast Asian migrant families), and to allocate and preserve public areas. Moreover, it suggests that a clean, cared for and pleasant space is more likely to inspire virtuous behaviour than a neglected one.

Although the relationship between political gardening and environmental political theories has not yet been thoroughly studied, the former clearly echoes some elements from the latter. For example, the gardeners can be compared to the eco-warriors of green anarchism (especially the guerrilla gardeners); the stress on organic choices is shared with green consumerism whereas the emphasis on responsibility is typical of the environmental ethics' perspective; the opposition to agribusiness and the support of traditional knowledge systems compare with the goals of neo-global movements; and the focus on place attachment originates from bioregionalism while the primacy of care does so from eco-feminist theory. In general, by adopting the classic "think globally, act locally" slogan of the first modern environmentalist wave, political gardening relies on the belief that "Every act of [. . .] gardening is a local tactic that also addresses a global crisis" (Tracey, 2007, p 28).

In addition to adopting many inspirational values and practices of traditional environmental movements and sustainability theory (Crane et al., 2013), several political gardening projects have gone even further and can easily be considered as post-environmentalist practices performed through "ordinary forms of environmentalism within processes of place-making and local responses to socio-environmental problems in the city" (Milbourne, this book, p. xx). As guerrilla gardener Dick Tracey provocatively wrote when criticising mainstream environmentalism:

> how [did] environmental politics get so earnest and dull? Has there ever been a rallying call more numbing that "sustainability"? Who decided that anyone working on environmental issues must appear grimmer than the consequences involved? If every worthwhile cause gets the dynamic visionaries it deserves, what's with Al Gore?
>
> (Tracey, 2007, pp. 26–27)

In line with the transformation of the political in the post-political age (see Chapter 1 of this book), post-environmentalism has been challenging mainstream environmental politics for the last ten years. Moreover, it has called for the re-politicization of the politics of nature, which, for a long time, had been reduced to a matter of general consensus and hampered by ambitious targets based on supposedly undisputable evidence. The term 'post-environmentalism' was originally coined by Young in 1990, in his book *Post-Environmentalism* (1990).

A few years later, Eder (1996) claimed to be part of a post-environmentalist age characterized by collective mobilization on environmental issues, where ecology is established as a non-controversial collective concern. The term became very popular with the publication of a pamphlet by US consultants Shellenberg and Nordhaus, entitled *The Death of Environmentalism. Global Warming Politics in a Post-Environmental World.* The authors stated that traditional environmental theory and movements are not able to address the current global ecological crisis because of their exclusive interest in technical solutions that weaken ideal aspirations but provide no increment of power (Schellenberger and Nordhaus, 2004). In this context, the main problem is that environmental politics seems to overlook the socio-political causes and effects of environmental issues. A deeper understanding of their implications will necessarily lead to the rejection of a consensus-seeking narrative which aims to guarantee both ecological conservation and economic expansion. According to the authors, environmentalism was thus reduced to a sort of special interest politics and lost its general relevance as a result of the literary interpretation of the objectives of environmental politics, the characterization of environmental issues as local, and the reluctance to form alliances with non-environmentalist groups. This has caused a progressive de-politicization of environmental politics whose constant attempt at broadening the consensus has unavoidably resulted in an increasing disengagement and disaffection. Although the critical analysis by Shellenberg and Nordhaus is insightful, the proposed solution entailing the realization of an environmental modernization blueprint is likely to lead to a further expansion of the ontological distance between humans and non-humans (Latour, 2008). In contrast, within the framework of material politics, post-environmentalism can re-politicize environmental issues. This starts from the recognition that the everyday making and unmaking of the world is a political activity (Featherstone, 2008) which requires the mobilization of the social, environmental, and techno-scientific dimensions all at once (Law, 2004).

While conventional political mechanisms, procedures, institutions, and theories often prove inadequate in dealing with environmental issues, post-environmentalism is able to re-politicize environmental facts by turning them into matters of concern, which is only possible through the formation of assemblages. These assemblages represent "a latent possibility of new politics and movements based on desire and becoming [. . .] ask[ing] us to consider how an alternative world might be assembled. Not by implying a particular content of alterity, whether socialist or otherwise, but through the concern with the *making* of alterity" (McFarlane, 2011, p. 211). Heterogeneous social actors can adopt a plurality of (linguistic and non-linguistic) means to exercise political agency by, for example, opposing resistance or practicing resilience, refusing assigned roles and dissolving or reshaping social formations in the re-creation of nature in the city, and engage in the transformation of urban space via a bodily form of politics (Certomà, 2017). Consequently, negotiations emerge through actual engagements, including recruiting allies into the network and utilizing powerful relationships to maintain them (Stanforth, 2006; Ghose and Pettygrove, 2014).

In the tradition of critical urbanism, assemblage thinking is "concerned with whether and how materialities might make a difference to the way in which poverty and inequalities are produced and experienced [and] how mundane micro-materialities [. . .] change their function through new interaction with assemblages, and have effects in terms of helping to structure and maintain resistance campaigns" (McFarlane, 2011, p. 221).

These interactions are precisely at the core of political gardening, which can thus be regarded as an exemplary expression of post-environmentalism. Political gardening unveils links and creates connections to address problems traditionally falling into distinct spheres of competence (e.g., environmental, social, political, economic, and health problems). It overcomes scales of governance and government, and mobilizes different technologies in order to make non-human things speak and make human beings heard in traditional political assemblies. It thrives on differences in styles, objectives, attitudes, tactics, and traditions in order to reconcile local knowledge with modern global mobility. It calls for a direct engagement with the materiality of daily life, the "stuff of politics" in material semiotic terms, to create alliances between different forms of living beings and non-living things, to negotiate common goals and to mobilize social actors toward their common concerns.

Within post-environmentalism, political gardening initiatives question the meaning of *politics* in several ways, for instance by showing how the environment can become the subject for assemblages to gather around and is continuously reconstituted through material practice in sometimes previously unthinkable configurations (Featherstone, 2008). The material politics-inspired reading of post-environmentalism proposed here is more a practice than a theory, performed in local places by social agents that are not necessarily interested in or knowledgeable about environmental thinking disputes because they would rather adopt a non-representational, non-discursive, materiality-oriented approach to environmental issues. Similarly, political gardening invites social actors to address socio-environmental political issues (such as the scarcity or poor quality of public spaces, the lack of green infrastructure, the need for better human relationships with nature, the urgency of providing marginalized social groups with dedicated spaces for self-improvement, etc.) by directly getting their hands dirty in an effort to create the world they want to live in. This implies a direct and non-mediated commitment to the local places because "you believe the entire city is worth the effort. And because you decided that, rather than wait for the world you want [. . .] to just appear, it was better to start making it yourself" (Tracey, 2007, p 29). Thus, gardeners forge alliances with plants, animals, bacteria, fungi, and so on to contest the shape of the city, to propose alternative planning solutions, and to bring about an alternative understanding of the public space where urban life unfolds. Cities are regarded as laboratories of politics, arenas for political experiments, spaces of rather unpredictable outcomes where heterogeneous actors interact. They are living battlegrounds for environmental issues to be addressed, and, most importantly, for a political gardener, they "are too important to leave to people who don't care" (Tracey, 2007, p. 15).

Notes

1 These effects include the redefinition of planning policies toward a collaborative exercise of collective imagination (Hou and Rios, 2003) for alternative uses of public space (Schmelzkopf, 1995); the provision of public and free health-supporting facilities (Wakefield et al., 2007); the transformation of food systems and the metabolic process in the city by contrasting current trading regimes and food insecurity (Pinkerton and Hopkins, 2009; Tornaghi, 2014); the possibility for marginalized social groups to become visible and active in city life with dedicated spaces for education self-improvement and rights protection (Flachs, 2010); and the re-creation of urban ecosystems and life-cycles (Irvine et al., 1999; Ferris et al., 2011).

2 Such studies include topics such as citizens' direct investment in (self)education (Flachs, 2010; Bendt and Barthel, 2013); the restoration of urban ecosystems (Bendt et al., 2013); the transformation of food production, distribution, and the consumption chain (McMichael, 2012); and support to the underprivileged in the face of economic crisis (Walliser, 2013; Emmett, 2011).

References

Allen, P.M., 1997. Cities and regions as evolutionary complex systems. *Geographical Systems* 4, 103–130.

Armstrong, D., 2000. A survey of community gardens in upstate New York: Implications for health promotion and community development. *Health Place* 6/4, 319–327.

Austin, J.L., 1962. *How to Do Things with Words: The William James Lectures Delivered at Harvard University, 1955*. London: Clarendon Press.

Barron, J., 2016. Community gardening: Cultivating subjectivities, space, and justice. *Local Environment* 22/9, 1142–1158.

Barry, A., 2001. *Political Machines: Governing a Technological Society*. London: The Athlone Press.

Bendt, P., Barthel, S., and Colding, J., 2013. Civic greening and environmental learning in public access community gardens in Berlin. *Landscape and Urban Planning* 109/1, 18–30.

Bonet-Martí, J., 2014. La participació ciutadana en l'urbanisme: potencials i límits. *Institut d'Estudis Regionals I Metropolitans de Barcelona* 57, 63–70.

Butler, J., 1993. *Bodies That Matter: On the Discursive Limits of "Sex"*. London: Routledge.

Certomà, C., and Notteboom, B., 2017. Hybrid planning in a transactive governmentality: Re-reading informal planning practices through Ghent's community gardens. *Planning Theory* 16/1, 51–73.

Certomà, C., and Tornaghi, C., 2015. Political gardening: Transforming cities and political agency. *Local Environment* 20/10, 1123–1131.

Clarke, P., 2010. Incredible edible: How to grow sustainable communities. *Forum* 52/1, 69–76.

Crane, A., Viswanathan, L., and Whitelaw, G., 2013. Sustainability through intervention: A case study of guerrilla gardening in Kingston, Ontario. *Local Environment* 18/1, 71–90.

Colding, J., Barthel, S., Bendt, P., Snep, R., van der Knaap, W., and Ernstson, H., 2013. Urban green commons: Insights on urban common property systems. *Global Environmental Change* 23/5, 1039–1051.

Coordinamento Parco, 2013. *Parco di Via delle Palme*. Available at www.parcodiviadelle palme.org/

Corsin Jimenez, A., 2014. The right to infrastructure: A prototype for open source urbanism. *Environment and Planning D: Society and Space* 32/2, 342–362.

Davies, J., 2011. *Challenging Governance Theory: From Networks to Hegemony.* Bristol: Policy Press.

Del Sesto, M., 2015. Cities, gardening, and urban citizenship: Transforming vacant acres into community resources. *Cities and the Environment* 8/2.

Dobson, A., 2003. *Citizenship and the Environment.* Oxford: Oxford University Press.

Eder, K., 1996. The institutionalisation of environmentalism: Ecological discourse and the second transformation of the public sphere. In S. Lash, B. Szerszynski, and B. Wynne (eds.), *Risk, Environment and Modernity: Toward a New Ecology.* London: Sage Publications.

Emmett, R., 2011. Community gardens, ghetto pastoral, and environmental justice. *Interdisciplinary Studies in Literature and Environment* 18/1, 67–86.

Ernwein, M., 2017. Urban agriculture and the neoliberalization of what? *ACME: An International Journal for Critical Geographies* 16/2, 249–275.

Evans, J., and Karvonen, A., 2010. Living laboratories for sustainability: Exploring the politics and epistemology of urban transition. In H. Bulkeley et al. (eds.), *Cities and Low Carbon Transitions.* London: Routledge, pp. 126–141.

Featherstone, D.J., 2008. *Resistance, Space and Political Identities: The Making of Counter-Global Networks.* Chichester: Wiley-Blackwell.

Ferris, J., Norman, C., and Sempik, J., 2011. People, land and sustainability: Community gardens and the social dimension of sustainable development. *Social Policy and Administration* 35/3, 559–568.

Flachs, A., 2010. Food for thought: The social impact of community gardens in the greater Cleveland area. *Electronic Green Journal* 1/30, 1–9.

Ghose, R., and Pettygrove, M., 2014. Actors and networks in urban community garden development. *Geoforum* 53, 93–103.

Hardman, M., and Larkham, P.J., 2014. *Informal Urban Agriculture: The Secret Lives of Guerrilla Gardeners.* Cham: Springer.

Hinchliffe, S., and Bingham, N., 2008. Securing life: The emerging practices of biosecurity. *Environment and Planning A* 40, 1534–1551.

Hinchliffe, S., and Whatmore, S., 2006. Living cities: Toward a politics of conviviality. *Science as Culture* 15, 123–138.

Holston, J., 1998. Spaces of insurgent citizenship. In L. Sandercock (ed.), *Making the Invisible Visible: A Multicultural Planning History.* Berkeley, CA: University of California Press.

Hou, J., and Rios, M., 2003. Community-driven place making. *Journal of Architectural Education* 57/1, 19–27.

Infobuild, 2013. *Riqualificazione del Giardino delle Palme.* Available at www.infobuild.it/progetti/riqualicazione-del-giardino-delle-palme/ [accessed 8 September 2016].

Ioannou B. et al., 2016. Grassroots movements: Towards cooperative forms of green urban development? In S. Bell, R. Fox-Kämper, N. Keshavarz, M. Benson, S. Caputo, S. Noori, and Voigt, A. (eds.), *Urban Allotment Gardens in Europe.* Abingdon, New York: Routledge.

Irvine, S., Johnson, L., and Peters, K., 1999. Community gardens and sustainable land use planning: A case-study of the Alex Wilson community garden. *Local Environment* 4/1, 33–46.

Kato, Y., Passidomo, C., and Harvey, D., 2014. Political gardening in a post-disaster city: Lessons from New Orleans. *Urban Studies* 51, 1833–1849.

Kurtz, H., 2001. Differentiating multiple meanings of garden and community. *Urban Geography* 22/7, 656–670.

Lanzi, A., 2013. *Anche a Roma Orti Sovversivi, Il Manifesto*, 26.4.2013. Available at https://ilmanifesto.it/anche-a-roma-orti-sovversivi/

Latour, B., 2004. *Politics of Nature: How to Bring the Sciences into Democracy*. Harvard: Harvard University Press.

Latour, B., 2005. *Reassembling the Social*. Oxford: Oxford University Press.

Latour, B., 2008. 'It's development, stupid !' or: How to modernize modernization. In J. Proctor (ed.), *Post-Environmentalism*. Cambridge, MA: MIT Press.

Law, J., 2004. *Enacting Naturecultures: A Note from STS*. Published by the Centre for Science Studies. Lancaster: Lancaster University. Available at www.comp.lancs.ac.uk/sociology/papers/law-enacting-naturecultures.pdf

Marres, N., 2005. No issue, no public: Democratic deficits after the displacement of politics. Unpublished doctoral thesis, Universiteit van Amsterdam, Amsterdam, the Netherlands.

Marres, N., 2012. *Material Participation: Technology, the Environment and Everyday Publics*. New York: Palgrave.

McClintock, N., 2014. Radical, reformist, and garden-variety neoliberal: Coming to terms with urban agriculture's contradictions. *Local Environment* 19/2, 147–171.

McFarlane, C., 2011. Assemblage and critical urbanism. *City* 15/2, 204–224.

McKay, G., 2011. *Radical Gardening*. London: Frances Lincoln Limited.

McMichael, P., 2012. The land grab and corporate food regime restructuring. *The Journal of Peasant Studies* 39, 681–701.

Mitchell, D., 2003. *Right to the City: Social Justice and the Fight for Public Space*. New York: Guilford Press.

Mol, A., and Law, J., 2002. *Complexities*. Durham: Duke University Press.

Nicholls, W., 2009. Place, networks, space: Theorising the geographies of social movements. *Transactions of the Institute of British Geographers* 34/1, 78–93.

OED Online, 2017. *Politics*. Oxford: Oxford University Press.

Parés, M., Marti-Costa, M., and Blanco, I., 2014. Geographies of governance: How place matters in urban regeneration policies. *Urban Studies* 51/15, 3250–3267.

Passatore, L., 2014. Il nuovo lago di Roma: qualità delle acque e rinaturalizzazione dell'area. In *Forum Territoriale Permanente (Ed.) eXSnia: la natura rigenera la città*, Seminar Proceedings, 24 may 2014, Casa del Parco delle Energie, Rome. Available at https://lagoexsnia.files.wordpress.com/2014/07/atti-convegno-exsniala-natura-rigenera-la-cittc3a0.pdf

Perkins, H.A., 2010. Green spaces of self-interest within shared urban governance. *Geography Compass* 4/3, 255–268.

Pinkerton, T., and Hopkins, R., 2009. *Local Food: How to Make It Happen in Your Community*. Cambridge: Green Books.

Pudup, M.B., 2008. It takes a garden: Cultivating citizen-subjects in organized garden projects. *Geoforum* 39/3, 1228–1240.

Purcell, M., 2002. Excavating Lefebvre: The right to the city and its urban politics of the inhabitant. *GeoJournal* 58/2–3, 99–108.

Purcell, M., 2013. Possible worlds: Henri Lefebvre and the right to the city. *Journal of Urban Affairs* 36/1, 141–154.

Quastel, N., 2009. Political ecologies of gentrification. *Urban Geography* 30/7, 694–725.

Reynolds, R., 2014. Disparity despite diversity: Social injustice in New York city's urban agriculture system. *Antipode* 47/1, 240–259.

Rose-Redwood, R., and Glass, M.R., 2014. *Performativity, Politics, and the Production of Social Space*. London: Routledge.

Rosol, M., 2012. Community volunteering as neoliberal strategy? Green space production in Berlin. *Antipode* 44/1, 239–257.

Schellenberger, M., and Nordhaus, T., 2004. *The Death of Environmentalism*. Available at http://gristmill.grist.org/

Schmelzkopf, K., 1995. Urban community gardens as contested space. *Geographical Review* 85, 364–381.

Schmelzkopf, K., 2002. Incommensurability, land use, and the right to space: Community gardens in New York city. *Urban Geography* 23/4, 323–343.

Searle, J., 1969. *Speech Acts: An Essay in the Philosophy of Language*. Cambridge: Cambridge University Press.

Smith, C., and Kurtz, H., 2003. Community gardens and politics of scale in New York city. *Geographical Review* 93/2, 193–212.

Staeheli, L., Mitchell, D., and Gibson, K., 2002. Conflicting rights to the city in New York city's community gardens. *GeoJournal* 58, 197–205.

Stanforth, C., 2006. Using actor-network theory to analyze E-government implementation in developing countries. *Information Technologies and International Development* 3, 35–60.

Tornaghi, C., 2014. Critical geography of urban agriculture. *Progress in Human Geography* 38/4, 551–567.

Tracey, D., 2007. *Guerrilla Gardening: A Manualfesto*. Gabriola Island, BC, Canada: New Society Publishers.

Travaline, K., and Hunold, C., 2010. Urban agriculture and ecological citizenship in Philadelphia. *Local Environment* 15/6, 581–590.

Wakefield, S., Yeudall, F., Taron, C., Reynolds, J., and Skinner, A., 2007. Growing urban health: Community gardening in South-East Toronto. *Health Promotion International* 22/2, 92–101.

Walliser, A., 2013. New urban activisms in Spain: Reclaiming public space in the face of crises. *Policy and Politics* 41/3, 329–350.

Weibel, P., and Latour, B. (eds.), 2005. *Making Things Public: Atmospheres of Democracy*. Karlsruhe: ZKM.

Weisman, E.L., 2009. Cultivating community: The governance of community gardening in Syracuse, NY. Paper presented at 2009 Joint Meeting of AFHVS and ASFS 2009, College Park, PA.

Whatmore, S., 2002. *Hybrid Geography*. London: Sage Publications.

Young, J., 1990. *Post-Environmentalism*. London: Belhaven Press.

Links

Giardinieri Sovversivi Romani, 2018, Available at www.facebook.com/GiardinieriSovversivi/
Nature en Ville, 2018, Available at http://ge.ch/nature/information-nature/nature-en-ville/concours-nature-en-ville

4 Cultivating food as a right to the city

Mark Purcell and Shannon K. Tyman

1. Introduction

There is a rich history of food cultivation in the city. Urban agriculture, community and school gardens, edible landscaping, and guerrilla cultivation of food in parking strips, vacant lots, and other interstitial and unused urban spaces are all longstanding practices that can bring people together, help them define common goals, and engage them in the process of negotiating physical space with their neighbours. This chapter argues that growing food also has the potential to be a more radical intervention in urban life. Specifically, growing food in the city has the potential to challenge dominant regimes that structure how urban space is produced and used. In contemporary cities, that dominant regime is neoliberalism, which values space predominantly for its exchange value, and prioritizes private property rights over other claims. Under neoliberalism, the priorities of the state have been greatly reoriented away from the needs of citizens, inhabitants, and users, and toward the needs of the market.

The act of cultivating urban land often emphasizes and develops social and ecological values rather than market logics. It can generate nodes of solidarity, relations of reciprocity, and networks of self-sufficiency among urban inhabitants. It can emphasize the use value of urban space rather than its exchange value, and it can prioritize the needs of inhabitants over the rights of owners. It can also inspire communities to become active as they engage in the project of producing food for themselves and actively appropriating the space (and other resources) needed to so. This process of becoming active can have important implications for justice, equity, and sustainability. None of these terms has a predefined meaning or practice; each must be defined and pursued in real contexts. Becoming active would open up the possibility of discussion (and even struggle) among inhabitants about what these terms mean in their context, and how they can best go about achieving them.

In this chapter, we understand and articulate the radical potential of food cultivation through the lens of Henri Lefebvre's concept of "the right to the city". Over the past ten years or so, there has been a renewed wave of interest in the idea of the right to the city (Mitchell 2003; UNESCO 2006; Harvey 2008; Marcuse 2009; UN-HABITAT 2010; Mayer 2012; Smith and McQuarrie 2012), but we think few of those who have engaged the idea have appreciated its full political potential. Discussions of the right to the city typically gesture at Lefebvre, but they rarely offer a sustained analysis of what he meant by the idea. We argue that Lefebvre's right to the city is, in its most fully developed form, a declaration by people that they intend to struggle for a radically democratized city beyond both capitalism and the state, a city where inhabitants directly produce and manage urban space for themselves through free activity. We argue that the struggle for the right to the city already exists, incipient but nevertheless real, in the everyday practices of urban inhabitants. In the chapter, we discuss the cultivation of urban land as an example of such emergent practices. We try to *see* these practices, and narrate them, in the hopes that they might grow and spread.

2. Henri Lefebvre[1] and the right to the city

In this section we offer a sustained account of how Lefebvre conceived of the right to the city. To do so, it is important *not* to begin where most do, with his book *The Right to the City* (1968, translated in Lefebvre 1996), which is vague and hard to decipher. Instead, we turn to one of his last works, from 1990, in which he outlines a "new contract of citizenship" (Lefebvre 1990, 2003a). In proposing this contract, Lefebvre is trying to reimagine the relationship between people and the state. The contract proposes several new rights, such as a right to information, to expression, to difference, to *autogestion*, and a right to the city. On its surface, this contract looks like nothing more than an addendum to existing liberal democratic rights guaranteed by the state. It seems only to want to expand existing rights but leave their logic fundamentally unaltered. However, Lefebvre is aiming at something far more revolutionary than that. That is because he is taking his cue here from the young Marx, and especially from "On the Jewish Question" (Marx 1994b). Marx's goal in that piece is to dissolve the relationship between citizens and the state. He imagines a process by which citizens will increasingly take up the work of governing themselves. Through this process, civil society will absorb the state, and the state will wither away. As this process unfolds, "citizens" will be transformed into merely "people" who are no longer subject to the sovereign authority of the state. They would become people who manage their affairs for themselves. Lefebvre shares this vision enthusiastically. It is an idea he articulated most strongly in the 1960s, and it is what his new contract of citizenship is designed to bring about.[2]

To achieve this transformation, the new contract begins by radically deepening and extending existing rights. But Lefebvre does not see rights as liberal-democracy does, as codified *protections* guaranteed by the state. Instead, he imagines rights to be political *claims* that are made through the action of mobilized groups. Rights are not an achievement that comes at the *end* of a struggle, as, for example, when the US Civil Rights movement resulted in the Civil Rights Act of 1964. Rather for Lefebvre, rights come at the beginning. He sees them as *declarations* of an intention to struggle. Rights consist of people voicing their commitment to become active and to move together in a particular direction, toward a particular horizon. Thus Lefebvre does not intend that his new contract and its rights will be enshrined into state law. The contract is instead a way to initiate a generalized political awakening among citizens in which they declare their intention to begin a struggle. Claiming the rights in the new contract is what touches off this awakening. He hopes it will launch a widespread and thoroughgoing mobilization of the population.

> The new political contract I propose will be only a *point of departure* for initiatives, ideas, even interpretations. This is not a dogmatic text. What is important is that this idea of contractual citizenship *gives rise to a renewal of political life*: a movement that has historic roots, roots in revolution, in Marxism, in production and productive labour. But the movement must go beyond ideology so that *new forces enter into action*, come together, and bear down on the established order. This movement would accomplish democratically a project that has been abandoned: the dictatorship of the proletariat. It would lead, without brutality, to the withering away of the state (1990, p. 37, emphasis added, our translation).

But what horizon does Lefebvre imagine this struggle would move toward? Notice in the quote Lefebvre proposes both the dictatorship of the proletariat and the withering away of the state. But he understands these terms differently than they were typically understood in Marxism. Lefebvre does *not* propose that a workers' party should seize the state and use it to achieve specific political ends. He vehemently rejects that option. Rather he imagines, with Marx in "On the Jewish Question", that the majority of society, which he understands to be the proletariat, becomes active and begins to manage their affairs for themselves. This is what he means by a dictatorship of the proletariat. It is for Lefebvre a movement that emerges from below, rather than one imposed from above by a workers' party that has seized the state. As people increasingly govern themselves, he suggests, as they gain experience and confidence at it, they will come to realize they are perfectly capable of managing their own affairs. The realization that self-management is possible spreads throughout society, more and more people begin to govern themselves, and the state becomes increasingly unnecessary, obsolete. It withers away.

This idea of self-management, of people governing themselves, is the meaning of Lefebvre's term *autogestion*. The French word means "self-management", and traditionally it refers to the factory, when workers take control of their workplace and begin to manage it themselves, without the factory owner and his or her hired managers. *Autogestion* is thus a quite radical project: workers reappropriate control of the means of production and thus strike directly at the system of property rights on which the capitalist economy rests. At its root, *autogestion* is a concrete practice of revolutionary struggle for an economy beyond capitalism. Lefebvre accepts this goal entirely. But he also thinks we can go further, that we can extend *autogestion* beyond the economy. He thinks we should struggle for *autogestion* in other arenas of life, like the family, the neighbourhood, the school, the barracks, and so on. And of course *autogestion* can be applied to the relation between citizens and the state as well. In that case it would mean, again recalling.

Marx's (1994b) arguments in "On the Jewish Question", that citizens of the state do not leave their affairs to be managed by state officials, rather they manage their affairs for themselves. As *autogestion* develops among citizens, as they increasingly show themselves capable of governing themselves, state officials will become obsolete, they will be "overcome" in Marx's sense, and the state will wither away. In a parallel way, as producers in the economy demonstrate to themselves that they are capable of managing economic production for themselves, capitalist relations of property and production will also wither away. "Each time a social group . . . refuses to accept passively its conditions of existence, of life, or of survival", he says, "each time such a group forces itself not only to understand but to master its own conditions of existence, autogestion is occurring" (Lefebvre, 2009, p. 135).

Lefebvre wants us to launch the struggle for autogestion, the struggle to remain aware, active, and in charge of our own affairs. This struggle has no end. It is perpetual. The revolution is continuous. Lefebvre imagines us moving toward a horizon, in the direction of autogestion, but we should not expect to arrive at that destination. Lefebvre is not proposing an ideal society that exists at the end of history, and so he is not a utopian in the traditional sense. He is saying that what we must do is to launch a struggle: a struggle *against* property, alienation, and the state, and a struggle *for* autogestion. Certainly this struggle will encounter difficulties. Capitalism and the state have thrown up barriers to autogestion in the past and will continue to do so. But we would insist, with Lefebvre, that we should think of this struggle not primarily as a struggle to destroy; its main activity is not to confront and smash the barriers that constrain us. It is, rather, *to develop our own powers*. The struggle must be to augment our own ability to manage our affairs for ourselves. We must realize the strength and delight that *autogestion* offers. We must put our energies toward building another polity, another economy, and another city. If we do that well, our own powers will grow and spread, and we will create viable new self-managed alternatives. At the same time, the current structures of state and capitalist power will increasingly appear unnecessary, then obsolete, and, ultimately, absurd.[3] The barriers they throw up to *autogestion* are formidable, but the way to overcome them is not so much to struggle *against* them as to struggle *away from* them, and struggle toward the horizon of *autogestion* instead.

3. The right to the city

So that is Lefebvre's right to *autogestion*. But recall that the new contract also calls for the right to the *city*. Thus far we have discussed political and economic relations, but we have said little about space. For Lefebvre, political struggle must necessarily also be spatial struggle as well. "Any revolutionary project today must, if it is to avoid hopeless banality, make the . . . reappropriation of space, into a non-negotiable part of its agenda" (1991, pp. 166–167). "Revolution", he goes on to say,

> was long defined either in terms of the political change at the level of the state or else in terms of the collective or state ownership of the means of production. . . . Today such limited definitions of revolution will no longer

suffice. The transformation of society presupposes a *collective ownership and management of space* founded on the permanent participation of the 'interested parties,' with their multiple, varied and even contradictory interests.

(1991, p. 422, emphasis added)

These interested parties, for Lefebvre, are the inhabitants of space, the people who use and rely on space for their daily survival. In the contemporary city, he argues, the production of space is not managed by inhabitants, by the users of space; it is managed by a relatively few elite corporate and state oligarchs (see especially 2003b). Those elite managers value urban space as a commodity and think of it as private property. This vision reduces the urban space to a single economic function, capital accumulation, and it sees urban inhabitants as merely passive consumers who help fuel that accumulation. The capitalist city segregates those consumers from each other, and it warehouses them in isolated, sterilized spaces Lefebvre calls "habitat".

Lefebvre's overall point here is that control over the city, over the production of its space, has been *alienated* from users (1991, p. 343). Here he draws again on the young Marx (1994a) to argue that urban space should be familiar to users because they inhabit it every day. But in fact it has been alienated, "made strange"[4] to them because it is produced not *by* them but *for* them by others. To counter this alienation, Lefebvre says, users must *reappropriate* the production of urban space, they must make it their own again.[5] They must reverse the process by which urban space is being made strange to them and reclaim the control of space for themselves, for *they* are its proper owners. This idea is quite similar to that of classic *autogestion*, whereby workers reappropriate their factory, its means of production, and the economic value that capitalism has been alienating from them. Similarly here, the inhabitants of urban space reappropriate the production of that space. It is an act of *spatial autogestion*. Inhabitants refuse to accept passively the existing system of spatial production in the city, and they decide to take up the challenge of understanding and mastering that production (Lefebvre 2009, p. 135). In short, they struggle to manage urban space for themselves.

As we saw with *autogestion* more generally, if inhabitants are able to become active, if they accept the challenge of managing urban space and they are able to do so effectively, the current corporate and state managers of space will increasingly become obsolete, no longer necessary, and they will wither away. The regime of private property, of state planning, of urban space valued primarily in terms of its exchange value: all of it withers away. And so for Lefebvre the right to the city is an *extraordinarily* radical proposal. It is "a cry and a demand" (1996, p. 158) by mobilized inhabitants that they intend to initiate a struggle to utterly transform urban life, to make the city entirely their own again.

It is important to reiterate that Lefebvre sees the right to the city, and the new contract more generally, as a *point of departure* for a new political struggle. Again, as with *autogestion*, the right to the city does not imagine a final utopia, a crystal palace of spatial self-management at the end of history. As with his politics more generally, Lefebvre conceives of spatial *autogestion* as a horizon we move toward but will never reach. The right to the city proposes a horizon beyond the contemporary city that is a transformed urban life, another city in which inhabitants themselves produce space in common. This other city is an urban community beyond capitalism and the state, a city that esteems use value over exchange value. It is a society where inhabitants are active participants rather than passive consumers. They struggle to make their activity increasingly free activity, which is the term Marx used to designate activity outside of capitalism, activity that is not labour-for-capital-accumulation. Free activity develops inhabitants' whole selves, their many different potentials as humans (Engels 1996). Spatial *autogestion* reverses the separation and segregation of inhabitants; it draws them together into common spaces where they would encounter each other and engage in meaningful discussions about the city and its future. As these engagements unfold, Lefebvre says, would make clear that users are not a homogeneous group, that they are marked by significant differences, and that they will have to negotiate those differences as they work out together what kind of city they want (Lefebvre 2003b, pp. 117–118; see also Schmid 2012).

Lefebvre argues that the struggle to become active and take up the challenge of spatial *autogestion* cannot be imposed, it must grow and proliferate on its own. It must come to pervade urban society so that it can eventually exercise "dominion" over the old order (1991, p. 348). That dominion must always remain immanent: it cannot be codified by seizing institutions, establishing new hierarchies, imposing new centres of power. The dominion of spatial *autogestion* can never be made permanent. It must be maintained by the active struggle of inhabitants to govern themselves. They must struggle actively and perpetually toward the horizon of spatial *autogestion*.

Lefebvre insists, unequivocally, that this struggle is not some wishful fantasy. Rather the struggle is *already going on now*, in the midst of the contemporary capitalist city. Even though the prevailing condition of inhabitants is often one of alienation and passivity, even though private property and economic competition tend to dominate political discourse, nevertheless there are also innumerable instances, in every city, of inhabitants taking up the struggle for spatial *autogestion*, the struggle for the right to the city as Lefebvre understands it. That struggle is going on here, now, all around us, even if it is often fledgling and overwhelmed by the capitalist city. Lefebvre says that what we must do in this situation is to seek out that struggle, we must learn to *see* it in the midst of the capitalist city, and we must do what we can to help it grow and spread. We could choose to fix our attention on the structures of power that seek to stifle spatial *autogestion*, but for Lefebvre the key is to focus instead on the always-emerging struggle, and to spend our energy cultivating it however we can.[6]

In the remainder of the chapter, we try to follow this method: to seek in contemporary practices of urban agriculture the kinds of desires and struggles among inhabitants that Lefebvre's right to the city imagines. The capitalist city may work to suffocate spatial *autogestion*, to prevent it from growing. But we can, if we choose, seek out and learn to recognize the many struggles for a right to the city. We can narrate them, augment them, and try to help them flourish. In that way, they can continue and strengthen the ongoing struggle to create another city. If that struggle becomes strong enough, it will eventually overcome the capitalist city. The latter will be rendered obsolete, and it will wither away.

4. Two cases of urban gardens in the Global North

Recently there has been a resurgence of interest in practicing, studying, and legitimizing urban agriculture, and so there are many examples we might turn to in hopes of discovering fledgling struggles for a right to the city in the practice of growing food. This chapter focuses its attention on two struggles over urban space: community gardens in New York City and South Central Farm (SCF) in Los Angeles. We do not present these cases as paradigmatic; they are not necessarily more important or more resonant with Lefebvre than other cases. Neither case is particularly new or unknown. What we are trying to do in presenting these cases is to discover spatial *autogestion* in practices of urban agriculture. The chapter does not report original research, and it has not uncovered new findings. Rather it reads the original research of others in order to revisit and represent two well-known cases through the lens of Lefebvre's right to the city. We are trying to flesh out what spatial autogestion would mean in the context of struggles over urban agriculture, what it looks like, what difficulties it encounters, what successes it has had. We hope to augment the struggle for the right to the city by seeking out, learning to recognize, and nurturing, however we can, emerging instances of spatial *autogestion* in the contemporary capitalist city.

4.1 A note on cultivating urban space

Neither the network of community gardens in New York nor South Central Farm are exclusively sites of food production.[7] They also provide access to open and green space in urban areas where such spaces are rare. They afford an opportunity to cultivate non-food plants like flowers and other ornamentals. In contrast to the capitalist logic of property ownership and exchange, urban agriculture engages the complexity of cultural, social, economic, ecological, and spatial aspects of urban land and human labour.

As it is usually practiced, urban agriculture has a distinctly social quality that can catalyse community organization (Staeheli et al. 2002; Lawson 2007; Barraclough 2009; Irazábal and Punja 2009; Shillington 2012). The social coordination and physical labour required to establish and maintain sites of cultivation is immense. Preparing an urban site for planting intimately involves the participants in urban metabolism, it helps them learn about the "circulatory processes that underpin the transformation of nature into essential commodities such as food, energy and potable water" (Gandy 2004, p. 374, quoted in Shillington 2012, p. 104). Soil, for example, must be tested and often remediated. Gardeners often refer to the process of "building" soil, increasing its living matter and nutrient content over the course of many cycles of planting, cultivating, and harvesting. This process can take years to refine and speaks to the long-term nature of the project to cultivate gardens well. This process is starkly different from a capitalist approach to urban land, which conceives of it as property, reduces its value to exchange value, and is only able to imagine a financial return on investment.

People join together into communities of mutual interest in order to understand and manage the complex task of building and maintaining their gardens. This task requires collective effort that typically engenders social relations like cooperation, solidarity, and mutual respect for the space of others, though of course it also highlights differences as well. In most cases, gardeners produce and manage their garden largely outside of the circuits of capitalist accumulation and commodity production. Urban agriculture is therefore often an experiment that tends more toward free activity rather than capitalist labour. Moreover, it has significant potential to work against the alienation of people – from their labour, from other people, from food, from ecological processes, and from urban space – and it very often offers people an opportunity to reappropriate food production, urban ecologies, and urban space. Urban food cultivation is, in short, fertile ground for the development of spatial *autogestion* among urban inhabitants.

4.2 Community gardens in New York

In New York City, a struggle has been underway since at least the 1970s to create and maintain community gardens in the face of pressures to realize profit through commercial development (Ferguson 1999; Staeheli et al. 2002; Smith and Kurtz 2003; Shepard 2009; Marcuse and Morse 2008; Eizenberg 2013). In the 1970s, the City of New York was facing an economic recession and fiscal collapse. It was also receiving an increasing number of properties through default, but it did not have the capacity to manage them effectively. Partly as a result, a group called the Green Guerillas began to take matters into their own hands. They were soon joined by other inhabitant groups, and they set about transforming vacant lots into garden spaces, most of which were managed by the gardeners themselves Green Guerrillas, 2013). This initiative emerged from the activity of inhabitants, who had very little support from City government. As Sara Ferguson observes, "the diverse patchwork of over 800 community gardens that have taken root in New York since the 1970s [was] born not out of government support, but rather its neglect" (1999, p. 83). Participants in this surge of activity had diverse motives. Some considered themselves activists in a movement, engaging in civil disobedience against private property, or struggling against a capitalist economy of endemic crisis. Others were less overtly and consciously political. They saw themselves simply as taking necessary steps to meet the need for food and for green space in the city. Either way, the community garden initiative emerged largely from the activity of the inhabitants themselves. The "genius" of these community gardens, observes one interviewee on the gardens in New York City, is "*the community deciding* to put [empty space] to use" (Staeheli et al. 2002, p. 201, emphasis added). And the initiatives grew and spread, as inhabitants decided to begin producing and managing garden spaces all over the city.

Near the end of the 1970s, the City became increasingly involved in managing community gardens. In 1978 it created the Green Thumb programme, which was a way to regularize and manage the insurgent garden activity. Most of the gardens were illegal initially because the gardeners did not own the land they were cultivating. Green Thumb helped establish leases for the gardens, and it provided limited public resources for their operation. As one might expect, Green Thumb also imposed some controls and conditions on gardeners' activity, trying to manage their energy in a way the City was comfortable with and could control. Green Thumb's governance and funding structure is designed to manage that activity. But at the same time, the gardeners' activity fundamentally shaped Green Thumb. The programme's very existence is evidence of a reactive City: it was searching for a way to respond to the initial activity of inhabitants, who were producing garden spaces for themselves. The gardeners were a new force actively transforming not only the land itself, but the political management of it. Jane Weissman, the former director of Green Thumb, describes this era of New York City as a time when "people were beginning to take control of their own environment" (Brooks and Marten 2005).

Today, Green Thumb still exists and administers the 250-plus community gardens that continue to operate on City-owned land. It offers some useful protection and legitimization to the gardens, and so it allows gardeners to focus more on necessary and everyday tasks. But this protection is by no means iron clad: the leases contain the stipulation that gardens can be removed with 30 days notice (Smith and Kurtz 2003, p. 197), and, historically, long-term leases have been difficult to secure for any garden on land valued over $20,000 (Ferguson 1999, p. 86). Consequently, many gardens have been lost to real estate development over the years. In 1999, for example, under Rudolph Giuliani's administration, and in the midst of a housing crisis, the City put more than 100 community gardens up for auction (Smith and Kurtz 2003, p. 193). Though these were not the first gardens to face eviction, the sheer number of properties for sale attracted widespread attention.

So while Green Thumb has provided some stability to the gardens, it also imposes new limits on gardeners' activity. As a result, the gardens remain very much contested spaces. The perceived limits of Green Thumb have led inhabitants to create their own organizations to defend and manage the gardens. The New York City Community Garden Coalition (NYCCGC), for example, was founded in 1996 "to promote the preservation, creation and empowerment of community gardens through education, advocacy and grassroots organizing" (NYCCGC 2013). More Gardens! was formed in 1999 to collectively organize the defence of the gardens. It is "a group of community people, community gardeners, and environmental and social justice activists who promote the development and preservation of community gardens as well as the cultivation of fallow land in NYC" (More Gardens! 2013). These inhabitant groups have defended individual gardens, procured needed resources for gardeners, and helped inhabitants learn about urban land use politics. Such activism operates both within formal institutions and outside them, through tactics like information campaigns and public demonstrations. It also provides opportunities to link the politics of gardening to other political causes such as land use development and environmentalism (Smith and Kurtz 2003).

For many activists the struggle to save neighbourhood gardens is part of a broader struggle to control their neighbourhoods and communities. As one interviewee put it,

> there are people, young kids, who through nothing more than gardening, are now becoming community activists, are standing up for a right. Because of the fact that if it's a community garden today, it's your apartment tomorrow. It's your school the next day. So it all interrelates. And as a community, you must take a stand. You must take a stand for the control of how your community is run.
>
> (Staeheli et al. 2002, p. 200)

As the above quote suggests, for many involved in the struggle, it is about more than saving a specific garden; it is also about a struggle to increase the control inhabitants have over the production of urban space.

Interviews conducted by both Smith and Kurtz (2003) and Staeheli et al. (2002) reveal that the gardens had a very different meaning for City officials than they did for gardeners and many inhabitants. The former saw community gardens as an interim use for the land until development could occur, whereas the latter saw the gardens as long-term investments in their neighbourhoods that they hoped would return social, cultural, economic, and ecological benefits.[8] The struggle to save the gardens was also a struggle about the meaning of urban space and how it should be used. The City maintained that financial, market-driven values should take priority. Urban inhabitants, through more traditional political organizing and through the act of cultivating land, insisted on a different way to understand the urban landscape, one rooted in inhabitance and use value, and they struggled to make this meaning manifest in the space of the city.

In New York, this struggle over space also involved an important dimension of racial inequity. In their interviews, Staeheli *et al.* found a common sentiment expressed by NYC gardeners that land use policies under Giuliani's administration promoted the interests of white, middle-class New York, rather than the public interest more generally. Moreover, gardeners felt the policies implicitly (and sometimes more explicitly) excluded some communities, especially those in non-white neighbourhoods that had been historically ignored by the City (2002, p. 200). They felt the City had much less desire to defend gardens in such non-white neighbourhoods. Interviewees thus remind us that the politics that structure the relations between the City and inhabitants, not to mention the relations among inhabitants themselves, are shaped by race. The same could be said, of course, for a politics of gender and sexuality. Political battles over land, as the New York experience suggests, are defined by historical and place-specific social conflict. It is sometimes through the process of struggle that inhabitants come to realize inequities, understand those inequities as unjust, and begin to develop responses to change the situation. In this manner, struggles for racial justice, for equitable access to urban resources, including decision-making power, can arise from and be bound up with struggles for the right to the city.

The case of community gardens in New York City thus offers us a sustained look at a concrete example of the desire for spatial *autogestion* that forms the core of Lefebvre's idea of the right to the city. In New York, many urban inhabitants are engaging in a long struggle to produce and manage for themselves spaces that are useful and meaningful to them. While the intensity of this activity has certainly waxed and waned, the spaces created in the initial wave of gardening, even after they came under the Green Thumb programme, have continued to serve as the impetus for wider political activation among inhabitants.

4.3 South Central Farm

The South Central Los Angeles Community Garden, known as South Central Farm (SCF), was a community garden that for over a decade provided almost six hectares of gardening space for more than 350 predominantly Latino families (Lawson 2007; *The garden* 2008; Barraclough 2009; Irazábal and Punja 2009; Foust 2011). Begun in 1994, SCF was conceived of as a peace offering from the City of Los Angeles to non-white communities in the wake of the 1992 beating of Rodney King, the subsequent outrage at the acquittal of the officers responsible, and the violent urban uprising that followed (Lawson 2007). SCF was initially proposed by the Los Angeles Regional Food Bank's Urban Gardening Programme. They hoped the farm would improve community health by providing better access to fresh, nutritious produce. The City of Los Angeles, through its Harbour Department, happened to own land adjacent to the food bank in a highly industrial area. It supported the project by issuing a revocable permit for the Food Bank to use the land as a community garden.

The land in question, at South Alameda and East 41st Street, had a contested history long before 1994. The City had originally seized it in the mid-1980s under eminent domain, intending to build a trash incinerator. The incinerator, known as the Los Angeles City Energy Recovery Project (LANCER), was opposed stridently by the local residents. The area's population at the time was predominantly low income and African-American. It had some of the highest toxic pollution rates in Los Angeles County and the fewest number of public parks. This situation prompted claims of environmental injustice (Barraclough 2009, p. 183). Organized protests against LANCER by Concerned Citizens of South Central Los Angeles (CCSCLA) eventually forced the City to abandon the plan for the incinerator in 1987. At that time, the permit to use the land was issued to the Food Bank. However, the fate of the land remained uncertain. After LANCER was abandoned, the City faced legal pressure from the original owners, who wanted to buy it back. Despite a protracted legal struggle, the City was never ordered to sell the land (Philpott 2006). In 1994, SCF began operating, growing food and providing a gathering space for local inhabitants.

The legal struggles over the land continued, and they became more acute after 2002, when construction was completed on the Alameda Corridor, a rail-cargo expressway from Los Angeles to the Ports of Los Angeles and Long Beach, which greatly increased the land value of the SCF property (Philpott 2006). Eventually the City decided to sell the land to one of the previous owners. It entered into negotiations with Ralph Horowitz and in 2003 they reached an agreement for Horowitz to buy back the land for just over $5 million (Lawson 2007). The SCF farmers were not invited to participate in the negotiations, even though many of them had worked the land for almost ten years.

As was the case in New York, the City of Los Angeles thought of SCF as a temporary land use, one that should properly give way when the market value of the land rebounded. The lease given to the food bank was never permanent – it could be revoked with 30 days' notice. Most of the gardeners, by contrast, saw SCF as a long-term economic, ecological, and cultural investment. They did not just plant annual crops; they also planted fruit and nut trees that take years to reach their full harvest potential. They did the considerable initial work of clearing the land, removing what one farmer described as "barrels and barrels of concrete and glass and metals" from the site, and preparing it for cultivation (Hoffman and McCracken 2006). Through their considerable labour, the farmers thus reclaimed what had been vacant land, and they transformed it into a space that played a vibrant role in the life of local inhabitants (Lawson 2007; *The garden* 2008). In addition, the farmers and other area inhabitants participated actively in governing the garden. As one of the farmers put it:

> The original process [of giving the land to the farmers] was done through the Food Bank. Then in 1994 the Food Bank said, "We can't afford to hire a person [to manage the project]", and they were gonna close this place down. But the community came together and told the Food Bank, "Let us run it". We have an internal government. We have a general assembly and representatives from different sections. It's based on the Mexican ejido system, the communal-land structure, where they have a junta and all of the general assembly come for decision-making and all that.
>
> (Hoffman and Petit 2006)

When the land was sold back to Horowitz in 2003, this governance structure had been in place and running effectively for nine years. Residents had been practicing, for some time, the political habits and skills they subsequently used to defend the property as a working farm. They formed South Central Farmers Feeding Families (SCFFF), a group described by Foust (2011, p. 351) as a "self-governing advocacy organization". It was SCFFF, not the Los Angeles Regional Food Bank, that led the struggle to defend the farm against Horowitz's attempts to remove them. The farmer-activists insisted that the space was serving the needs of more than 350 families who had, by their gardening practice, demonstrated their commitment to the land and their ability to manage and care for it effectively. Moreover, through the cultivation and managing of the farm, inhabitants had become active and developed their ability to govern themselves and manage the land. They also came to "articulate an alternate vision of community ownership based on self-determination and years of labour spent improving the land, both at the farm itself and in the larger industrial districts of South Central Los Angeles" (Barraclough 2009, p. 180). For the farmers, the value of the land lay not in its market value as property, but in its productive capacity, in the plants that they cultivated, in the physical structures they had built, and in the shared sense of achievement and well-being the work had engendered. SCF was also an important source of nutrition in a low-income neighbourhood where affordable fresh produce was difficult to find. For the participants, the land was made valuable through their use and stewardship of it.

In their effort to defend the farm, activists engaged in letter writing campaigns, marches, protests, and civil disobedience, including an occupation of the land. They were even able to secure the help of the Annenberg Foundation to raise $16 million, which they used to make an offer to buy the land from Horowitz. He refused their offer at the last minute, citing what he perceived to be harassment and character attacks on the part of those defending the farm (*The garden*, 2008)

As in New York, racial inequity also played a role in the politics of South Central Farm. Barraclough's research (2009) finds a perception among non-whites in Los Angeles that City land use policies systematically benefit white neighbourhoods more than non-white ones. This observation closely mirrors that of the interviewees cited by Staeheli et al. (2002) and Rosenthal (2003) who identified a similar perceived racial bias in New York. Moreover, it is important to note that the community of gardeners in South Central was itself marked by difference, and that difference had a strong racial component. South Central Farmers Feeding Families represented a primarily Latino constituency, and it sought to defend the land as a working farm (LeGreco and Leonard 2011). Concerned Citizens of South Central Los Angeles, who had previously led the fight against LANCER, was a predominantly African-American group that was less concerned with the farm per se and more concerned with other sorts of community benefits, like jobs and a soccer field (Irazábal and Punja 2009). This difference should be understood in context: South Central was historically an African-American area of the city that over the last decades has become primarily Latino. This internal community conflict exemplifies the real challenges embedded in direct communal organization of space. It is easy to assume that inhabitants are undifferentiated and will entirely agree on how to produce space. But Lefebvre always insisted that that inhabitants and their interests are plural and marked by difference. When they become active and encounter each other in the course of their struggle to manage space for themselves, they will be made aware of, and will need to negotiate, the differences that exist among them (see especially Lefebvre 2003b, p. 38ff). This case in particular shows us that actual land use decisions involve a multitude of perspectives that must be accounted for. Doing this work of negotiating inevitable disputes together amidst difference is part of the continual work of defining and enacting (and re-enacting) the right to the city.

In the end, the effort to save SCF failed. It was bulldozed on July 5, 2006. At the time, it was an actively tended, ecologically-diverse, working farm in the midst of an industrial warehouse district. It was also the largest urban community garden in the United States (Irazábal and Punja 2009, p. 2). Various plans for the property have been proposed since the bulldozing, but none have been implemented and the land remains vacant. Nevertheless, seven years later, the farmers remain active. Some of them farm a smaller community garden space that was offered by the city. Others began a Community Supported Agriculture operation. They operate a cooperative farm outside the City and deliver boxes of organic produce to members weekly. South Central Farmers Feeding Families remains an active organization that advocates for access to healthy food and more democratic food systems. Though the South Central Farm itself is no longer operating, it did serve as something like what Lefebvre would call a point of departure, as the beginning of a larger political awakening among many inhabitants of South Central Los Angeles who now struggle for greater control over the production of food and of urban space in their local area. Even those inhabitants in CCSCLA, who favoured uses of the site other than farming, were active and engaged in the politics of land use in their local area. They advocated other kinds of uses that inhabitants also desired. Though the farm is gone, the local inhabitants are not the same inhabitants they were before. Through the acts of cultivating an agriculturally productive space, struggling to produce space in their local area, and learning more about how and why to govern themselves, they realized that they were more capable than they imagined. Many have carried this feeling on into other activities and struggles.

If Horowitz had accepted the $16 million offer to buy the land, farmers would have been able to continue their experiment. Instead, the farmers have had to redirect their activity, to seek other creative ways to cultivate land, grow food, and manage urban space for themselves. To be sure, this activation among inhabitants is not total. Some have remained active in the struggle over the Alameda property, others have put their energy into other pursuits, still others have given up and become passive. We only want to highlight the fact that, even in a case where a flourishing community garden was lost to the regime of private property and exchange value, there remains a glow of spatial *autogestion*, a persistent desire among many inhabitants to produce, cultivate and manage urban space for themselves, together, on their own terms.

Conclusion: cultivating a renewal of political life

Cultivating land in the city is an extremely complex process that is always made up of many different actors, agendas, and desires. In our account of the two cases, we have focused on those elements that resonate with Lefebvre's idea of the right to the city, and in particular the way inhabitants became active and began producing and managing urban space for themselves. This activation was certainly partial: not every inhabitant became active. And inhabitants' spatial *autogestion* was also partial. They did not create a city in which urban space was entirely produced and managed by inhabitants, without the state and capitalism. Yet in both cases, inhabitants *did* become active, and they did achieve a considerable measure of spatial *autogestion*. We highlight this element of these stories in order to gain practice doing what Lefebvre's method would have us do: seek out and learn to recognize the fledgling struggle for spatial *autogestion* that is already taking place in the contemporary city.

In both cases, inhabitants actively produced and managed urban space for themselves. They cleared and planted the gardens, they managed the subsequent cultivation and distribution of food, and they undertook the task of governing the everyday affairs of the gardens as well. This activity required them to understand and act effectively in many areas: the dynamics of soil, water, and nutrients; the particular needs and strengths of different plants; the complex process of community governance; the equally complex process of city permits and regulations; strategies of collective political action; how to write successful grant applications; and so on. Gardeners drew on their existing abilities in these areas, and they often also had to develop new abilities very quickly.

The state tended to be more of a hindrance than a help in this process. But from Lefebvre's perspective, the state's action is not what matters. For Lefebvre, the right to the city is not a struggle to build better government institutions, institutions that in this case would create and manage spaces for urban agriculture. In the short term, the state can assist urban farmers in their work (e.g. more secure leases, zoning changes, public grants) or it can hinder them (e.g. selling the land and bulldozing the garden), but in the long term it should not produce and manage the gardens on behalf of inhabitants. Inhabitants should. The right to the city is, for Lefebvre, a struggle by inhabitants to become such capable managers of urban space that the state becomes obsolete.

In addition to inhabitants becoming active as cultivators of land, they also became active as agents in a wider city politics. They were especially engaged in issues of land use, zoning, and economic development. Their struggles to defend and cultivate their gardens produced mobilized groups of inhabitants with high levels of solidarity. The struggle for the farms intensified the degree to which inhabitants considered themselves capable and legitimate participants in urban politics. As they gained experience, they became increasingly aware of their power, of what they were capable of – as farmers, as community members, and as political activists. For some, and at times, it was the kind of political awakening Lefebvre envisions.

Through the act of producing and managing space for themselves, inhabitants developed their own understanding of urban space and their own way of valuing it. Against the dominant idea that reduces urban space to private property and thinks of it as a commodity whose exchange value must be maximized, inhabitants developed a much more complex idea. In addition to the exchange value it might hold, inhabitants added a whole range of use values as well. For them urban space is an ecosystem where soil, water, sun, plants, insects, animals, and people interact in a dynamic system. It is a green space where human and non-human organisms intermingle. It is a space for culture, for preserving and exchanging seeds, crops, cultivation practices, and recipes. It is an open space that provides inhabitants relief from the densely built city. It is a site and a stake of struggle between owners and inhabitants. And it is a shared space where community members encounter each other.

This last element of urban space, as a site of encounter, bears particular attention. For Lefebvre the capitalist city segregates inhabitants and separates them from each other in an effort to produce passive consumers instead of active citizens. So it is essential for inhabitants to overcome segregation by creating spaces of encounter, spaces in which they can come together to interact, to play, to share experiences, and to work out how they want to live together in the city. Lefebvre refers to such spaces rather vaguely, as "the street" (1970, p. 18ff). Urban gardeners offer a much more vibrant understanding of what such spaces might be like. In addition to all the other functions they serve, urban gardens are a centre, a gathering space, a hub around which inhabitants' common project is constructed. It is a place they can gather to make decisions about the production and management of space. In his research on New York's community gardens, Shepard observes that

> without such spaces where citizens can meet, share a moment, where citizens can act together, democratic publics dwindle. Without a space where people share conversations, differences and pleasures, it is difficult to imagine citizens linking their needs to political participation.
>
> (2009, p. 293)

In both New York and Los Angeles, community gardens serve as key spaces of encounter. They are places that encourage (and force) people not only to gather, but also to become aware of and negotiate differences and govern their shared space.

One axis of the differences, of course, is race. Communities of colour are often marginalized by a city's dominant land use regime, and so the struggle of inhabitants for greater control over land use can intermesh with the struggle of those communities against their marginalization. But as we saw, race can also be an axis of difference *within* a community of inhabitants. In Lefebvre's idea of the right to the city, the community of inhabitants tends to get reduced to the proletariat. These cases demonstrate that inhabitants are far more than just their class identity. So it is crucial to be attentive to how communities of inhabitants, as they become active and advocate for their interests, become aware of racial and other differences, how they narrate them, and what kinds of practices they use to engage with those differences.

Certainly community gardens are not the only urban spaces where spatial *autogestion* is occurring. Even if they are a particularly compelling example, Lefebvre would caution us to look not only for the obvious cases like SCF where people are struggling to preserve a space they have produced. He would tell us to also seek out the more mundane, less visible spaces where inhabitants are producing spaces for themselves. Such spaces exist, both spectacular and quotidian, even in the contemporary capitalist city. They were there in US cities wading through the flotsam of the crash of 2008. They were there in Southern Europe in 2011, in cities where harsh austerity policies intensify the burden on inhabitants. And they are there in the mega-cities of the Global South, where urbanization and proletarianization is taking place at an almost unimaginable speed. The right to the city, *Lefebvre's* right to the city, calls us to seek out these spaces, narrate them, learn their contours, discover what inhabitants are doing, what they are capable of, what spaces they are producing. The project must be to help these acts of spatial *autogestion* to grow and spread, to proliferate so that they become the norm, so that they might constitute, one day, the world's primary motor of urbanization.

Notes

1 Like other French intellectuals on the left in the late 1960s and 1970s (e.g. Cornelius Castoriadis, Guy Debord, Gilles Deleuze, Felix Guattari, and Michel Foucault), Lefebvre was deeply critical of both the totalitarian state socialism that came to exist in the Soviet Union, Eastern Europe, and China, and the state-managed capitalism the reigned in France at the time. As a result of this experience, the work of all these thinkers (we would argue) is just as much a reaction against the *state* and bureaucratic domination as it is against capitalism.

2 Lefebvre's eager return to "On the Jewish Question" is most pronounced in his 1964 work "The Withering Away of the State" (see Lefebvre 2009), and was no doubt spurred by his years-long struggle against Stalinism and, more generally, state socialism. But Marx's text continued to strongly influence his thought and politics, and it is still very much a presence even in the 1990 piece.

3 Lefebvre (2009, pp. 194–195) writes: "But how can we limit and suppress the ownership of space? Perhaps by remembering the writings of Marx and Engels: one day, which will indeed come, the private ownership of land, nature and its resources, will seem as absurd, as odious, as ridiculous as the possession of one human by another".

4 Marx's term *Entfremdung* literally means "a making strange (or foreign or alien)". We typically translate this as "alienation".

5 This is the literal meaning of the word reappropriate. The Latin means *re* = again, *a* = to, and *proprio* = one's own.

6 On this point see Gibson-Graham (1996) who make a compelling argument that resonates quite strongly with Lefebvre's.

7 It is worth noting, though, that growing food provides unique opportunities in the context of urban space that speak to issues of sustainability. Unlike growing non-food plants, urban food cultivation can increase food security and sovereignty, and it can support community health by providing fresh and healthy food and mitigating malnutrition and hunger. This is particularly important in low-income neighbourhoods termed "food deserts" that lack sufficient access to a grocery store (USDA 2013, Grow NYC 2010). In many communities, the fruits, vegetables, herbs, and roots cultivated on urban land are used as medicine in addition to food (Shillington 2012; Barraclough 2009). Such medicinal plants play an especially important role for community members without access to affordable healthcare. The role urban agriculture can play in securing bodily health is thus a reminder of the literal truth of Lefebvre's insistence that inhabitants rely on urban space for their daily survival.

8 According to a 2011 report by Grow NYC (see Gittleman et al. 2011), approximately 80% of community gardens in New York City grow food. A citizen-science survey revealed that 67 gardens inventoried in 2010 grew around (87,690 pounds) of food, worth approximately $214,060USD (Gittleman et al., 2012, p. 6).

References

Attoh, K., 2011. What Kind of Right Is the Right to the City? *Progress in Human Geography*, 35(5), 669–685.

Barraclough, L., 2009. Land Use Policy and Relational Racialization in Los Angeles. *The Professional Geographer*, 61(2), 164–186.

Brooks, S. and Marten, G., 2005. Green Guerillas: Revitalizing Urban Neigborhoods with Community Gardens (New York City, USA) [online]. The Eco Tipping Points Project. Available from: www.ecotippingpoints.org/our-stories/indepth/usa-new-york-community-garden-urban-renewal.html [Accessed 14 June 2013].

Eizenberg, E., 2013. *From the Ground Up: Community Gardens in New York City and the Politics of Spatial Transformation*. Burlington, VT, Ashgate Publishing Company.

Engels, F., 1996 [1845]. The Great Towns. *The City Reader*. Edited by R. LeGates and F. Stout. New York, Routledge, pp. 46–55.

Ferguson, S., 1999. A Brief History of Grassroots Gardening on the Lower East Side. *Avant Gardening: Ecological Struggle in the City and the World*. Edited by P.L. Wilson and B. Weinberg. Brooklyn, NY, Autonomedia, pp. 80–90.

Foust, C., 2011. Considering the Prospects of Immediate Resistance in Food Politics: Reflections on the Garden. *Environmental Communication*, 5(3), 350–355.

The garden, 2008. Film. Directed by Scott Hamilton Kennedy. Los Angeles, CA, Black Valley Films.

Gandy, M., 2004. Rethinking Urban Metabolism: Water, Space and the Modern City. *City*, 8(3), 363–379.

Gibson-Graham, J.K., 1996. *The End of Capitalism (As We Knew It)*. Cabridge, MA, Blackwell.

Gittleman, M., Jordan, K., and Brelsford, E., 2012. Using Citizen Science to Quantify Community Garden Crop Yields [online]. *Cities and the Environment*, 5(1), 1–12. Available at: http://digitalcommons.lmu.edu/cgi/viewcontent.cgi?article=1095&context=cate [Accessed 14 June 2013].

Gittleman, M., Librizzi, L., Stone, E., 2011. *Community Garden Survey, New York City: Results 2009/2010* [online].

GrowNYC and GreenThumb. Available at: https://www.grownyc.org/blog/community-gardens-survey-released [Accessed May 18, 2018].

Green Guerrillas, 2013. Our History [online]. Available at: www.greenguerillas.org [Accessed June 14, 2013].

Harvey, D., 2008. The Right to the City. *New Left Review*, 53(September–October), 23–40.

Hoffman, J. and McCracken, A., 2006. Voices from the South Central Community Garden. *Clamor*, 36(Spring). Available at: http://clamormagazine.org/issues/36/webfeature.php [Accessed 14 June 2013].

Hoffman, J. and Petit, C., 2006. 14 Acres: Conversations across Chasms in South Central Los Angeles [online]. *Clamor*, 36(Spring). Available at: http://clamormagazine.org/issues/36/people.php [Accessed 14 June 2013].

Irazábal, C. and Punja, A., 2009. Cultivating Just Planning and Legal Institutions: A Critical Assessment of the South Central Farm Struggle in Los Angeles. *Journal of Urban Affairs*, 31(1), 1–23.

Lawson, L., 2007. The South Central Farm: Dilemmas in Practicing the Public. *Cultural Geographies*, 14, 611–616.

Lefebvre, H., 1968. *Le Droit à la Ville*. Paris, Anthropos.

Lefebvre, H., 1990. Du pacte social au contrat de citoyennete. *Du contrat de citoyennete*. Editions Syllepse et Editions Periscope. Paris, Groupe de Navarrenx, pp. 15–37.

Lefebvre, H., 1991 [1974]. *The Production of Space*. Cambridge, MA, Blackwell.

Lefebvre, H., 1996. *Writings on Cities*. Cambridge, MA, Blackwell.

Lefebvre, H., 2003a [1990]. From the Social Pact to the Contract of Citizenship. *Henri Lefebvre: Key Writings*. Edited by S. Elden, E. Lebas, and E. Kofman. New York, Continuum, pp. 238–254.

Lefebvre, H., 2003b [1970]. *The Urban Revolution*. Minneapolis, MN, University of Minnesota Press.

Lefebvre, H., 2009. *State, Space, World: Selected Essays*. Minneapolis, MN, University of Minnesota Press.

LeGreco, M. and Leonard, D., 2011. Building Sustainable Community-Based Food Programs: Cautionary Tales from the Garden. *Environmental Communication*, 5(3), 356–362.

Marcuse, F. and Morse, J., 2008. Saving Community Gardens in NYC: Land Trusts and Organizing [online]. *Race, Poverty & the Environment: Who Owns Our Cities?*, 15(1). Available at: http://urbanhabitat.org/node/1827 [Accessed 14 June 2013].

Marcuse, P., 2009. From Critical Urban Theory to the Right to the City. *City*, 13(2–3), 185–197.

Marx, K., 1994a [1844]. Economic and Philosophic Manscripts. *Karl Marx: Selected Writings*. Edited by L. Simon. Translated by L. Easton and K. Guddat. Indianapolis, Hackett.

Marx, K., 1994b [1844]. On the Jewish Question. *Karl Marx: Selected Writings*. Edited by L. Simon. Indianapolis, Hackett, pp. 1–26.

Mayer, M., 2012. The "Right to the City" in Urban Social Movements. *Cities for People, Not for Profit*. Edited by N. Brenner, P. Marcuse, and M. Mayer. New York, Routledge, pp. 63–85.

Mitchell, D., 2003. *Right to the City: Social Justice and the Fight for Public Space*. New York, Guilford Press.

More Gardens!, 2013. Available at: www.moregardens.org/ [Accessed 14 June 2013].

New York City Community Garden Coalition, 2013. Available at: http://nyccgc.org/ [Accessed 14 June 2013].

Philpott, T., 2006. Neoliberalism at the Garden Gate [online]. *Counterpunch*. Available at: www.counterpunch.org/2006/03/16/neoliberalism-at-the-garden-gate/ [Accessed 14 June 2013].

Rosenthal, C., 2003. New York City's Community Gardens: Follow Up. *The Drama Review*, 47(1), 8–9.

Schmid, C., 2012. Henri Lefebvre, the Right to the City, and the New Metropolitan Mainstream. *Cities for People, Not for Profit*. Edited by N. Brenner, P. Marcuse, and M. Mayer. New York, Routledge, pp. 42–62.

Shepard, B., 2009. Community Gardens, Convivial Spaces, and the Seeds of a Radical Democratic Counterpublic. *Democracy, States, and the Struggle for Global Justice*. Edited by H. Gautney, O. Dahbour, A. Dawson, and N. Smith. London, Routlege, pp. 273–295.

Shillington, L., 2012. Right to Food, Right to the City: Household Urban Agriculture, and Socionatural Metabolism in Managua, Nicaragua. *Geoforum*, 44(2013), 103–111.

Smith, C. and Kurtz, H., 2003. Community Gardens and Politics of Scale in New York City. *Geographical Review*, 93(2): 193–212.

Smith, M.P. and McQuarrie, M., Eds., 2012. *Remaking Urban Citizenship: Organizations, Institutions, and the Right to the City*. New Brunswick, NJ, Transactions.

Staeheli, L.A., Mitchell, D., and Gibson, K., 2002. Conflicting Rights to the City in New York's Community Gardens. *Geo Journal*, 58, 197–205.

UNESCO, 2006. *International Public Debates: Urban Policies and the Right to the City*. Paris, UNESCO.

UN-HABITAT, 2010. *The Right to the City: Bridging the Urban Divide*. World Urban Forum, Rio de Janeiro, United Nations.

United States Department of Agriculture (USDA), 2013. Food desserts [online]. USDA. Available at: http://apps.ams.usda.gov/fooddeserts/foodDeserts.aspx [Accessed 14 June 2013].

5 Public-access community gardens

A new form of urban commons? Imagining new socio-ecological futures in an urban gardening project in Cologne, Germany

Alexander Follmann and Valérie Viehoff

1. Introduction

In the summer of 2011 local media reported that in Cologne a "green smartmob" of more than 170 people had gathered on a vacant plot south of the city centre.[1] Sneaking through the fence and embellishing the brownfield site with marigolds, sunflowers, pumpkins, and palm trees, they staked their claims to more political involvement of local residents in the future of this site, which had lain barren for years. This unauthorized greening of an urban brownfield site sounds like a typical act of "guerilla gardening" – rebellious, subversive and immanently political.

"Community garden", on the contrary, whiffs of tame and conservative staidness. Yet, within a few months, the gardeners had founded a community garden on the 8,000 m² of wasteland,[2] were holding regular meetings, and had set up a legal body called *Kölner NeuLand*.[3] Despite the landowning North-Rhine Westphalia property management and development department (BLB) initially being highly suspicious of the group's motives, the gardeners of *NeuLand* commenced growing vegetables, fruits, and flowers in transportable planting boxes in March 2012. After covering the (probably) contaminated ground with specialist webbing materials (obtained from discarded scaffolding covers) and a thick layer of red sand (obtained from tennis clay courts) they set out to realize their dream of a new urban common, of a "public-access community garden" (Bendt et al. 2013).

This chapter argues that urban gardening has the potential to be explicitly political, if it strives for an ecologically and socially more sustainable, just, and fair, potentially even radically different city. Tracing the development of *Kölner NeuLand* from a green flash mop of guerrilla gardening to an established public-access community garden with individual (private) planting boxes, we investigate the "political" in this project with a particular focus on its experiments in "urban commoning" and, we analyse the practicalities and everyday challenges, as well as the utopian and transformative potential of creating, cultivating, and maintaining an "public-access community garden and common". In particular, the chapter focuses (1) on the role of this public-access community garden in relation to urban land access struggles, mediated by and instrumentalized through the spatiality of the garden and (2) the forms of "the Political" manifested and negotiated in and through this gardening project. Situated within a wider right to the city discourse, grounded mainly in the work of Lefebvre, in this chapter "the Political" in urban gardening is predominantly understood to lie in its attempts to place the (social) production of space back into the hands of the citizens: First, this refers to new forms of political participation and engagement outside of existing formal participatory models in urban planning and, second, it also refers to new ways of getting involved in shaping the physical and material form of urban space through the medium of gardening (Lefebvre 1991; also Harderer 2017).

Following a brief review of urban gardening literature, focusing on urban gardens as actually existing commons, the case study will be presented and situated within the specific urban planning history of Cologne. The chapter concludes with a discussion of the potential lessons to be drawn from this experiment in urban communing, outlining the pitfalls and inspirations it might provide for other projects fighting for greater urban justice. This chapter is grounded in empirical research (i.e. participant observation, interviews, media analysis) and presents the results of a continuous dialogue between the authors – with Alexander Follmann, as member of the gardening project representing the inside view, and Valerie Viehoff contributing the critical perspective of an external investigator.

2. Urban gardens as actually existing commons in the neoliberal city

Urban gardening has been interpreted as a form of protest against neoliberal urbanization or even explicitly as a political movement (e.g. Certoma 2011; McKay 2011; Quastel 2009; Schmelzkopf 2002; Staeheli et al. 2002), while others have shown how community gardens are being co-opted to actually advance neoliberal urbanization, for instance, as a strategy of outsourcing previously publicly provided services (see: Rosol 2006, 2010, 2012; Pudup 2008; Quastel 2009). While praised by some as being subversive, conducive for creating a fairer and greener society, and helpful in promoting community adhesion, urban gardening has also been attacked for fostering individualism and sustaining the status quo of capitalism. Especially those gardening projects that focus on food production, maintenance of green space, or beautification of neighbourhoods, have been severely criticized for fostering neoliberal agendas, often despite their best intentions to the contrary (McClintock 2014; Rosol 2012). Pudup (2008, p. 1229), for instance, sees gardening projects in San Francisco very critically as "spaces of neoliberal governmentality". By engaging in various forms of cushioning the adverse effects of austerity measures these projects contribute to diluting social conflict, obviating more radical forms of social protest, individualizing responsibility for citizens' well-being, and, hence, advancing neoliberal governmentalities. In her nuanced discussion of community gardens' potential for resistance to neoliberalism, Jennifer Barron points out that gardening projects could potentially also enforce "neoliberal subjectivities", if their focus lies on food production and overcoming hunger based on the assumption that the source of the problem is "consumers' inability to procure sufficient food" (Barron 2016, p. 6).

This dualistic view on the transformative and radical potential of urban gardening practices has recently been critically reflected (Ernwein 2017; Kumnig et al. 2017; McClintock 2014; Ghose and Pettygrove 2014, Tornaghi 2014).[4] Kumnig et al. propose that urban gardening and agriculture projects are necessarily contradictory and inconsistent in their struggles for a socially and ecologically more just and sustainable urban future, because they operate within and against a neoliberal system that is neither coherent nor static. Rina Ghose and Margaret Pettygrove also suggest that community gardens can "simultaneously contest and reinforce local neoliberal policies" (Ghose and Pettygrove 2014, p. 1092). And Nathan McClintock opines that urban agriculture is "not simply radical or neoliberal, but both, operating at multiple scales" (2014, p. 145) since urban agriculture and gardening projects operate within the "contradictory processes of capitalism, [which] both create opportunities for urban agriculture and impose obstacles to its expansion" (McClintock 2014, p. 157).

In addition to its complex interweaving with the neoliberal city, the phenomenon of urban gardening often stands in an unclear position with regards to the dichotomous concepts of public and private space. While in some cases the installation of community gardens in public green spaces could be interpreted as a (partial) privatization and occupation of public space by certain social groups (Sondermann 2017, also Ernwein 2017) in other cases the creation of new gardening projects opens up previously inaccessible public or private spaces (e.g. Crossan et al. 2016). In this context, community gardens have been interpreted as experiments in, and testing grounds for, new forms of commons, providing practical examples of "actually existing commoning" (Eizenberg 2012). Framed as urban commons they might provide new alternatives on a theoretical level for thinking about urban futures and for developing practical solutions for achieving greater social justice (see among others Barron 2016; Colding et al. 2013; Colding and Barthel 2013; Follmann and Viehoff 2015; Kumnig et al. 2017; Linn 1999; McClintock 2014; Müller 2011, 2012a, 2012b; Viehoff and Follmann 2017; Tornaghi 2012, 2014).

Although the idea that commons might provide alternatives to and an escape from the oft proclaimed false dichotomy between either the dominant capitalist world system based on private property or a system of state-dirigisme managing all public assets is not new, it was initially predominantly discussed by economists and political scientists.[5] According to Michael Hardt and Antonio Negri, the way that the conflict between the private and the public and the "equally pernicious political alternative between capitalism and socialism" is often pitched, is not only simplistic, it also neglects the fact that both are "regimes of property that exclude the common" (Hardt and Negri 2009, p. ix). Yet, it is exactly the *instituting of the common* that they intend, because commons have the potential to cut "diagonally across these false alternatives – neither private nor public, neither capitalist nor socialist" and to provide opportunities to open "new space for politics" (Hardt and Negri 2009, p. ix). Instituting the commons as a valid political, social, and economic alternative has also been the intention of a series of publications of the critical thinktank Heinrich-Böll-Stiftung[6] (see: Helfrich and Heinrich-Böll-Stiftung 2009, 2012; Heinrich-Böll-Stiftung 2009, 2010). The idea that commons do not necessarily result in the "tragedy of the commons" (Hardin 1968) and instead provide a – sometimes the only – feasible solution for the management of many common-pool resources stands also at the heart of Elinor Ostrom's Nobel Prize–winning work (e.g. Ostrom 1990).

Not just activists, but also critical social scientists have recently discovered the value of commons and discussed them as an important tool in the fight against neoliberal urbanism. For example, David Harvey highlights that "[t]he role of the commons in city formation and in urban politics is only now being clearly acknowledged and worked upon, both theoretically and in the world of radical practice" (Harvey 2012, p. 88); and Paul Chatterton explains "the quest for greater spatial justice [. . .] can be sharpened and deepened further through the use of the 'common' as both a political imaginary and vocabulary, and also as a material aspiration and organizing tool" (Chatterton 2010, p. 626). Linking Edward Soja's recent work on spatial justice, especially the claim that spatial justice concerns "greater control over how the spaces in which we live are socially produced" (Soja 2010, p. 7) with literature on the commons, Chatterton concludes that claims for spatial justice can only "be fully realized if they are embedded in a deep desire to (re)build the urban common" (Chatterton 2010, p. 626).

Chatterton outlines three areas of potential of the urban common aiding in the fight for greater urban justice of academics and activists: First, urban commons provide us with a new perspective to understand the city itself as "the ultimate contemporary common" and the site of "resistance and struggle and articulations of alternatives" (Chatterton 2010, p. 627). Second, through its "rich encounters and activities", urban life also provides an exemplary setting for people to exchange ideas, share resources, etc. (see Hardt and Negri 2009, p. 250) and thereby de-commodify urban life. Third, urban commons open up "new political imaginaries", to "control and imagine governance in new ways" (Chatterton 2010, p. 627). Understanding the city as an urban common also means addressing the perpetual threats to which it is being exposed, ranging from the degradation and banalization of the "culturally creative common" of the city through "excessive abuse" (Harvey 2011, p. 103) to the destruction of the "city as a social political and liveable commons" through capitalist urbanization (Harvey 2012, p. 80). Urban commons, although continuously being produced through the social practice of "commoning" are "just as continuously being enclosed and appropriated by capital in its commodified and monetary form" (Harvey 2011, p. 105).

Against the background of "actually existing neoliberalism", Eizenberg proclaims that actually existing commons have "multiple modalities, mechanisms of development and 'diverse socio-political effects' (Brenner and Theodore 2002, p. 353)" (Eizenberg 2012, p. 765).

> Actually existing commons are live relics of the ideal of the commons; they are never complete and perfect and may even have components that

contradict the ideal type. Nevertheless, even in the face of pervasive neoliberal ideology and practices, 'alternatives do exist' and they pave the road to new politics and another possible world (De Angelis 2003, p. 2).

(Eizenberg 2012, p. 765)

While adopting Eizenberg's understanding of community gardens as "another manifestation of actually existing urban commons" and "a paradigmatic example of counter-hegemonic spaces" (2012, p. 765), we propose that her account of a transition from gardening to activism is not applicable one-to-one to newer, politically motivated gardening projects such as *NeuLand* in Cologne. Due to the recent media hype and the burgeoning body of academic publications on urban gardening in general, and on recent gardening projects in Germany in particular, it may be assumed that any more recent projects are aware of the opportunities that community gardens provide to intervene in urban politics. The question we will critically engage with is whether these new gardening activities are intentionally designed to demonstrate that commons are a liveable alternative to the current dominant form of neoliberal urbanism and whether they are purposefully utilized for a general fight for a *right to the city*, i.e. the gardeners' right to be involved in the shaping of their city and raising a voice in the struggles about the redevelopment of centrally-located high-value land.

3. Urban gardening in Germany

The phenomenon of urban agriculture has, of course, existed for a long time, in German cities. However, new forms of urban gardening like public-access community gardens – as opposed to traditional allotment gardens (in German *Kleingärten* or *Schrebergärten*) – are a relatively recent phenomenon in Germany. They have seen an explosive development in the last decade and are expected to further increase in the future. Overall, public-access community gardens share some features with allotment gardens, but they differ considerably in terms of their organizational structure (Fox-Kämper et al. 2017). In particular, they are open to the public at all times – like a public park – and "formal obstacles for immediate participation by the public are absent to low" (Bendt et al. 2013, p. 19).

The existing about 1 million allotment gardens in Germany are a clearly defined form of urban land use, namely as gardens for the purpose of non-commercial gardening (specifically for self-subsistence), for leisure and recreational activities and located within a compound with shared facilities. They are formally organized[7] with strict rules (minimum 30% of the surface for production of food), socially enforced norms regarding "proper" gardening, an expectation of long-term commitment and regular attendance, and an entry hurdle in form of an average takeover premium of 1,900€ to be paid to the previous plot holder for facilities installed (Appel et al. 2011, p. 54).

Allotments in Germany are hence generally not perceived as counter-hegemonic spaces, but rather, as spaces of escapism from modern (urban) life and political engagement. German allotments contrast with the openness and temporality of new forms of urban gardening, which are characterized by a higher degree of openness, inviting participants to participate and contribute to their design (Müller 2012b).

In Germany, the most prevalent and probably best known community gardens are the intercultural gardens, first introduced in Göttingen in 1995 (Müller 2002; Appel et al. 2011).[8] Berlin has been a traditional stronghold of urban gardening in Germany (cf. Gröning 2000; Rosol 2006; Appel et al. 2011; Meyer-Renschhausen 2011) and is today one of the pioneer cities in Germany with regards to new forms of community gardens with *Prinzessinnengärten* in Berlin receiving by far the most extensive media coverage. In 2017, more than 620 community and intercultural gardens existed in Germany (Anstiftung 2017).

This recent proliferation of urban gardening projects in Germany – following similar developments in other parts of the world with a certain delay – has not only created a media hype followed by a growing public interest, but it has also inspired a burgeoning body of academic publications (e.g. Bendt et al. 2013; Kumnig et al. 2017; Fox-Kämper et al. 2017; Follmann and Viehoff 2015; Müller 2011, 2012a, 2012b; Rosol 2005, 2006, 2010, 2012). In line with the discussion of urban gardens worldwide, German projects have been discussed as sources of "social capital" and empowerment and as spaces of (cultural) diversity, intercultural engagement, progressive gender politics or learning and knowledge exchange and community building in general (Meyer-Renschhausen 2002; Müller 2002). They have attracted interest as an instrument (or a problem) in urban and regional planning, for instance, as interim use of vacant plots in shrinking cities or to improve the image of a neighbourhood (Appel et al. 2011; Eißner and Heydenreich 2004; Rosol 2005). From a critical perspective, German community or urban gardens have also been interpreted as sites where conflicts between public and private land use become evident, where the battle for a right to the city or for urban justice might be fought out implicitly or explicitly (e.g. Halder et al. 2011; Werner 2011). Most recently, they have been reviewed in the context of the neoliberal city (see Follmann and Viehoff 2015, Kumnig et al. 2017, Rosol 2012).

The community gardens that have emerged across Germany in the last few years show different engagements with the idea of commons. In intercultural gardens, each family is generally responsible for their own plot. At *Prinzessinnengärten*, volunteers are welcome to help during open gardening hours; however, the garden's products are sold in the café. In other projects like *Allmende-Kontor*[9] gardeners have their individual planting containers whilst sharing common infrastructure and equipment. In contrast, *NeuLand* stood out for being intended as a *common in every respect*. Therefore, the gardeners put strong emphasis on the garden as an urban common with only common planting boxes and no individual seed beds. However, ever since its first season in 2012, the *NeuLand* gardeners have had intensive debates on the purity of their garden as a common and finally decided to allow individual planting boxes from 2015 onwards. In the following, we will trace these transformations within the garden starting with an analysis of the history of the site, which needs to be understood in order to grasp the political motivation of the gardeners, and outline the genesis of *NeuLand*.

4. NeuLand – a new urban common in Cologne

4.1 History of the site

Separated from the dense and relatively affluent residential quarters of Cologne's *Südstadt* (South City) by a railway line, *NeuLand* is located in a neighbourhood that used to be dominated by various industrial uses, including the city's wholesale market (to be relocated by 2023). To the south, predominantly affluent residential areas with detached houses dominate in Bayenthal and Marienburg (see Figure 5.1). The South of Cologne has substantially changed over the last 15 years, especially since the construction of new high-end office and residential water-front developments in *Rheinauhafen*, a former dockyard on the river Rhine in the 1990s.

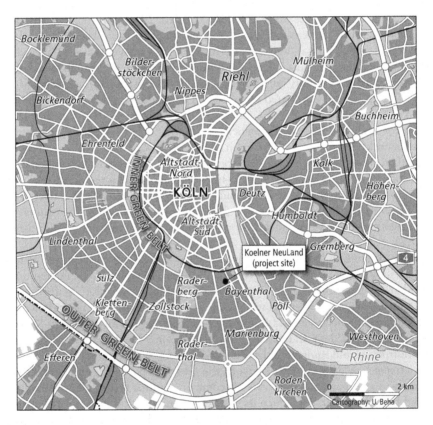

Figure 5.1 The location of *Kölner NeuLand* in Cologne

Source: cartography U. Beha

Today's garden is located on an industrial brownfield site. After the closure of a local brewery, a developer had bought the land for a large-scale housing and retail development. However, these plans fell through and in 2008 the constructing of a new engineering campus for the Cologne *Fachhochschule* (polytechnic) was envisaged on the site. Without acquiring final approval for the plan, the BLB spent more than €88 million on the acquisition of land in south Cologne (see Figure 5.2), including the former brewery site. The acquisitions were put through different subsidiary companies of BAUWENS, a building developer with strong local networks, and then sold on to the BLB, resulting in BAUWENS making almost €25 million profit.[10] Paul Bauwens-Adenauer, one of the managing directors of BAUWENS and grandson of the former German chancellor Konrad Adenauer, is also president of Cologne's Chamber of Industry and Commerce and chairman of a local business society (*Unternehmer für die Region Köln e.V.*). In 2007, it had been this local business society that had commissioned a new urban master plan for Cologne outlining the urban development priorities for the next two decades. This new master plan included the proposal of relocating the engineering department of the Cologne's *Fachhochschule* to a new campus on the former brewery site, even though this idea[11] collided with the city's long-term strategic plans for this area, which envisioned a continuous green belt of accessible public space (see Figure 5.1).[12] In July 2011, the federal state government, holding the ultimate responsibility for schools and universities, rejected the plans for the new campus of the *Fachhochschule*. The irregularities around these land speculations – which later were also subject to a legal court case and investigation by a fact-finding commission of the state parliament (Parlamentarischer Untersuchungsausschuss des Landtags NRW) – could be considered as the spark that caused local protest, initiated a "green smartmob" and finally lead to the creation of *NeuLand*.

4.2 Genesis of NeuLand

From the onset, the creation of *NeuLand* served the dual purpose of drawing attention to the ongoing land speculation and to demonstrate alternative (temporary) uses of the vacant plot. To pursue these two ambitions, the activist-gardeners soon formalized their activities by registering a charitable society, *Kölner NeuLand e.V.*[13] They were granted a temporary concession to use the site by the landowning BLB, on condition of a deposit of €20,000 and the gardeners' promise to vacate the land whenever necessary. In March 2012, the gardeners arrived onsite with their first transportable planting boxes, made from wooden pallets. The foundation of the garden was financially supported by various sources, including *Stiftungsgemeinschaft anstiftung & ertomis*, and *KlimaKreis Köln*, a foundation supporting innovative projects for climate protection and sustainable resource use. The *KlimaKreis Köln* grant initially provided up to €189,000 to be matched either in cash (donations) or in-kind (through volunteer work). At the end of the funding period, only 160.000 € of the grant had been spent, mostly on staff salaries (one full-time and four part-time), but

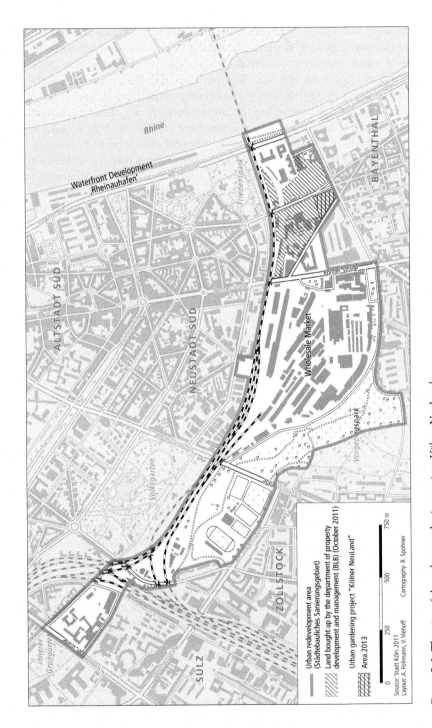

Figure 5.2 The site of the urban gardening project *Kölner NeuLand*

Source: own figure based on Stadt Köln 2011, cartography R. Spohner

also on the installation of infrastructure (e.g. water and electricity connections, mobile toilets) and the purchase of four containers used as lockable gardening sheds and a garden kitchen.

4.3 Characterization of NeuLand – initial motives and motivations

The initial trigger for creating *NeuLand* was not the intrinsic desire to garden, but rather the growing anger about the perceived powerlessness of local residents in the face of a coalition of interest between private and public developers. The gardeners of *NeuLand* used the medium of the garden as a tool to voice their claims for a greener, more sustainable and socially and economically just city. In doing so, they "deliberately play with the urban space" (Werner 2011, p. 58). Inspired by other urban gardening projects, the *NeuLand* gardeners promoted their project very effectively via their homepage, via different social media, and through an active engagement with local and national media.

New gardeners joining the project at a later stage, however only knew the site as a "garden already in the making" or through a range of other activities, including barbecues, beekeeping workshops, a "food exchange station", etc. These *second generation* gardeners are often not aware of, or interested in, the history of the site or the original political motivations. For example, when Frank, a rose lover in his mid-70s, joined the garden in 2012, his love for roses seemed strangely out of place.[14] However, over time, Frank became increasingly involved, participated in the management and development of the garden, and in spring 2013 coordinated his first workshop. Nevertheless, Frank remains a gardener, not an activist. Political gardening remains alien to him. Yet, by contributing their time and knowledge to *NeuLand*'s creative common of shared knowledge and skills, the rose lover and other non-political gardeners are participating in the evolution of the garden as a common (see Eizenberg 2012).

Although gardeners are free to pursue their own interests, the garden charity's main objective remains the intervention in the urban development process within and beyond the existing modes of public participation. Therefore, the *NeuLand* gardeners are active members of a larger citizens' network,[15] actively participate in the public participation process of the urban redevelopment area Parkstadt SÜD,[16] are involved in the Cologne's Food Policy Council (*Ernährungsrat Köln und Umgebung*, founded March 2016), and take part in different other local and regional initiatives.

4.4 Challenges for urban commons – NeuLand's transformation 2012–2017

Whilst *NeuLand* is still a relatively recent urban gardening project, some (future) challenges and issues are already observable. The gardening project has gone through a transformation of its understandings and practices towards the garden as an urban common. We argue that some of the challenges and transformations actually stem from the (political) agenda of the project to be an "actually existing urban common" (in the making), others might be superimposed on the project by the dynamic urban restructuring in south Cologne.

According to Eizenberg (2012, p. 765), *actually existing commons* are "live relics of the ideal of the commons", which "are never complete and perfect and may even have components that contradict the ideal type". This implies that *NeuLand* is, and might remain, an *unperfected common* in the making for a long time. Additionally, some of the challenges *NeuLand* is facing might be analysed as a result of the dominant neoliberal practices of both private and public actors adversely affecting and eventually destroying commons (Hardt and Negri 2004; Eizenberg 2012; Harvey 2012). Finally, some of the challenges might be traced back to the confusion "over the relationship between the commons and the supposed evils of enclosure" described by Harvey (2012, p. 70). Harvey argues in this respect that "some sort of enclosure is often the best way to preserve certain kinds of valued commons" (2012, p. 70) and that local autonomy – in other words self-determination – "is actually a demand for some kind of enclosure" (2012, p. 71) in a positive sense.

Against the backdrop of these debates we will focus on two major challenges *NeuLand* is facing with respect to its nature as a *new urban common in the making*: 1) Communicating *NeuLand* as an open and inclusive urban, and 2) *NeuLand* as an enclosure.

1) Communicating NeuLand as an open and inclusive urban common

The *NeuLand* community arose out of a politically motivated green flashmob, which later employed a professional PR-campaign to promote the garden with three journalists onboard. Starting in the second season in spring 2013, *NeuLand* had already more than 1,500 fans on Facebook. These numbers keep rising and in July 2017 *NeuLand* had more than 4,500 likes. Despite some attempts to activate people from the neighbourhood through flyers and posters as well as regular reports in local newspapers, even radio and TV, the key means of communication has been the internet. The second form of advertising for the project was via a snowballing system of word-of-mouth, as gardeners introduced the project to their friends and colleagues. The numbers of people participating during the open gardening hours and attending workshops, presentations, and garden festivals remains uncounted.

In the first three gardening seasons (2012–2014), *NeuLand* comprised of a community of about 40–50 regular gardeners – usually more at a start of the season and fewer by the end of the year. As a result, a core-group of committed gardeners often worked at their limits, cared for the common planting boxes and kept the garden running beyond the direct gardening work (organizing workshops, etc.). Regarding their level of responsibility and involvement, the gardeners could be tiered into five groups: (1) the paid members of staff (one full-time and four part-time jobs), (2) the elected members of the steering committee of the charitable association[17] (three people, including part-time staff), (3) the members of the charitable association 'Kölner NeuLand e.V.' (15 people),

(4) a "quorum" regularly attending the weekly meetings to discuss the everyday business and future perspectives of the project (about 30 to 40 people), and (5) those who are solely involved in various levels of practical gardening without any further involvement in the management of the project.

Strategic decisions about the garden, its organization, management, and future, for instance, were all open to discussion at weekly public meetings and the steering committee members strived to avoid creating hierarchical structures or taking unilateral decisions. Yet, the contrast between paid-work and volunteer work – with fluid boundaries – created tensions within the group. In retrospective, the substantial amount of financial support by *KlimaKreis Köln* created complex internal governance structures and might have discouraged people from joining on a more regular basis.

Another point of contention was whether the "purity" of the common was tainted by its dependency on external sponsoring, in particular the grant from *KlimaKreis Köln*. Is it sustainable to use these funds to cover the expenses for utility bills (electricity, water, sewage, etc.), PR-campaigns, and public events, knowing that this large-scale sponsoring will run out one day? The majority of gardeners at the weekly meetings agreed that the funding presented a unique opportunity and that it would neither restrict the autonomy of the project, nor "taint" the purity of the common despite the source of the funds being *RheinEnergy*, an energy provider. Addressing disagreements over the distribution of the funds and the potential conflicts arising between personal interests and the interests of the common have, nonetheless, been challenging.

Most challenging was, however, the day-to-day work in the garden, which had continuously grown to about 400 planting boxes in 2014. Especially in the heat of the summer of 2014, several adverse factors combined, when the number of active gardeners was dropping and the school holidays prevented some of the remaining gardeners from attending regularly. Watering rotas were not adhered to, resulting in many parched planting boxes. These experiences and the fact that the KlimaKreis funding was coming to an end, resulted in a change of mind and a growing support for the introduction of individual planting boxes in private hands (Viehoff and Follmann 2017).

Initially, *NeuLand* showed a much stronger emphasis on the garden as a *common* than in most other projects. Despite the fact that it might potentially alienate certain groups of potential gardeners, individual planting boxes were not allowed in order to protect the "pure" nature of the garden as a true common. However, after the disastrous experience of the drought in the summer of 2014, the gardeners sought advice from other gardening projects at the annual Urban Gardening Camp Germany and eventually called in an extraordinary meeting to decide on the option of individual (private) planting boxes. A majority of the members voted for the introduction of a dual system (for more details on the internal debate see Viehoff and Follmann 2017). This new dual system is based on the principle that every gardener is allowed to lease a maximum of two private planting boxes per year, under the condition that they also take responsibility for an equal number of common boxes.

2) NeuLand as an enclosure

Since any common needs a group of commoners, who care for the common – a community (De Angelis 2007) – some form of enclosure could be regarded as a (pre)condition of a common. The management of a common based on a resource with limited and rivalling character may require the exclusion of outsiders, who are not part of the community. However, the core question then is – as Elenor Ostrom (1990) had succinctly pointed out – how can the community implement rules which protect the urban common from misuse by *outsiders*, whilst also encouraging those *outsiders* to become commoners? This is a dilemma which an open-access community garden like NeuLand inevitably faces. Theft of vegetables/fruits and vandalism emerge here as the main problems.

Even though the garden is permanently accessible to the public, vandalism had not been a big issue in the first years of NeuLand. However, over time vandalism has increased, spurring repeated calls for locking the garden after dark. Yet – and although on one occasion the police had to be involved – the majority of gardeners are still upholding their believe in an open public space and the garden remains open around the clock. Theft of vegetables/fruits remains a recurring problem and has even resulted in frustration of some gardeners, who have ended the lease of their individual boxes.

The question of enclosure also applies to the second pillar of NeuLand's identity as a common: its creative common or free exchange of knowledge and skills. Currently, any workshops organized by gardeners for other gardeners and "outsiders" alike, are free and the instructors receive no salary. Conversely, sharing collective knowledge with outsiders is considered an acceptable way to generate funds. For instance, members usually charge small fees for talks held outside the garden and the project's photographers sell their pictures to the media. Although no formal rules exist, usually a certain amount of these revenues is donated to the project.

These examples underline Harvey's argument that it is acceptable or even necessary for community gardens to sell some of their production (e.g. produce or knowledge) and thus generate funds for upkeep (Harvey 2012), while simultaneously highlighting Eizenberg's conclusion that community gardens might always remain a *common in-the-making* and never achieve the ideal form of the commons.

The common knowledge generated within the community of the gardeners "is both a collective resource for protecting the commons and a mechanism that defines, shapes and produces the commons" (Eizenberg 2012, p. 778). Whether gardeners and other commoners around the world – not just in New York – have morphed into activists trying to protect their commons and gardens, or whether they have started from the perspective of *activist* or *political gardeners*, the hope of the NeuLand project is that being exposed to this experiment with commoning even less political NeuLand gardeners of the second generation (people like Frank, who initially consider themselves simply as gardeners, not political activists) will make this transition, should the garden be threatened one day.

To recognize community gardens as positive enclosures to protect the *common in-the-making* helps us to better understand this transformation of gardeners into activists. These second-generation gardeners may become aware citizens developing critical knowledge and skills in order to "outsmart" the neoliberal city for the protection of their common (Eizenberg 2012, p. 778). This is anything but atypical for an enclosure, because an "[e]nclosure is a temporary political means to pursue a common political end" (Harvey 2012, p. 79).

Finally, the organizational structure of the project as a charitable organization has initially also deliberately designed as an enclosure. A small group of seven members, who submitted the initial project concept, justified their desire to limit membership access to the charitable organization with a need to keep the community of decision-makers small as to not risk diluting the political agenda and the concept of the garden as an urban common. Only once their project outline had been accepted and funding been secured, was the organization opened and new members welcomed. Yet, although membership of the charitable organization *Kölner NeuLand e.V.* is open to everyone, applications are only permissible under the condition that the terms and conditions set by the founders are accepted, in particular the character of the garden as a common – based on the sharing of land and knowledge. While offering open-access to everybody who is interested in the project of creating a new urban common, the project initiators seem wary of a larger community managing the common. Hence, the *urban common in-the-making* has been initially protected via various deliberately designed forms of enclosures. Today, everyone interested is welcome to become a member of the charitable organization.

However, it seems that the project's concept is alien to many first-time visitors, creating a certain barrier to engagement with the project. This barrier protects the common, because only people who actively engage with the idea of the common and find it appropriate for the garden get involved. Yet, one could argue that it also limits the potential for engaging with a wider and more inclusive public.

5. Claiming the right to the city through actually existing urban commons

We have argued that the establishment of the *NeuLand* community garden could be interpreted as an example of an *actually existing urban common in-the-making*. The project uses the creative and space-(re)making practice of gardening as a unifying vehicle to bring together people from a variety of backgrounds. Therefore, the practice of gardening – which has indeed been both a social and a productive common adventure – has established a new claim to the *city* through a rediscovery and appropriation of a neglected brownfield site. Through their day-to-day gardening and incremental space-making, the gardeners have shaped their neighbourhood "more and more after their own particular needs and hearts' desire" (Harvey 2012, p. 24). In the Lefebvrian sense, what has been established by the gardeners is space – a common urban space made up of the oeuvre of the gardeners' work (Lefebvre 1991).

What emerges to be new is the way in which gardening and the community garden as collective action have been explicitly and intentionally instrumentalized by the *NeuLand* pioneers to claim their right to the city. Whereas urban gardens on once-derelict lands in New York and elsewhere have often become political issues only retrospectively, the creation of *NeuLand* has been a political issue right from the beginning. Thus, *NeuLand* could be interpreted as a new generation of urban gardening initiatives. The garden is used as a tool to make people aware of the negative effects of real estate speculation and of the interconnectedness and dependencies between private interests and state agencies (here at the federal state level).

Clearly, the previous real estate speculation and the profits already realized in some of the transactions will continue to be a heavy burden on the future of the site. The entanglement of politics and business interests, especially the role of the developer Bauwens-Adenauer playing philanthropic benefactor of the city while being head of the Cologne Chamber of Commerce and Industry, one of the financiers of the master plan and founder of the *Kölner Grün Stiftung*, shows once more that it is a "small political and economic elite who are in a position to shape the city more and more after their own particular needs and hearts' desire" (Harvey 2012, p. 24). By creating an actually existing urban common, *NeuLand* rebels against this "capitalist urbanization", which "tends to destroy the city as a social, political and liveable commons" (Harvey 2012, p. 80).

As a result, the relationship between *NeuLand* and the city administration (non-elected) and local politicians (elected part of city management) is complex. While some policy makers have sporadically visited *NeuLand's* events, municipal support for the project has been sparse. Interviews with some of the garden founders suggest that they are being perceived as an unpredictable new actor in an already complex urban setting. To the chagrin of the city authorities, this new actor is not just suggesting the creation of an urban common, but is already creating facts. The dynamic of the urban gardening project and the ensued creation of a new citizens' movement demanding more public consultation and participation in the early stages of the planning process has to a certain degree challenged the city.

We argue, therefore, that politically motivated urban gardening projects like *NeuLand* are deliberately designed as urban commons in order to tease out the protective interest of the (gardening) community, which has created the common in the first place. The initiators of *NeuLand* knew about the collective power of gardening projects around the world and wanted to activate these forces by utilizing the garden as a political tool to engage in the remodelling of the new quarter of the city. Rather than just vocally protesting against the continuous neoliberalization of urban policy and urban space (e.g. Brenner and Theodore 2002a, 2002b, 2005) and arguing against privatization and other new forms of urban governance (see, e.g. Peck and Tickell 2002; Jessop 2002; Mayer 1996), the gardeners have created an actually existing urban common and a counter-hegemonic space as a showpiece of citizen engagement. Thus, by creating and managing the garden as an actually existing common, the gardeners challenge the city to renounce the neoliberal logic that seems to invariably drive the redevelopment of south Cologne. The garden therefore is a claim for a right to more "productive" urban green space and more direct citizen involvement in the remaking of the city.

Yet, some have cautioned that projects claiming such rights to the city, which are driven largely by a (young and well educated) urban middle class risk diluting Lefebvre's original intention of mobilizing those most marginalized and disadvantaged by existing urban policies, to claim their rights to the city (Holm 2011; Mayer 2009). Holm warns that without making a clear reference to the social question the call for "the right to the city" might end up as "lifestyle-revolts" of the middle class (Holm 2011, p. 97).

We argue that *NeuLand* has shown a hybrid character with regard to these debates. While the key aims of the garden project, which included protest against land speculation and to engage in and campaign for an earlier, more comprehensive, and opener citizen participation in urban planning processes, are laudable, a more detailed analysis also shows that the gardeners' involvement stemmed from a range of different motivations, ranging from altruistic ideals of creating a green and sustainable city to more NIMBY-syndrome affiliated feelings against the building of a new judicial centre in this neighbourhood. Similarly, while the gardeners were obviously interested in urban and political questions and strived to disseminate information and to engage citizen in political and public participation through workshops on a range of topics (e.g. gentrification, plans for the extension of Cologne's green belt, co-housing concepts), there could maybe have been more reflection on how citizens' openness and capability for political participation might be shaped by their social capital – or lack thereof.

Undoubtedly, the gardener-activists have significantly contributed to forcing the city of Cologne to provide more opportunities for local residents to be informed and express their opinions, i.e. through a "participatory process" on the Parkstadt SÜD. Yet, in retrospective the gardeners' disillusioned conclusion is that the final outcome of this remains disappointingly void of any of the constructive interventions made by *NeuLand* and other groups over the course of the "participatory process". The plans for the Parkstadt SÜD might now be compatible with creating a continuous green belt, *NeuLand* itself might have been promised a more permanent site within the new development, but whether overall the gardening project has advanced "the right to the city" or made urban panning in Cologne more democratic remains difficult to assess.

Conclusion

With their request "cities for people, not for profit" Brenner et al. (2009) emphasize "the urgent political priority of constructing cities that correspond to human social needs rather than to the capitalist imperative of profit making". Harvey similarly argues that the right to the city falls increasingly "into the hands of private or quasi-private interests" (Harvey 2012, p. 23). Following the understanding of urban gardening projects to represent actually existing urban commons (Eizenberg 2012), we have demonstrated that the recent proliferation of urban gardening initiatives in Germany includes, among others, politically motivated community gardens, which emphasize the creation of urban commons in order to create powerful "counter-hegemonic spaces" (Eizenberg 2012) to claim their right to the city. In doing so, they use the urban common as a tool to rebel against "hypercommodificated urban spaces" and the "propaganda of market fundamentalism" (Brenner et al. 2009, pp. 180–181).

Born out of the residents' feeling of powerlessness, when relying only on existing democratic institutions and mechanisms of public participation, *NeuLand* was founded to raise awareness and to re-politicize discussions about and germinate opposition to the neoliberal logic of urbanization in Cologne. Although not using direct references to Lefebvre's right to the city (Lefebvre 1996a, 1996b), the gardening project is effectively evoking his work in spirit when protesting against land speculation and the amalgamation of the public and the private and when promoting the creation of a socially and environmentally just city. However, like other social movements, community gardening is under threat of being co-opted by the neoliberal agenda of those in power (Brenner et al. 2009, p. 180). As Attoh injects, it remains a difficult question, whether the claim to "a collective right for gardeners [. . .] to a piece of land" is to be viewed as "a right against democratically elected officials that see such a use of land as inappropriate" (2011, p. 677).

Considering the paradoxical and contradictory processes of which neoliberalism is composed (Harvey 2005; Brenner and Theodore 2002), it is not surprising that many of these contradictions are also evident in urban gardening projects (McClintock 2014; Kumnig et al. 2017). Through various processes and at different scales, urban gardening may be neoliberal as well as radical. The chapter has outlined the various ways in which the urban gardeners in Cologne have engaged with and developed solutions to these challenges. For instance, the critical engagement of the gardeners with the "purity" of the commons and the protective enclosures created around their common in-the-making seem to have protected the project from being co-opted so far. Yet, our detailed analysis of *NeuLand* also reveals that we still need a better understanding of urban commons in order to analyse the interdependencies between gardening and political activism in recent gardening initiatives. Whereas (first generation) community gardens often made the transition towards politicization when the land was under threat of official development (see e.g. for New York Staeheli et al. 2002; Schmelzkopf 2002; Eizenberg 2012), community gardening of the second generation is used as a political tool from the outset (Certomà and Tornaghi 2015). This second generation of community gardens hence needs to be understood as an inherently political project. Rather than retreating from post-political politics (Werner 2011; Crouch 2004), creative new actors attempt to develop new counter-hegemonial urban futures (Purcell 2013, p. 560). Therefore, we conclude that claiming a right to the city through the creation of a community garden in the form of an "actually existing common" can support demands for more democratic governance of the city. Politically motivated community gardening is thus able to initiate major changes, even if the gardens may remain *unperfected commons in-the-making*. However, we argue that realizing Lefevbre's ideal of general public participation in "making the city", may only be achieved through a combination of social change and unrelenting pressure on urban planners and political representatives. Gardening projects such as *NeuLand* may only have the potential to make a small contribution to this incremental process, but occasionally they can provide the catalyst or stage for the appearance and promotion of an alternative urban future.

Despite their contradictory elements, urban gardening projects such as *Neu-Land* demonstrate that it is possible and necessary to develop commons as real alternative to the current hegemonial model of neoliberal and post-democratic urban space production, to experiment and think with and through commons for a fairer, greener, and more sustainable urban future.

Notes

1 E.g. *Die Welt (newspaper)*, Mobile Gärten für die Brache, 1st August 2011 (see: Kaufmann 2011), *WDR Lokalzeit Köln* (radio): Streit ums Südstadt-Filet, 3rd August 2011, Koelnarchitektur (online magazine), Zucchini zur Zwischenmiete, 12th August 2011 (see: Lisakowski 2011).

2 Initially, the garden was envisaged to cover 16,000 m². However, based on other temporary uses of the northern part of the site, the garden was limited to about 8,000 m².

3 *NeuLand* means "new land" or new "territory" in German.

4 See also other papers in the Special Issue on Darly, S. and McClintock, N., 2017. "Urban Agriculture in the Neoliberal City: Critical European Perspectives" *ACME*, 16 (2).

5 In Germany, for instance, the Max-Planck-Institut für das Recht der Gemeinschaftsgueter (Max-Planck-Institute for the Right to the Commons) already exists since 1990 (see: Helfrich 2009, p. 19).

6 The Heinrich-Böll-Stiftung (Foundation Heinrich Böll) is a thinktank linked to the left-wing political party Bündnis 90/Die Grünen (green party).

7 All allotments are members of the National Association of Allotments, a charitable, non-profit, non-religious, politically-neutral organization (www.kleingarten-bund. de).

8 More than 110 intercultural gardens exist all over Germany (Müller 2002), supported by the Stiftungsgemeinschaft Anstiftung & Ertomis. The Stiftungsgemeinschaft Anstiftung & Ertomis as a foundation supports innovative civil society activities including urban gardening. See: www.anstiftung-ertomis.de/die-stiftung

9 The project Allmende-Kontor, dedicated to the promotion and networking of urban gardening, runs a community garden of the same name as one of the pioneer projects on the former airfield Tempelhofer Feld. Between 2011 and 2013 more than 300 individual mobile planting containers have been erected by about 900 gardeners (www. allmende-kontor.de:81/index.php/gemeinschaftsgarten).

10 Hohengarten, D. and Wassily, N., 2012. Chronologie eines dubiosen Geschäfts. *In*: Meine Südstadt. www.meinesuedstadt.de/dombrauerei-brache-und-fh-umzug/chronologie-eines-dubiosen-gesch%C3%A4fts 28/04/2012 [accessed 15 June 2013].

11 Unternehmer für Köln e.V., 2008. Master plan Köln. p. 86. www.masterplan-koeln.de/ pool/files/Bericht_Masterplan/04_Masterplan_Innenstadt_K_F6In_AS_P_GmbH. pdf [accessed 15 June 2013].

12 The city's development plans draw here upon the early twentieth-century idea of creating a two continuous green spaces around Cologne, the inner and outer green belt.

13 The larger goals of *Kölner NeuLand e.V.* are to promote popular education (Volksbildung), conservation of the environment and citizens' involvement for public benefit.
14 Names changed.
15 The citizens' network is called 'BÜSIE – *Bürgernetzwerk Südliche Innenstadterweiterung*', named after the city's development concept (Entwicklungskonzept Südliche Innenstadt Erweiterung), literally meaning Citizens' Network Southern City Centre Extension.
16 For more information on the urban redevelopment project Parkstadt SÜD see www.stadt-koeln.de/leben-in-koeln/planen-bauen/projekte/parkstadt-sued/ [accessed 15 January 2018].
17 As the garden is a registered charitable association, it has to abide to certain legal rules regarding its management, including the election of a steering committee or council.

References

Anstiftung, 2017. *Die urbanen Gemeinschaftsgärten im Überblick. Stiftungsgemeinschaft anstiftung & ertomis gemeinnützige GmbH.* Available from: https://anstiftung.de/urbane-gaerten/gaerten-im-ueberblick [Accessed 25 July 2017].

Appel, I., Grebe, C., and Spitthöver, M., 2011. *Aktuelle Garteninitiativen. Kleingärten und neue Gärten in deutschen Großstädten.* Kassel: Kassel University Press. Available from: www.uni-kassel.de/upress/online/frei/978-3-86219-114-7.volltext.frei.pdf. [Accessed 25 June 2013].

Attoh, K.A., 2011. What kind of right is the right to the city? *Progress in Human Geography*, 35 (5), 669–685.

Barron, J., 2016. Community gardening: Cultivating subjectivities, space, and justice. *Local Environment*, 1–17. http://dx.doi.org/10.1080/13549839.2016.1169518.

Bendt, P., Barthel, S., and Colding, J., 2013. Civic greening and environmental learning in public-access community gardens in Berlin. *Landscape and Urban Planning*, 109 (1), 18–30. http://dx.doi.org/10.1016/j.landurbplan.2012.10.003.

Brenner, N. and Theodore, N., eds., 2002. *Spaces of Neoliberalism: Urban Restructuring in Western Europe and North America.* Oxford: Blackwell.

Brenner, N. and Theodore, N., 2002a. Cities and the geographies of "actually existing neoliberalism". *Antipode*, 34 (3), 349–379.

Brenner, N. and Theodore, N., 2002b. Preface: From the "new localism" to the spaces of neoliberalism. *Antipode*, 34 (3), 341–347.

Brenner, N. and Theodore, N., 2005. Neoliberalism and the urban condition. *City*, 9 (1), 101–107.

Brenner, N., Marcuse, P., and Mayer, M., 2009. Cities for people, not for profit. *City*, 13 (2–3), 176–184.

Certoma, C., 2011. Critical urban gardening as a post-environmentalist practice. *Local Environment*, 16 (10), 977–987.

Certomà, C. and Tornaghi, C., 2015. Political gardening: Transforming cities and political agency. *Local Environment*, 20 (10), 1123–1131. http://dx.doi.org/10.1080/13549839.2015.1053724.

Chatterton, P., 2010. Seeking the urban common: Furthering the debate on spatial justice. *City*, 14 (6), 625–628.

Colding, J. and Barthel, S., 2013. The potential of "urban green commons" in the resilience building of cities. *Ecological Economics*, 86, 156–166.

Colding, J., Barthel, S., Bendt, P., Snep, R., Van der Knaap, W., and Ernstson, H., 2013. Urban green commons: Insights on urban common property systems. *Global Environmental Change*, 23 (5), 1039–1051.

Crossan, J., Cumbers, A., McMaster, R., and Shaw, D., 2016. Contesting neoliberal urbanism in Glasgow's community gardens: The practice of DIY citizenship. *Antipode*, n/a–n/a. doi:10.1111/anti.12220.

Crouch, C., 2004. *Post-democracy*. Cambridge: Polity.

Darly, S. and McClintock, N., 2017. Introduction to urban agriculture in the Leoliberal city: Critical European perspectives. *ACME*, 16 (2), 224–231.

De Angelis, M., 2007. *The Beginning of History: Value Struggles and Global Capital*. London: Pluto Press.

Eißner, C. and Heydenreich, S., eds., 2004. *Baulücke? Zwischennutzen! Ein Ratgeber für den Weg von der Brachfläche zur Stadtoase*. Bonn: Verlag Stiftung Mitarbeit.

Eizenberg, E., 2012. Actually existing commons: Three moments of space of community gardens in New York city. *Antipode*, 44 (3), 764–782.

Ernwein, M., 2017. Urban agriculture and the neoliberalization of what? *ACME*, 16 (2), 27.

Follmann, A. and Viehoff, V., 2015. A green garden on red clay: Creating a new urban common as a form of political gardening in Cologne, Germany. *Local Environment*, 20 (10), 1148–1174. http://dx.doi.org/10.1080/13549839.2014.894966.

Fox-Kämper, R., Wesener, A., Münderlein, D., Sondermann, M., McWilliam, W., and Kirk, N., 2017. Urban community gardens: An evaluation of governance approaches and related enablers and barriers at different development stages. *Landscape and Urban Planning*. http://dx.doi.org/10.1016/j.landurbplan.2017.06.023.

Ghose, R. and Pettygrove, M., 2014. Urban community gardens as spaces of citizenship. *Antipode*, 46 (4), 1092–1112.

Gröning, G., 2000. Kampfesmutige Laubenpieper. Kleingärten und Politik in Berlin zwischen 1985 und 1995. In: Holl, A. and Meyer-Renschhausen, E. (Eds.), *Die Wiederkehr der Gärten*. Innsbruck: Studien Verlag, 140–161.

Halder, S., Jahnke, J., Mees, C., and von der Haide, E., 2011. Guerrilla Gardening und andere politische Gartenbewegungen. Eine globale Perspektive. In: Müller, C. (Ed.), *Urban Gardening. Über die Rückkehr der Gärten in die Stadt*. Munich: Oekom Verlag, 266–278.

Harderer, M., 2017. Recht auf Stadt! Lefebvre, urbaner Aktivismus und kritische Stadtforschung. Eine Rekonstruktion, Interpretation und Kritik. In: Kumnig, S., Rosol, M., and Exner, A. (Eds.), *Umkämpftes Grün. Zwischen neoliberaler Stadtentwicklung und Stadtgestaltung von unten*. Bielefeld: Transcript Verlag, 63–78.

Hardin, G., 1968. The tragedy of the commons. *Science*, 162, 1243–1248.

Hardt, M. and Negri, A., 2004. *Multitude*. New York: Penguin.

Hardt, M. and Negri, A., 2009. *Commonwealth*. Cambridge, MA: The Belknap Press of Harvard University Press.

Harvey, D., 2005. *A Brief History to Neoliberalism*. New York: Oxford University Press.

Harvey, D., 2006. *Space of Global Capitalism: Towards a Theory of Uneven Geographical Development*. New York: Verso.

Harvey, D., 2008. The right to the city. *New Left Review*, 53 (September, October), 23–40.

Harvey, D., 2011. The future of the commons. *Radical History Review*, 2011 (109), 101–107.

Harvey, D., 2012. *Rebel Cities. From the Right to the City to the Urban Revolution*. London, New York: Verso.

Heinrich-Böll-Stiftung, ed., 2009. *Gemeingüter stärken. Jetzt!*. Available from: www.boell.de/downloads/gemeinguetermanifest.pdf [Accessed 20 June 2013].

Heinrich-Böll-Stiftung, ed., 2010. *Gemeingüter – Wohlstand durch Teilen. Ein Report von Silke Helfrich, Rainer Kuhlen, Wolfgang Sachs und Christian Siefkes*. Available from: www.boell.de/downloads/Gemeingueter_Report_Commons.pdf [Accessed 20 June 2013].

Helfrich, S., 2009. Einleitung. In: Helfrich, S., and Heinrich-Böll-Stiftung (Eds.), *Wem gehört die Welt? Zur Wiederentdeckung der Gemeingüter*. Berlin: oekom Verlag. Available from: https://www.oekom.de/nc/buecher/gesamtprogramm/buch/wem-gehoert-die-welt.html [Accessed 22 May 2018].

Helfrich, S. and Heinrich-Böll-Stiftung, eds., 2009. *Wem gehört die Welt? Zur Wiederentdeckung der Gemeingüter*. Berlin: Oekom Verlag. Available from: www.boell.de/downloads/Netzausgabe_Wem_gehoert_die_Welt.pdf [Accessed 20 June 2013].

Helfrich, S. and Heinrich-Böll-Stiftung, eds., 2012. *Commons. Für eine neue Politik jenseits von Markt und Staat*. Bielefeld: Transcript Verlag. Available from: www.boell.de/downloads/2012-04-buch-2012-04-buch-commons.pdf [Accessed 20 June 2013].

Holm, A., 2011. Das Recht auf die Stadt. *Blätter für deutsche und internationale Politik*, 2011 (8), 89–97.

Jessop, B., 2002. Liberalism, neoliberalism, and urban governance: A state-theoretical perspective. In: Brenner, N. and Theodore, N. (Eds.), *Spaces of Neoliberalism: Urban Restructuring in Western Europe and North America*. Oxford: Blackwell.

Kaufmann, S., 2011. Mobile Gärten für die Brache. *Die Welt*, 1st August 2011. Available from: www.welt.de/print/welt_kompakt/koeln/article13518801/Mobile-Gaerten-fuer-die-Brache.html

Kumnig, S., Rosol, M., and Andreas Exner, A., eds., 2017. *Umkämpftes Grün: Zwischen neoliberaler Stadtentwicklung und Stadtgestaltung von unten*. Bielefeld: Transcript Verlag.

Lefebvre, H., 1991. *The Production of Space*. Oxford: Blackwell.

Lefebvre, H., 1996a [1968]. The right to the city. In: Kofman, E. and Lebas, E. (Eds.), *Writings on Cities*. Cambridge, MA: Blackwell, 63–181.

Lefebvre, H., 1996b [1973]. Space and politics. In: Kofman, E. and Lebas, E. (Eds.), *Writings on Cities*. Cambridge, MA: Blackwell, 185–202.

Linn, K., 1999. Reclaiming the sacred commons. *New Village Journal*, 1 (Community revitalization), 42–49. Available from: www.newvillage.net/assets/docs/linn.pdf [Accessed 23 June 2013].

Lisakowski, V., 2011. Zucchini zur Zwischenmiete. *Koelnarchitektur Magazin*, 12th August. Available from: www.koelnarchitektur.de/pages/de/home/news_archiv/2627.htm

Mayer, M., 1996. Postfordistische Stadtpolitik: Neue Regulationsweisen in der lokalen Politik und Planung. *Zeitschrift für Wirtschaftsgeographie: Regulationstheoretische Ansätze in der Geographie*, 40 (1–2), 20–27.

Mayer, M., 2009. The "right to the city" in the context of shifting mottos of urban social movements. *City*, 13 (2–3), 362–374.

McClintock, N., 2014. Radical, reformist, and garden-variety neoliberal: Coming to terms with urban agriculture's contradictions. *Local Environment*, 19 (2), 147–171.

McKay, G., 2011. *Radical Gardening: Politics, Idealism and Rebellion in the Garden*. London: Francis Lincoln.

Meyer-Renschhausen, E., ed., 2002. *Die Gärten der Frauen – Zur sozialen Bedeutung von Kleinstlandwirtschaft in Stadt und Land weltweit*. Herbolzheim: Centaurus-Verlag.

Meyer-Renschhausen, E., 2011. Von Pflanzerkolonien zum nomadisierenden Junggemüse. Zur Geschichte des Community Gardening in Berlin. In: Müller, C. (Ed.), *Urban Gardening. Über die Rückkehr der Gärten in die Stadt*. Munich: Oekom Verlag, 319–332.

Müller, C., 2002. *Wurzeln schlagen in der Fremde. Die Internationalen Gärten und ihre Bedeutung für Integrazionsprozesse.* Munich: Oekom Verlag.

Müller, C., ed., 2011. *Urban Gardening. Über die Rückkehr der Gärten in die Stadt.* Munich: Oekom Verlag.

Müller, C., 2012a. Practicing commons in community gardens: Urban gardening as a corrective for homo economicus. In: Bollier, D. and Helfrich, S. (Eds.), *The Wealth of the Commons: A World Beyond Market & State.* Amherst, MA: Levellers Press. Available from: http://wealthofthecommons.org/essay/practicing-commons-community-gardens-urban-gardening-corrective-homo-economicus

Müller, C., 2012b. Reiche Ernte in Gemeinschaftsgärten. Beim Urban Gardening findet der Homo oeconomicus sein Korrektiv. In: Helfrich, S. and Heinrich-Böll-Stiftung (Eds.), *Commons. Für eine neue Politik jenseits von Markt und Staat.* Bielefeld: Transcript Verlag, 267–272.

Ostrom, E., 1990. *Governing the Commons: The Evolution of Institutions for Collective Action.* Cambridge: Cambridge University Press.

Peck, J. and Tickell, A., 2002. Neoliberalizing Space. *Antipode*, 34 (3), 380–404.

Pudup, M.B., 2008. It takes a garden: Cultivating citizen-subjects in organized garden projects. *Geoforum*, 39 (3), 1228–1240. http://dx.doi.org/10.1016/j.geoforum.2007.06.012.

Purcell, M., 2013. To inhabit well: counterhegemonic movements and the right to the city. *Urban Geography*, 34 (4), 560–574.

Quastel, N., 2009. Political ecologies of gentrification. *Urban Geography*, 30 (7), 694–725.

Rosol, M., 2005. Community gardens: A potential for stagnating and shrinking cities? Examples from Berlin. *Die Erde*, 132 (2), 23–36.

Rosol, M., 2006. *Gemeinschaftsgärten in Berlin. Eine qualitative Untersuchung zu Potentialen und Risiken bürgerschaftlichen Engagements im Grünflächenbereich vor dem Hintergrund des Wandels von Staat und Planung.* Dissertation in Geography, Berlin, Humboldt-University Berlin.

Rosol, M., 2010. Public participation in the post-fordist urban green space governance: The case of community gardens in Berlin. *International Journal of Urban and Regional Research*, 34 (3), 548–563.

Rosol, M., 2012. Community volunteering as neoliberal strategy? Green space production in Berlin. *Antipode*, 44 (1), 239–257.

Schmelzkopf, K., 2002. Incommensurability, land use, and the right to space: Community gardens in New York city. *Urban Geography*, 23 (4), 323–343.

Soja, E., 2010. *Seeking Spatial Justice.* Minneapolis: University of Minnesota Press.

Sondermann, M., 2017. Gemeinschaftsgärten, Gemeinwohl und Gerechtigkeit im Spiegel lokaler Planungskulturen. In: Kumnig, S., Rosol, M. and Exner, A. (Eds.), *Umkämpftes Grün. Zwischen neoliberaler Stadtentwicklung und Stadtgestaltung von unten.* Bielefeld: Transcript Verlag, pp. 209–232.

Stadt Köln – Amt für Stadtentwicklung und Statistik [City of Cologne], 2011. *Vorbereitende Untersuchung und Entwicklungskonzept (Entwurf) südliche Innenstadt-Erweiterung in Bayenthal/Raderberg/Zollstock*, Oktober 2011, Cologne.

Staeheli, L.A., Mitchell, D., and Gibson, K., 2002. Conflicting rights to the city in New York's community gardens. *GeoJournal*, 58 (2/3), 197–205.

Tornaghi, C., 2012. Public space, urban agriculture and the grassroots creation of new commons: Lessons and challenges for policy makers. In: Viljoen, A. and Wiskerke, J. (Eds.), *Sustainable Food Planning: Evolving Theory and Practice.* Wageningen: Wageningen Academic Publishers, 349–364.

Tornaghi, C., 2014. Critical geography of urban agriculture. *Progress in Human Geography*, 38 (4), 551–567.

Viehoff, V. and Follmann, A., 2017. Das Politische eines Gemeinschaftsgartens – NeuLand in Köln als Experimentierort für urban commoning? In: Kumnig, S., Rosol, M., and Exner, A. (Eds.), *Umkämpftes Grün. Zwischen neoliberaler Stadtentwicklung und Stadtgestaltung von unten*. Bielefeld: Transcript Verlag, 233–261.

Werner, K., 2011. Eigensinnige Beheimatungen. Gemeinschaftsgärten als Orte des Widerstandes gegen die neoliberale Ordnung. In: Müller, C. (Ed.), *Urban Gardening. Über die Rückkehr der Gärten in die Stadt*. Munich: Oekom Verlag, 54–75.

6 Challenging property relations and access to land for urban food production

Gerda R. Wekerle and Michael Classens

1. Introduction

A Portuguese-Canadian retiree, originally from the Azores, singlehandedly cleans up an empty lot designated for luxury condominiums near his house in downtown Toronto and plants beans, corn, and tobacco. An Afro-Caribbean director of a food security organization transforms his suburban backyard into a demonstration farm cultivated by local youth. They grow callaloo, yams, and other vegetables for the Afri-Can Food Basket. A young, socially and environmentally conscious entrepreneur convinces urban homeowners to share their backyards with her to grow vegetables and herbs for sale at a farmers' market. These projects and dozens of others like them springing up throughout cities of the Global North challenge our experiences of where food comes from and complicate our notions of private property and urban land use. Typically, within cities of the Global North, public lands have been the terrain upon which urban agriculture activists struggle (Lawson 2005). However, in an era of continued public divestment and unimaginative, often regressive public land management, urban food activists are increasingly looking to the agrarian potential of privately owned land. This signals an evolution in the dynamics of urban food activism, as emphasis shifts from public to private land. This is no simple swap, but instead, as we describe below, food activists are increasingly engaged in actively challenging the material and discursive limits of private property and associated land uses in the neoliberal city.

This chapter addresses initiatives that involve renegotiating access to land for growing food between private property owners and landless growers. Often unheralded, these shifts are based on relations of trust between individuals rather than public battles over lands lost to urban agriculture through political decisions and urban policies. We argue that growing food on private lands in the city is no less political: by presenting alternative options for urban agriculture, the initiatives challenge urban residents to redefine what it means to "enact" private property through urban food growing. We document the ways in which urban residents with limited access to land negotiate usufruct rights to urban land. Usufruct rights, a millennia-old concept, bestow non-owners with access to land and the spoils it yields (Goldie 1985; Pierce 2010). We discuss three cases in Toronto, Canada, that problematize the notion of *private* property through usufruct rights: a downtown, squatted urban farm; suburban backyards, transformed into farm demonstration plots; and central city backyards conscripted into a quasi-commercial, non-contiguous urban farm. These initiatives articulate alternative visions of sustainability, food security, and access to urban land. They challenge prevailing notions of private property, land ownership, and land use in the neoliberal city.

We argue, as others have (Blomley 2004), that property is much more than simply a "thing"; it is a socially enacted relation between "owners" and "non-owners". If private property is defined on the basis of exclusionary rights, then what are we to make of ostensibly private property that is shared amongst urban farmers? Drawing on feminist scholarship (Gibson-Graham 2006; MacGregor 2006; Wekerle 2013), we outline how urban food activists confront and redefine conventional enactments of private property through personal relationships based on an ethic of care for the land and others. We utilize the powerfully optimistic analysis of community economies developed by Gibson-Graham (2006) and subsequent elaborations of the concept and practices of commoning (Gibson-Graham et al. 2016; Foster and Iaione 2016) and the idea of a sharing economy (Botsman and Rogers 2010; Davies et al. 2017). Currently, scholars are too-hastily dismissing urban agriculture projects as regressive, neoliberal enterprises, simply filling the gaps of state retrenchment (Guthman 2008; Pudup 2008). These are in sharp contrast with more nuanced and optimistic perspectives elaborated by Alkon (2012) and McClintock (2010). In North American cities, access to land is *the* political project of urban agriculture. We demonstrate that engaging with private property for the purposes of food production, even if only temporarily, is a profoundly political expression of challenging the contemporary neoliberal condition by "starting where you are" (Gibson-Graham 2006, p. 195). The urban food activists and projects we discuss represent an emerging expression of the politics of urban food – a pragmatic politics that is subtly altering our food system, and the private property relations it is built on.

We briefly discuss the politics of land – as distinct from property – within the context of global neoliberal capitalism. Next, we draw on legal scholars and critical geographers to elaborate on our contention that struggles over urban food growth must be understood as struggles over the enactment of different property relations. This is illustrated by three examples of urban agriculture in Toronto that rely on access to privately owned land. Finally, we conclude with some reflections on the politics of urban food, private property, and potential future directions for research on urban agriculture.

2. The politics of land

Access to land for growing food in cities of the Global North has become a critical issue as concerns increase about the sustainability of the long-haul food system (Mikulak 2013). Urban expressions of sustainable agriculture include a range of experimental activities, such as community gardens, school gardens, rooftop gardens, and urban farms. Despite the many differences among these initiatives, they are united in their dependence on land or related infrastructure such as rooftops. Although land may be set-aside for urban food production, as in allotments, or it may be surplus or in low demand, it remains either private or public property. In either case, community gardens and urban farms are often at the mercy of landowners and state agencies looking to sell the land for more profitable use. Security of tenure and property rights continue to be key policy and political issues for urban agriculture across North America as local production of food is brought into conversation with the global forces of real estate development and transnational circuits of capital.

As Nicholas Blomley (2004) has argued, property is a crucial basis for political claim-making and creative opposition. When land that has been used communally for food production is taken back by the state or transformed back into private property, there is often public opposition. The "politics of gardens" is portrayed as the resistance and mobilization of marginalized communities to preserve community gardens against capitalist urban development. Research has focused on the subaltern and grassroots struggles that create counter-publics through their ongoing renegotiations of private and public space in the city, including the work on urban squatters (Chatterton 2002) and community gardeners in various cities (Schmelzkopf 2002; Staeheli and Mitchell 2008). (For the Toronto context, see Baker 2005; Wekerle 2004). The stories popularized in newspaper headlines, videos, and books are framed as battles between urban food growers, rapacious landowners, and acquiescent city politicians/bureaucrats.

One of the most widely documented battles for urban gardens occurred in New York City, in 1999, when the Guiliani government sought to sell or develop 131 of the more than 700 community garden sites within the city limits. The battle for community gardens was framed as a contestation between community needs and the right of the city as the owner of the lands to develop them either for affordable housing or to maximize assessments through urban development. While the city argued that it was operating within a market economy, garden advocates countered that community gardens represent use values (Schmelzkopf 2002). Scholars and activists alike framed this as a contestation between the *rights to the city* and the *right of the city* to balance its budget (Staeheli and Mitchell 2008). The resolution was for the city to sell 100 community gardens to the Trust for Public Land and the New York Restoration Project.

The overwhelming bulk of the literature detailing the dynamics of access to land to grow food has focused on peasant land struggles in the Global South and the emergence of landless rural workers' movements (Desmarais 2007; Mezaros 2000; Wolford 2003). Tactics have focused on seizing unfairly owned lands or on land redistribution "to break the nexus between land, agriculture, power and profit" (Field and Bell 2013, p. 88). Most recently popular resistance has challenged "land grabs" by large-scale land-based investment by foreign companies often supported by active state involvement, coercion, and violence (Borras et al. 2012; Fairbairn 2014) in areas as geographically disparate as South America, Africa, and China. The land grab literature highlights issues of livelihood, private property, and alternative forms of land tenure. Land wars taking place around the world remind us that access to land to grow food is both an issue of social justice but also integral to global capitalist practices of capital accumulation by processes of accumulation by dispossession.

In cities of the Global North, the very visible garden battles are the exceptions in the politics of gardens, not the rule. The politics of gardens for food production are played out on a daily basis across a multitude of sites, communities, and cities (McClintock 2013). The politics of the uses of scarce urban lands for urban food production in ever-larger and denser cities of the Global North are part of the everyday life of urban dwellers (Classens 2014). Gardens in cities have taken on a new political significance as the visible representation of urban sustainability and responses to climate change and food insecurity. With their tomatoes, corn, and zucchini flourishing amid public housing projects and on the rooftops of commercial buildings, food gardens, no matter how vestigial, located in city centres or around apartment towers, challenge our preconceptions of neoliberal urbanism.

Blomley (2005, p. 281) notes that gardening is an "interstitial activity" that though traditionally private and associated with the domestic home, often crosses the boundaries into public space. Conversely, urban food production on public or institutional lands introduces a domestic element, thereby forcing us to re-examine our notions of commerce and domestic caring work and the separation between private/domestic activities and the public uses of land (Wekerle 2005). When new commercial gardening ventures are based on privately owned domestic gardens, as in backyard-sharing projects, this further complicates the separation of public and private space, domestic and employment lands. These types of sharing arrangements are associated with hybrid forms of property rights (Turner 2017) such as the recent popularity of new relational forms of property based on practices of commoning that may involve community-controlled resources or the shared use of lands between formal property owners and others.

3. (Re)negotiating property and access to land in urban food production

The ways in which property relations have been restructured as part of neoliberal urbanism have been well-documented (Blomley 2004; Hackworth 2007). In urbanizing areas, land for growing food is being squeezed out by uneven capitalist development that seeks to convert present uses of land to more lucrative and capital-intensive uses. Access to land for growing food in cities of the Global North has been identified as a nexus of conflict (Schmelzkopf 1995, 2002; Staeheli and Mitchell 2008) due to contradictions in property regimes that separate access to food, land, and property ownership.

Neoclassical liberal conceptions of property ownership are predicated on notions of the self-interested, possessive individual (Singer 2000). As Blomley (2005, p. 283) notes, "One of the most consequential of categorical boundaries relating to the spatial order of property is that which separates the realm of private ownership from the sphere of public ownership". In practice, property is dynamic and not definitively either private or public – as demonstrated by the usufruct rights – a politicized set of relations between property owners and others, including people with no access to land, who actively claim rights of use. Blomley (2004) points out how the formal enactment of property bestows the right of use or benefit and the power to exclude others. Both property (Blomley 2004) and food (McMichael 2009) are much more than discrete, physical entities, but are instead entanglements of continually enacted power relations, which become solidified as "things" through the consolidation and maintenance of particular constellations of power. Private property ownership enables the control of valued resources through the erasure of competing and contrasting claims. Yet "property is not a static, pre-given entity, but depends on a continual, active, 'doing' notes Blomley (2004).

How land is deemed useful and valuable in a specific legal and social sense changes over time (Wiebe et al. 1998). Bromley (1998) observes that property in land has multiple meanings that are both separate and overlapping, depending on the circumstances. The multiple claims to land as property include viewing land as a commodity to be traded and sold; the personal attachments to land through history, culture, and symbolic meaning; land as community property; and the conception of land tied to a land ethic and caring practice. According to Graham (2011), the ownership model of property assumes that owners are detached from the places that are owned, i.e. that people have no relationship, attachment, or responsibility with the land that is owned. Within this property regime, land is considered a commodity that can be bought and sold and its resources used to generate profit.

New theoretical frameworks applied to property law account for "the non-ownership interests in land privately owned by others. . . . and the creative ways they are reshaping land use law" (Van Wagner 2013, p. 2). According to Van Wagner (2013), while property law makes a clear distinction between the property rights of owners and non-owners, in many conflicts over land use, non-owners, whether neighbours or advocacy groups, assert their interests over private lands and make claims regarding the uses of such lands. Ribot and Peluso (2003) develop a theory of access that argues that property is only one set of access relationships among others and that it is important to study closely who actually benefits, through what processes and social relations. They argue that we must pay attention "to property as well as the illicit actions, relations of production, entitlement relations, and the histories of all of these" (Ribot and Peluso 2003, p. 157).

Legal scholarship on property law examines wider community interests by focusing on the nature of rights in land and the balance between public and private interest in land when there are challenges over property rights and ecosystem protection. Legal scholar Joseph Sax (1993) has argued that land is not only defined by its potential for development and profit. Land is already in use and the ecological function of the land is what will determine any level of development. This legal position draws upon Aldo Leopold's (1966, pp. 238–239) concept of a land ethic: "An ethic, ecologically . . . simply enlarges the boundaries of the community to include soils, water, plants and animals, or collectively the land".

In ecosystems planning, where plans often cross many ownership boundaries and forms of tenure, the concept of stewardship challenges traditional views of the rights of private property ownership and individual entitlements (Logan and Wekerle 2008).

One might argue that landless peasants squatting on vacant lands not only assert the interests of the non-owner in the productivity of the land and their own livelihood, but also demonstrate an interest in maintaining the care of the land. Similarly, urban farmers who develop productive gardens in urban parks, on vacant lands or in shared backyards see themselves as improving the soil and the land's productivity and use value, as well as contributing to urban food security.

Garden sharing schemes, where private homeowners allow others to cultivate their lands in exchange for certain benefits, reflect a dual interest in caring for the land *as place and as property*. Intensively gardening the property may result in the land's "improvement", thereby potentially increasing its exchange value as a commodity. In backyard sharing schemes, the landowner foregrounds the use value of the land. The urban farmer, as a non-owner, has a strong interest in the land's specificity – its location, the amount of sunlight, and the kind of soil. For the use of the land to grow food, he/she may engage in an exchange of produce that is either shared, donated, or sold in the marketplace. While property law has dealt extensively with encroachments of private owners of gardens into the public street as crossing the boundary between defined private and public spaces, such encroachments are provisionally viewed as a privilege that can be removed at will rather than a right (Blomley 2005). Garden sharing reverses this dynamic: private gardens become shared space, and, in some cases, commercial space. Although the increasing numbers of garden sharing schemes for urban food production, some of which are based on formal contracts, may challenge conventional notions of private and public space, these have not yet attracted the attention of legal scholars or by-law enforcement officers concerned with the uses of property.

In recent years, renewed attention has been directed to what has been called the "sharing economy" or the "collaborative economy" (Botsman and Rogers 2010). While much of the focus has been on web-facilitated new consumer behaviours and services such as car and ride sharing, and tool libraries, collective use and exchange based on relations of trust are ideas that have travelled from one sector to another. Viewing backyards as an underutilized asset that can be shared through collaborative consumption to supplement income and innovate new business models is part of this wider trend. Business journalists view the sharing economy as an opportunity for peer-to-peer businesses (*The Economist* 2013). Environmentalists emphasize the challenge to the market economy posed by sharing of resources that cultivates sustainability by conserving resources (cf. special issue of *Alternatives Journal*, April 2014 www. alternativesjournal.ca). Davies et al. (2017) point out that there are diverse sharing economies, some of which contribute to new ways of living and labouring. They define this as "transformational sharing" that "seeks to change power and social relations around who benefits, who owns and controls the processes through which sharing takes place" (Davies et al. 2017, p. 211). Community-based urban agriculture initiatives offer some prime existing examples of sharing economy activities.

4. Urban agriculture in Toronto

Toronto has been described as "Canada's food capital" (Cockrall-King 2012) due to the plethora of food security initiatives extending over several decades and the networked nature of many of these programmes and projects (Classens et al. 2015; Levkoe 2014; Blay-Palmer 2009; Wekerle 2004). There are an estimated 226 known community gardens, some on public lands and in parks spread across the city, and 1,674 plots in allotment gardens (Cockrall-King 2012). Home gardening is a popular activity: 40% of people in Greater Toronto live in households that produce some of their own food (City Farmer 2004). In a study of 125 residents in two Toronto neighbourhoods 54% grew food (Kortright and Wakefield 2011). Even in the downtown core of the city, there are neighbourhoods of single family houses with private front and backyards. In the post-war suburbs, single family houses on large lots predominate. High rise apartment towers, with substantial lands around them, line the arterial roads of post-war suburban neighbourhoods. These are some of the spaces identified as a potential resource for the scaling up of urban agriculture in Toronto (Nasr et al. 2010). As a city with large numbers of international migrants, the pressures to find land to grow food resonate with those desiring to work the land to grow culturally specific foods and connect with a homeland.

The stories of urban gardeners in this chapter surfaced over three decades and in different contexts, rather than as findings generated by one defined research project. Both Wekerle and Classens are activist scholars engaged in community-based research. Wekerle founded the first political action group focused on urban agriculture in Toronto and was an active participant in several urban agriculture organizations, including initiatives to incorporate urban agriculture into planning documents. Classens initiated an urban agriculture project in Calgary. His research has focused on the political ecology and changes over time of a peri-urban farming community and on food security organizations. In this chapter, we highlight experiments and innovations in urban agriculture, adaptations to land scarcity in a fast-growing and high-priced city, and emergent trends in commoning and the sharing economy. A funded research project headed by Gerda Wekerle on land use conflicts in the contested countryside underpins our focus on the renegotiation of land and property and changing ideas of property law. A case study, based on observation and interviews over a ten-year period, is drawn from Wekerle's research project on immigrants and their gardens in Toronto, conducted with Vincenzo Pietropaolo, a social documentary photographer, that culminated in a two-year (2000–2002) exhibit at Toronto's Royal Ontario Museum. Through walking the city, Wekerle discovered an immigrant gardener who squatted on downtown land and this became the focus of an ethnographic study. Conversations with a university student surfaced her entrepreneurial initiatives in garden sharing. Hence, our cases are grounded in our immersion in the urban agriculture movement in Toronto.

5. Sharing private lands for urban food production: some stories

5.1 *Appropriating waste lands from downtown redevelopment*

High-priced downtown redevelopment sites often lie idle for years, surrounded by intimidating signs designating them as private property. In the Queen West area of Toronto's centre city, an area known for its artists, boutiques, and music scene, a commercial laundry occupying a large block of land was torn down and surrounded by fencing for several years. In the summer of 2001, on a walk through the neighbourhood, Wekerle observed that half of the site was densely planted with vegetables and tobacco plants. It was cultivated by a 78-year old retired man, Manuel Raposo, an immigrant from Azores, Portugal. Wekerle and geographer Carlos Teixera (who translated from Portuguese to English) interviewed the gardener on two occasions and documented the plants grown (Manuel Raposo, personal communication with Wekerle, June 2001 and June 8, 2004). A short video was also made. Manuel had lived in a house in the neighbourhood for 50 years. Over one winter and spring, he singlehandedly cleaned up this large vacant lot to grow tobacco and food for his own use, to give as gifts to friends, and to sell to neighbours. Drawing upon his skills in working for the city's works department, he installed an extensive drainage system, and buried two bath tubs as water reservoirs. He built a small shed, a *casita*, to shelter him and his friends from the sun and rain.

In Manuel's view, land should not sit idle; productive use of land is distinguished from legal ownership. He said "I didn't know who was the owner, but I know this land for a long time. This place was abandoned, with a lot of garbage. I wanted to work and I said to myself, 'I have nothing more to do, and this one is abandoned.' But I don't know the owner of this land" (Raposo 2001). Despite his respect for private property and the law, Manuel's desire to work hard, create order, and improve the land for cultivation overcame his misgivings about squatting on land that was not his own. When the owner of the property, a young professional man in a suit, showed up one day, he was surprised to find Manuel hard at work on his now-cleared lot. "What are you doing on my land?" he asked. "Just cleaning up so I can plant some things", said Manuel. "Are you going to give me trouble for planting this land?" "No", said the owner, "If you want to work the land, do it".

The next time the owner came, he told Manuel that there was a development application to build on the land, but that Manuel could plant it until it was approved. Manuel laid out his position: "This land is not mine. You will not pay me anything for the cleaning I did for the land. I also don't pay anything to you. What I get from it is mine. The land is not mine. It's yours. Anytime you want it, take it". Manuel knew that he had no legal rights to the land. But his usage of the land gave him the benefits of his own labour. Out of a derelict space,

Manuel created a productive small urban farm. This vernacular landscape of food production was in sharp contrast with the rapidly gentrifying neighbourhood of trendy restaurants and expensive boutiques. Manuel created a place where his Portuguese male friends could hang out and play cards, where neighbours could obtain or buy fresh vegetables, and where he could grow tobacco, beans, potatoes, tomatoes, cabbages, and squash.

After three years, in the summer of 2004, a fence surrounded the site and billboards announced a new townhouse condominium development – the Gardens of Queen Street – where each unit was designed with private access to a small patio. Manuel was able to temporarily retain a ten-foot long and three-foot wide area, which he densely planted with wooden poles to train runner beans. By the fall of 2005, however, the buildings were up and the garden was gone. Ever resourceful, Manuel had only moved 100 feet away to the backyard of a house owned by an Italian family where he cultivated peas and beans, potatoes and more tobacco within view of the luxury condominiums. Manuel's garden reflected the survival of an agrarian tradition and the resistance of the subalterns in the cracks of the neoliberal city. Manuel Raposo died in a garage fire in November 2010 and is still remembered by his neighbours for his many vegetable gardens.

Manuel knew that his claim to the land was tenuous, but he managed to access land for growing crops through his personal relationship with the landowner, and animated it with an ethic of care for the land. His transformation of the derelict land into a working farm and community gathering point, however temporary, represents both a symbolic and material incursion into the hegemonic property relations of downtown Toronto. Squatting and guerilla gardening are often celebrated as acts of resistance or denigrated for breaking the law and violating private property rights (Winne 2010). Manuel's form of "soft squatting" demonstrates that these are not the only options. A landowner can cede temporary use of a development site to a gardener who agrees to relinquish claims when development permits are granted. In an age when guerrilla gardeners play into the logic of municipal devolution by openly organizing clean-up projects online (see www.guerillagardening.ca/), the radical *bone fides* of these kinds of "resistance" projects should be scrutinized. Similarly, while it might be easy to dismiss Manuel's garden as a prototypical example of citizens temporarily beautifying warehoused land in the service of global capital, there is something more going on here. As Gibson-Graham's (2006) political strategy – equal parts pragmatic and revolutionary – suggests, starting "where you are" and with what you have is the only rational way of building survival strategies in the era of late capitalism.

6. Redesignating suburban yards for community-based food production

Toronto's post-war suburbs attract new immigrants, people of colour, and the working class. A suburban neighbourhood, Jane-Finch, often labelled as high crime and low income, is developing local networks to deal with food security. The focal point for these activities is the Afri-Can Food Basket, headquartered in a rented, 1960s suburban single-family bungalow. Founded in 1995, it started as a food-buying club in response to the rising costs of imported culturally specific foods from the Caribbean. As observed at an initial site visit in 1999 to the home and office of Anan Lololi, Executive Director, the private backyard of the house was transformed into an intensive urban farm with training centred on food production by local youth. This backyard garden has become an experimental and demonstration plot for attempts to extend the season on tropical vegetables like okra, amaranth, and callaloo, sometimes referred to as "world foods" in Toronto, which might be grown commercially in the city. When the garden was first visited, half the produce went to the volunteers who worked in the garden; the rest went into the food box programme (Lololi 2000). In 2013, Anan Lololi (Figure 6.1), Executive Director of the African Food Basket, noted that

> My backyard garden (BYG) has been productive as ever with food for the home, family friends and the foodbanks. This year I decided to start my own little social enterprise and grossed over $3,000 from the sale of onion, garlic, kale, radish, peas, chard, calaloo, cilantro, mix-salad, bitter-melon, pak-choi. It was a good harvest.
>
> (Personal communication, Lololi 18 Dec 2013)

Through collective usage, the private backyard attached to the single family suburban house was transformed into a site for an education programme, workspace,

Figure 6.1 Anan Lololi, Executive Director, African Food Basket in suburban backyard
        garden

Source: Gerda R. Wekerle

experimental growing centre, and a source of fresh vegetables for volunteers from the neighbourhood and the food box programme. When asked whether this intensive urban farm and the introduction of neighbourhood youth and other volunteers created difficulties with the house's property owner and neighbours, Lololi (2014) replied: "It was no problem; this was an Italian neighbourhood and my landlord, same as now, encouraged this/no problem. None of my neighbours had a problem; the most consistent and focused urban gardener I know is my Italian neighbour, a woman who has been a great inspiration to me".

The mandate of the African Food Basket (AFB) is to work with the most marginalized low income communities, especially people living in social housing in the suburban west end of Toronto. According to Lololi (2014), the city has supported the AFB in several ways: it has worked in one housing project, Lawrence Heights, since 2003, with an office and access to city-owned lands – the school yard, parks, and land adjacent to a community centre – for growing food. At this site, the urban agriculture programme encompassed 5,000 square feet of growing space in five community gardens. Some gardens were planted in bulk to produce organic garlic, onions, parsley, peppers, and celery. The community garden coordinator within the city's Parks Department served as a mentor, providing training in horticulture for four consecutive years for about ten members of AFB. The city also funded a food animator from the AFB for five years, providing support to establish community gardens. This is documented in a 25-minute video (www.youtube.com/watch?v=GszkB11cc).

In several neighbourhoods, the AFB established more than 60 backyard gardens and involved around 150 gardeners and their families. "Most of the food from these gardens was consumed by gardeners and their families; a portion was also donated to family and friends or cooked in community kitchens" (Lololi 2005). Reflecting on this project, Lololi (2014) reports that the intention was to empower the community to run their own show through giving tenants seeds, tools, a hose, and perhaps seedlings. People may receive help with planting out and weeding.

> Folk who have land benefit because they get some food; their backyard is pretty and there are no weeds. Growing food is a good way to engage the space that is available. People often put a lot of chemicals on the lawn. Growing food is a win-win situation. It creates income and you can do good organically. People in cities always want to have access to green space to grow food.

Lololi (2005), a veteran food activist, notes that there needs to be more access to land. "But the emphasis is on real estate, not the values of a garden. There is competition for access to land. We end up in church yards or school yards". AFB now has two farm plots, one at the Black Creek Community Farm owned by the Toronto Region Conservation Authority in the same neighbourhood as the headquarters house. The second is a peri-urban farm, a two-acre plot farmed by seven farmers – the Ujama Farmers Collective. This is part of the larger McVean

Incubator Farm, a 25-acre farm owned by the Toronto Region Conservation Authority in Brampton, Ontario, north of the city of Toronto. Here, an organization founded to develop farming skills, FarmStart, supports immigrant farmers from India, the Caribbean, Africa, South America, and elsewhere with access to land, a tractor, tiller, water, and compost, as well as a farmer who offers advice. Farmers regularly experiment with crops commonly produced in other countries but seldom grown in Ontario, including callaloo, okra, and Jamaican pumpkins. The African Food Basket sells what they grow both at the farm and at three farmers' markets, utilizing the produce from three backyards, the Black Creek Community Farm and the McVeen Farm. Sales average about $650 a week. In 2013, the AFB grossed about $20,000 from sales of food (Lololi 2014). Starting from an initial modest base of one suburban backyard, the AFB has expanded to create community gardens, private food gardens, and urban farms in several suburban low-income communities. It has raised issues of representation and race in the food movement; it has specialized in training and providing employment to youth in food production.

6.1 Shared backyards: combining exchange relationships and commercial enterprise

In the summer of 2010, a graduate student in the Faculty of Environmental Studies, York University, Erica Lemieux, created a brochure and went around her neighbourhood in the west end of Toronto, High Park, asking whether people wanted part of their backyard farmed (personal communication, Lemieux 2014). She distributed one hundred brochures; eight people called back right away. Lemieux had been inspired by an urban farmer growing food in backyards in Kelowna, British Columbia (Bolton 2014; Porter 2011). In a personal interview (Lemieux 2014), Erica said "I saw the opportunities in the neighbourhood I grew up in, those huge sunny backyards. It was a way to match up people with land and no time and others with time and no land. I loved the idea of turning over lawns to edible gardens". She had wanted to grow local food to sell at farmers' markets but found out that "you are not allowed to sell what you grow on public lands. With private yards, it is a faster process. There is no shortage of private lands" (Lemieux 2014). Lemieux called her sole-proprietorship business City Seed Farms. In the summer of 2013, she expanded her operation and cultivated 12 backyards bio-intensively, growing leafy greens, beets, radishes, carrots, spring onions, arugula, spinach, edible flowers, pea and radish shoots. A formal contract with the homeowner stipulated that this was a barter system in which homeowners who let her grow food in their backyards receive a weekly food basket in exchange. Homeowners were very satisfied with this arrangement, according to Lemieux, most of them returning the next year.

To reduce potential conflict, Lemieux carefully vetted the homeowners that she worked with to determine whether they were a good fit and that she and they had a shared vision. She observed that homeowners "didn't make a big deal of the backyard sharing aspect". There were no concerns about privacy or private property: "They got used to the crew, the four of us with volunteers. It was a good group. The homeowners were so respectful" (Lemieux 2014). She suggests that homeowners are open to sharing their garden space because they see positive gains. "They may see it as a value added thing. It can easily be transformed back to lawn. A lot of homeowners, they enjoy looking out the back window and seeing something useful" (Lemieux 2014). In the summer of 2013, City Seed Farms harvested approximately 3,000 pounds of vegetables (Bolton 2014). In an interview, Lemieux (2014), recounted that she sold her produce to restaurants and at two weekly farmers' markets. She provided part-time employment to three people, but needed to take an additional job herself. The work was physically taxing, especially since she travelled among gardens by bicycle. During the third growing season, Lemieux exited from the garden project and moved to Calgary. She reported that another group of six farmers and co-ordinators had examined the feasibility of a neighbourhood farm based on backyards. Although 90 homeowners responded enthusiastically to their preliminary notices, the farmers concluded that the work involved in coordinating such a large number of sites was prohibitive.

However, the idea of commercialized garden sharing has travelled and inspired others. In June 2017, a resident of the Brockton Village neighbourhood in Toronto launched a garden and produce sharing project with 12 neighbours (Brait 2017). Two hundred kilometres north of Toronto, in Huntsville, a town of 18,000, another woman gardener inspired by Erica Lemieux and the gardener from Kelowna was farming six large private garden sites and selling her greens, garlic, and potatoes at local farmers' markets in the summer of 2014. While some aim to professionalize and commercialize backyard sharing, other groups in Toronto incorporate backyard sharing into their larger projects to foster commoning and community ties. Shared backyards projects started out as non-profit and sharing economy/commoning projects without commercial benefits. There is an online map of the city of Toronto at SharingBackyards.com which brings together people with land for food production and gardeners seeking access to land. The harvest is equally shared between gardener and homeowner. This free programme exists in 20 cities across North America (Porter 2009). Another project, Grow-a-Row, Plant-a-Row asks a home grower to plant a row of vegetables for donation to a food bank. The Stop Community Food Centre in Toronto runs the Yes-in-My-Back Yard (YIMBY) programme that matches people with land and gardeners seeking land, including providing training and tool sharing. Targeting under-utilized assets in a sharing economy model, Not Far From the Tree, a charitable urban gleaning project in Toronto, harvests fruit trees on private lands and shares the fruit among volunteers and homeowners.

Backyard sharing arrangements of various kinds have received little scholarly attention. In a study of three garden partnerships, Blake and Cloutier-Fisher (2009) treat these as smaller scale variants of community gardening. In this chapter, we argue that garden sharing innovations are social enterprise projects that renegotiate private property rights as a strategy of increasing urban food production. Such projects open up access to private lands by engaging private landowners and gardeners/urban farmers in the renegotiation of property relations and introduce homeowners to the concept of local food. The non-profit garden sharing initiatives contribute to community development, skill development, and build social capital. These consensual relationships stand in stark contrast to the politics of mass protest, interest-based politics, legal challenges, and legislative remedies often targeted to gaining access to or security of tenure to public lands for urban agriculture. The emphasis in garden sharing projects is on partnerships among strangers that draw upon notions of shared benefits, trust, and altruism. Involving the home garden, the domestic space associated with caring relations, growing, making, and eating food may elicit a response that goes beyond the assumptions of private property ownership as commodity, resource, and exclusionary space suggested by the neoliberal city paradigm. In garden sharing schemes, the ethic of care (Tronto 1993) for home and family is extended to others that care for the garden and generate food for the household and others. While this "caring-practice" has been examined in community-supported agriculture (Wells and Gradwell 2001), it has not been studied as it relates to garden sharing schemes in urban agriculture – this constitutes a significant oversight given the growth of sharing arrangements in recent years.

Garden sharing initiatives are political in subtly challenging single-family zoning and residential land use designations. By introducing intensive food production to home gardens, they subvert the lawn culture (Robbins 2007) focused on private use and display of the typical middle-class Toronto single-family house, whether urban or suburban. By bringing in non-household members, either as volunteers or as paid employed cultivators of the land, the shared backyard garden becomes a worksite that challenges the separation of home and work and the segregation of residential homeowners from other kinds of urban residents. While residential zoning typically has restrictions on commercial uses, roomers or basement apartments that bring in non-family members, and strictly limits the kind and size of home occupations, these strictures are limited to the dwelling unit itself. Growing food on lands attached to a dwelling is generally not subject to such limitations, although backyard chicken raising in urban neighbourhoods has generated heated debate and new restrictive zoning regulations that permit chickens but limit their numbers (Johnson 2010). Food production, when expanded into backyard sharing schemes or the routine incorporation of commercial food production into the residential landscape, challenges our notions of private property, including exclusive access and use of the resources of the urban garden. In commercial garden sharing schemes, relations of exchange and profit are melded into a new hybrid relationship between property owner and food grower. Backyard sharing arrangements institutionalize and formalize this new use of lands in private ownership. In some cases, formal contracts between owner and grower, salaries for employees, and sales of produce at farmers' markets situate these urban agriculture projects squarely within the marketplace.

In Toronto, since the late 1990s, the political work of urban food networks and urban agriculture activists has been to direct their efforts to policy change at the municipal level to increase support for urban agriculture (Blay-Palmer 2009; City of Toronto 2013; Wekerle 2004). A report (Nasr et al. 2010) comprehensively outlines the many constraints on urban agriculture that could be addressed by changes to city policies or programmes. The city could revise guidelines to allow urban producers to sell home-grown food at farmers' markets. The city is urged to coordinate a land inventory of potential food growing spaces and to change land use regulation by inserting language into official plans and zoning to allow community gardens and fruit trees across all zoning designations. Recommendations include the possibility of a temporary use by-law to zone development land for agricultural use for a specific time period and changes to provincial policies that would allow urban agriculture sites to receive lower property taxation rates, as well as creating a new designation of food producing land trusts. One recent change is the creation of a Residential Apartment Commercial Zone for apartment tower sites that would allow urban agriculture in lands surrounding the towers. One recommendation (Nasr et al. 2010) is that the municipality could support garden sharing food production initiatives through providing a template contract and management of lease arrangements. The approval by City Council of a Toronto Agricultural Programme and Workplan in November 2013 signals strong support for scaling up urban agriculture in the city.

A different model is the farm subdivision (Gallant and Wekerle 2009) initiated by developers, non-profits, and government. Prairie Crossing, near Chicago, is a housing development that has 154 acres reserved for organic farming, a 40-acre family farm, farm education programmes, and a farmers' market. For homeowners, the farm is an amenity and one-quarter of residents volunteer on the farm. Qroe Farm Preservation, a US developer, has created farm subdivisions that combine estate lots with shared ownership of farmlands. Residents purchase their own housing site and a portion of the farmlands is held as an agricultural easement by all landowners. In Tsawwassen, British Columbia, the 350-acre Southlands development designates 30% as agricultural lands, including community gardens, smaller farms near a village, and large farms on the outskirts. These will be placed in a community land trust. While clearly designed as luxury housing developments, these farm subdivisions incorporate food production into residential development from the outset and develop new hybrid models of property ownership that reflect the mainstreaming of the local food concept.

7. Reflections

The search for arable urban lands has often ignored the millions of acres available in front and backyards of single family houses located in urban, suburban, and exurban areas of cities in the Global North or the land around apartment buildings, assuming that private property ownership puts these lands off limits to urban agriculture. We argue that the association of a practice and a land use – urban agriculture – primarily with publicly owned lands severely curtails the opportunities for food growing in cities. Assumptions about private property are challenged when property relations between property owners and urban growers are re-negotiated, or when the homeowners' "property" includes access to land to grow food. These initiatives are dependent on entrepreneurial individuals and NGOs who see opportunities to expand sustainable urban agriculture in inner cities, suburbs, and peri-urban areas by engaging directly with private property owners. These projects are often the outcomes of personal relationships dependent on trust and shared values. They offer a hybrid approach to property relations composed of elements of exchange and commerce that challenge conventional notions of private property based on exclusive control over resources and access.

Johnson (2010) argues that urban agriculture projects confront some of the tenets of neoliberal capitalism based on individualism, private property ownership, and speculative land investment. Urban food growing projects serve as useful precedents for relocalizing food production, community building, and local economic development. Their innovation lies in the restructuring of social relations between food producers and consumers, sometimes resulting in a new shared economy. They represent yet another example of goods and services produced outside the mainstream capitalist economy through operating in accordance with a social and environmental ethic of care. Garden sharing projects and the small number of farm subdivisions suggest that there is substantial variation and complexity in urban property relations and urban food production, particularly when it involves the single-family house and its associated lands. There is limited empirical evidence of how these projects alter either the politics of food or gardens. How do these urban food growers with one foot in caring work and the other in capitalist enterprise connect with the networks of food-based movements? As individual projects scattered throughout the city, are they individualistic entrepreneurs or will they develop networks and organized groups that engage in formal politics at the municipal level? Will they focus narrowly on issues of access to land for setting up more gardens and start-up funds for food entrepreneurs or will they frame their work as food-animated social change efforts? Garden sharing and new built forms that incorporate food growing have the potential to move food politics and urban agriculture out of the realm of marginal left-over urban spaces cultivated by the converted to reach out to more mainstream urban residents living in single-family houses or apartments in urban, suburban, and peri-urban locations. Can a partnership model that combines exchange with entrepreneurial urban agriculture tied to the market be the catalyst for expanding the urban agriculture movement spatially and politically?

References

Alkon, A.H. 2012. The socio-nature of local organic food. *Antipode*, 45 (3), 663–680.

Alternatives Journal. 2014. Special issue on sharing economy. April. Available from: www.alternativesjoiurnal.ca

Baker, E.L. 2005. Tending cultural landscapes and food citizenship in Toronto's community gardens. *The Geographical Review*, 94 (3), 305–325.

Blake, A. and D. Cloutier-Fisher. 2009. Backyard bounty: Exploring the benefits and challenges of backyard garden sharing projects. *Local Environment*, 14 (9), 797–807.

Blay-Palmer, A. 2009. The Canadian pioneer: The genesis of urban food policy in Toronto. *International Planning Studies*, 14 (40), 401–416.

Blomley, N. 2004. *Unsettling the city: Urban land and the politics of property*. New York: Routledge.

Blomley, N. 2005. Flowers in the bathtub: Boundary crossings at the public-private divide. *Geoforum*, 36, 281–296.

Bolton, R. 2014. Cities feed cities: Unearthing three unique urban agriculture projects in Montreal, Toronto, and Vancouver. *Spacing*, Summer, 60–63.

Borras, S.M. et al. 2012. Land grabbing in Latin America and the Caribbean. *The Journal of Peasant Studies*, 39 (3–4), 845–872.

Botsman, R. and R. Rogers. 2010. *What's mine is yours: The rise of collaborative consumption*. New York: Harper Collins.

Brait, E. 2017. Toronto's new agrihood. *Toronto Star*, June 3, L1.

Bromley, D. 1998. Rousseau's revenge: The demise of the freehold estate. In H. Jacobs, ed. *Who owns America? Social conflict over property rights*. Madison: University of Wisconsin Press, 19–28.

Chatterton, P. 2002. Squatting is still legal, necessary and free: A brief intervention in the corporate city. *Antipode*, 34 (1), 1–7.

City Farmer. 2004. Ipsos-Reid poll on behalf of City Farmer. [online] Available from: http://cityfarmer.org/40percent.html. [Accessed 6 June 2004].

City of Toronto. 2013. *Toronto agricultural program and workplan*. Toronto: City of Toronto November 13.

Classens, M. 2014. The nature of urban gardens: Toward a political ecology of urban agriculture. *Agriculture and Human Values*. 32 (2), 229–239.

Classens, M., J.J. McMurtry, and J. Sumner. 2015. Doing markets differently: FoodShare Toronto's good food markets. In J. Quarter, S. Ryan, and A. Chan eds. *Social purpose enterprises: Case studies for social change*. Toronto, ON: University of Toronto Press, 215–235.

Cockrall-King, J. 2012. *Food and the city: Urban agriculture and the new food revolution*. Amherst, NY: Prometheus Books.

Davies, A., B. Donald, M. Gray and J. Knox-Hayes. 2017. Sharing economies: Moving beyond binaries in a digital age. *Cambridge Journal of Regions, Economy and Society*, 10 (2), 209–230.

Desmarais, A. 2007. *La via campesina: Globalization and the power of peasants*. Halifax, NS: Fernwood Publishing.

The Economist. 2013. The rise of the sharing economy. March 9. Available from: www.economist.com/news

Fairbairn, M. 2014. Like gold with yield: Evolving intersections between farmland and finance. *The Journal of Peasant Studies*, 41 (5), 777–795.

Field, T. and B. Bell. 2013. *Harvesting justice: Transforming food, land and agricultural systems in the Americas*. New York: U.S. Food Sovereignty Alliance.

Foster, S.R. and C. Iaione. 2016. The city as a commons. *Yale Law and Policy Review*, 34 (2), 281–350.

Gallant, E. and G.R. Wekerle. 2009. Farm subdivisions: Preserving farmland and/or exurban amenity space. *Plan Canada*, August, 29–32.

Gibson-Graham, J.K. 2006. *A postcapitalist politics*. Minneapolis, MN: University of Minnesota Press.

Gibson-Graham, J.K., J. Cameron, and S. Healy. 2016. Commoning as a post-capitalist politics. In A. Amin and P. Howell, eds. *Releasing the commons*. London: Routledge, 192–212.

Goldie, L. 1985. Title and use (and usufruct): An ancient distinction too oft forgot. *American Journal of International Law*, 79, 689–714.

Graham, N. 2011. *Lawscape: Property, environment, law*. New York: Routledge.

Guthman, J. 2008. Neoliberalism and the making of food politics in California. *Geoforum*, 38, 1171–1183.

Hackworth, J. 2007. *The neoliberal city: Governance, ideology, and development in American urbanism*. Ithaca: Cornell University Press.

Johnson, L. 2010. *City farmer: Adventures in urban food growing*. Toronto: D&M Publishers.

Kortright, R. and S. Wakefield. 2011. Edible backyards: A qualitative study of household food growing and its contributions to food security. *Agriculture and Human Values*, 28, 39–53.

Lawson, L.J. 2005. *City bountiful: A century of community gardening in America*. Berkeley: University of California Press.

Lemieux, E. 2014. Personal interview with author, December 10.

Leopold, A. 1966. *A sand county Almanac*. New York: Ballantine Books.

Levkoe, C. 2014. The food movement in Canada: A social movement network perspective. *The Journal of Peasant Studies*, 41 (3).

Logan, S. and G.R. Wekerle. 2008. Neoliberalized environmental governance? Land trusts, private conservation and nature on the Oak Ridges Moraine. *Geoforum*, 39, 2097–2108.

Lololi, A. 2000. Personal interview with author, September 29.

Lololi, A. 2005. *Presentation, food for talk series, Faculty of environmental studies*, York University, December 2.

Lololi, A. 2013. Personal communication with author, December 18.

Lololi, A. 2014. Personal communication with author. September 9.

MacGregor, S. 2006. *Beyond mothering earth: Ecological citizenship and the politics of care*. Vancouver: University of British Columbia Press.

McClintock, N. 2010. Why farm the city? Theorizing urban agriculture through a lens of metabolic rift. *Cambridge Journal of Regions, Economy and Society*, 3, 191–207.

McClintock, N. 2013. Radical, reformist, and garden-variety neoliberal: Coming to terms with urban agriculture's contradictions. *Local Environment*, 1–25. DOI 10.1080/13549839.2012.752797

McMichael, P. 2009. A food regime genealogy. *Journal of Peasant Studies*, 36 (1), 139–169.

Mezaros, G. 2000. Taking the land into their hands: The landless workers' movement and the Brazilian state. *Journal of Law and Society*, 27 (4), 517.

Mikulak, M. 2013. *The politics of the pantry: Stories, food and social change*. Montreal and Kingston: McGill-Queen's University Press.

Nasr, J. et al. 2010. *Scaling up urban agriculture in Toronto: Building the infrastructure*. Toronto: The Metcalf Foundation.

Pierce, J. 2010. Reinvigorating the concept of land tenure for American urban geography. *Geography Compass*, 4 (12), 1747–1757.

Porter, C. 2009. Garden-sharing program bears fruit. *Toronto Star*. [online] Available from: www.thestar.com/news/gta/2009/07/10/gardensharing_program_bears_fruit.html. [Accessed 3 September 2013].

Porter, C. 2011. Backyard farming in the GTA. *Toronto Star*. [online] Available from: www.thestar.com/news/gta/2011/04/06/porter_backyard_farming. [Accessed 28 November 2013].

Pudup, M.B. 2008. It takes a garden: Cultivating citizen-subjects in organized garden projects. *Geoforum*, 39, 1228–1240.

Raposo, M. 2001. Personal interviews by the G. Wekerle and Carlos Teixeira, June.

Raposo, M. 2004. Personal interview by G. Wekerle, June 8.

Ribot, J.C. and N.L. Peluso. 2003. A theory of access. *Rural Sociology*, 68 (2), 153–181.

Robbins, P. 2007. *Lawn people: How grasses, weeds, and chemicals make us who we are.* Philadelphia: Temple University Press.

Sax, J.L. 1993. Property rights and the economy of nature: Understanding Lucas vs. South Carolina Coastal Commission. *Stanford Law Review,* 45, 1433–1455.

Schmelzkopf, K. 1995. Urban community gardens as contested space. *Geographical Review,* 85, 364–381.

Schmelzkopf, K. 2002. Incommensurability, land use, and the right space: Community gardens in New York City. *Urban Geography,* 23, 323–343.

Singer, J.W. 2000. *Entitlement: The paradoxes of property.* New Haven: Yale University Press.

Staeheli, L. and D. Mitchell. 2008. *The people's property? Power, politics, and the public.* New York: Routledge.

Tronto, J. 1993. *Moral boundaries: A political argument for an ethic of care.* New York: Routledge.

Turner, M.D. 2017. Political ecology III: The commons and commoning. *Progress in Human Geography,* 4 (6), 795–802.

Van Wagner, E. 2013. Putting property in its place: Relationship theory, environmental rights and land use planning. *Revue Generale de Droit,* 43, 271–311.

Wekerle, G.R. 2004. Food justice movements: Policy, planning and networks. *Journal of Planning Education and Research,* 23 (4), 78–86.

Wekerle, G.R. 2005. Domesticating the neoliberal city: Invisible genders and the politics of place. In W. Harcourt and A. Escobar, eds. *Women and the politics of place.* Bloomfield, CT: Kumarian Press, 86–89.

Wekerle, G.R. 2013. Interrogating gendered silences in urban policy: Regionalism and alternative visions of a caring region. In L. Peake and M. Rieker, eds. *Rethinking feminist interventions into the urban.* New York: Routledge, 142–158.

Wells, B.L. and S. Gradwell. 2001. Gender and resource management: Community-supported agriculture as caring-practice. *Agriculture and Human Values,* 18, 107–119.

Wiebe, K.D., A. Tegene and B. Kihn. 1998. Land tenure, land policy and the property rights debate. In H. Jacobs, ed. *Who owns America? Social conflict over property rights.* Madison: University of Wisconsin Press, 79–93.

Winne, M. 2010. *Food rebels, guerilla gardeners, and smart cookin' mamas: Fighting back in an age of industrial agriculture.* Boston: Beacon Press.

Wolford, W. 2003. Families, fields, and fighting for land: The spatial dynamics of contention in rural Brazil. *Mobilization,* 8 (2), 201–215.

7   UK allotments and urban food initiatives

(Limited?) potential for reducing inequalities

Wendy M. Miller

1. Introduction

The number of urban and peri-urban food initiatives has increased significantly in many regions of the world in recent years, notably Europe and the US. For example, in the UK, from just one farmers' market in the city of Bath in 1997, there were over 800 by 2013.[1] The Federation of City Farms and Community Gardens (FCFCG) now represents around 200 city and school farms, 1,000 community gardens, and more than 70 school farms, with an estimated three million visitors a year.[2] Further unknown numbers take part in other food ventures such as school gardens, food banks, abundance initiatives and foraging, or guerrilla gardening.[3] There are also around 330,000 individual allotment plots in the UK, and an estimated 23 million domestic gardens (Buck 2016), although no data exists on how many of the latter are used for growing food.

This chapter aims to examine how these different forms of food-related activities can contribute to the values of social and environmental justice, reducing inequalities. It starts with an overview of the burgeoning number of food-related activities within (peri-)urban areas, of the outcomes evidenced for them, and the different analytical perspectives applied in academic literature. It then outlines the development of the UK allotment system to provide the context for these newer urban food initiatives. This illustrates how the impacts acknowledged for allotments in the nineteenth century were the same as those acknowledged in the present day for the newer urban food initiatives. The next section introduces the conceptual frameworks of diverse economies and capital-assets framework used to help identify the contingent factors and social-ecological impacts of different food ventures. Findings from empirical research on allotments and other food activities in Plymouth are then used to illustrate how the frameworks presented can be applied to provide evidence of outcomes in an accessible form. The chapter concludes with discussion of how this research helps to inform understandings of the potential of food-related activities to reduce inequalities, or enhance social and environmental justice, and offers suggestions for further research.

2. Unpacking (peri-)urban food initiatives

The wide range of urban food-related activities have diverse characteristics in the nature of their activities, scale, and purpose or guiding values (see e.g. Kirwan et al. 2013). Brief descriptions of these activities, urban space arrangements, and requirements, and examples of impacts evidenced for them are given below (Table 7.1).

Table 7.1 Different types of urban food activities, their land/space requirements, and key impacts

	Description/example claims
Community supported agriculture	Land (owned or leased) in peri-urban region with food produced on a "shared-risk" basis with consumers, through subscription arrangements that may involve commitment of time as well as money to ensure a sustainable enterprise. Quality food, learning and skills development.
Urban agriculture	Commercial-scale growing in cities on owned or leased land. Provides incomes, skills, jobs, food, and builds communities.
Allotments	Statutory duty of local authority to provide individual plots, on average 250m2, at "reasonable rent" on 12-month renewable leases to residents. Quality food for households, self-reliance, social cohesion, increased biodiversity.
Community gardens	Neighbourhood sites for residents to garden and interact with others often on local authority land with range of tenancy arrangements/lengths. Builds social capital, reduces isolation, improve local environments, increases food security.
Farmers' markets, farm shops, independent retailers, mobile outlets, vegetable box schemes, buyers cooperatives	Local outlets for local produce. Requirements of retail/market venues or parking for deliveries. Short supply chains that reconnect producers and consumers. Builds social capital and local economies. Quality food assurance.
Fair trade, local in supermarkets	Outlets for ethical or local produce. Shelf space. Consumer choice.
School gardens	Often run by individual teacher outside "the day job" involving allocation of space within school grounds. Learning opportunities for all aspects of food on school grounds, in curricula, practical skills, and input to school meals.
Guerilla gardening	Planting of spaces without agreement of landowner. Improving biodiversity and providing food. Reclaiming "rights" to space.
Abundance initiatives, foraging	Harvesting of unused crops and wild food, with permission of owner if on private land or tacit agreement by local authority.
Food policy councils or urban food partnerships	Coordination of different food actors/interests across urban areas. Requirements normally of meeting and events spaces.

Source: Author

The grouping of the different food activities suggested above is offered as a means to achieve conceptual clarity with which to situate analyses. While allowing for their diverse characteristics, it also indicates potential similarities according to their function and area of operation. The key focus for this chapter, of impact on inequalities, is signposted by requirements for urban land, but also by the outcomes suggested in a wide range of literature.

Many analyses situate community gardens, farmers' markets, and other urban food-related activities under the umbrella term of "alternative food networks" (AFNs), as a means of distinguishing their alterity or difference to food activities within conventional food networks or systems (see e.g. Sonnino and Marsden 2006; Jarosz 2008; Goodman and Goodman 2009; Harris 2009). For example, Goodman *et al.* (2012: 48) explore alternative food networks as:

> processes that integrate new complexes of production-consumption, with their distinctive material, cultural and moral economies – organic, local, fair trade, or animal-friendly foods, for example – into the practices and routines of daily life.

Other terms for similar processes and networks are also used, including local food networks (LFNs) (Kirwan et al. ibid.), food sovereignty movements (Leventon and Laudan 2017), sustainable food systems (Blay-Palmer *et al.* 2016), and diverse food economies (DFEs) (Dixon 2010). Literature that compares these DFEs to conventional food systems has explored how the former represent a "quality turn" (Ilbery and Kneafsey 2000), an "ethics of care" with outputs of "good food" (Sage 2003; Dowler *et al.* 2010), and how they involve "reconnecting producers and consumers" (Kneafsey *et al.* 2008) alongside a reflexivity, or feedback loops, involving different values and knowledges (Goodman *et al.* 2012). The variety of ventures considered under the rubric of DFEs ranges from large-scale commercial organic agriculture, locality and terroir food networks, to the urban projects listed above, which are the focus of this chapter.

A growing academic literature presents evidence on the impacts of these varied food ventures for human populations and wider ecosystems (see for example Stocker and Barnett 1998; Holland 2004; Mougeot 2005; Levkoe 2006; Seyfang 2006; Alaimo *et al.* 2008; Sherriff 2009; Kortright and Wakefield 2011; Hawkes and Acott 2013; Kirwan *et al.* 2013). Empirical research has demonstrated how specific food initiatives contribute to nutritional intakes (Kortright and Wakefield 2011), food justice and food security (Pothukuchi 2004; Wekerle 2004; Levkoe 2006; Kirwan and Maye 2013), economic development (Marsden 2010; Choo 2011), community building (Kingsley and Townsend 2006), and resilience or sustainability (Morgan and Sonnino 2010). Other analyses discuss the (often limited) potential of these projects to enhance food sovereignty, rights to the city and spatial justice (Soja 2008; Ladner 2011; Colasanti *et al.* 2012; Darly and McClintock 2017; Clair *et al.* 2017). Goodman *et al.* (*ibid*: 24) suggest that local food movements have ignored the tensions between universal and particular values (global-local) as acknowledged in theories of justice, whilst Edwards-Jones *et al.* (2008) contend that the focus on "local" does not necessarily provide social or ecological advantages, especially in terms of food miles. An increasing literature questions the usefulness of the term "alternative food networks" pointing to the blurring of boundaries or co-optation (see Goodman *et al. ibid.*), the fact that urban food projects facilitate the continuation of a neoliberal rolling back of state welfare (Perrons and Skyers 2003; Harris 2009; McClintock 2014), that the word "alternative" perpetuates a dualism and the hegemony of "conventional" (Gibson-Graham 2002; Wilson 2013), or even that the word alternative can be seen as pejorative (Venn *et al.* 2006). Tregear (2011) states the need for future work to break the impasse between these positions, and suggests there is often inconsistent use of concepts, and conflation of spatial/structural characteristics of AFNs with outcomes. The focus taken in this chapter is to build on findings presented in the literature relevant to urban inequalities rather than engage in these many debates *per se*.

Given the diversity of activities discussed in analyses of AFNs, it is problematic to make generic assertions about their impacts, whether over food justice, sustainability, or social cohesion. However, the research on which this chapter is based suggests that the greater conceptual clarity which Tregear (*ibid.*) calls for can be attained through applying the capital-assets framework. It uses the case of UK allotments, whereby households produce food on land rented "at a reasonable rate", as a comparator for impacts of other food-related activities in (peri-) urban areas. In order to provide the context to discussion of the current and future impacts of the diverse present day food initiatives, an historical perspective is required (see e.g. Wainwright 2005; Ekers *et al.* 2009), and a brief outline of the development of the UK allotment system is given next.

3. Allotments

An estimated total of 330,000 individual allotment plots exist in the UK, varying in size, albeit with a norm of $250m^2$, and are made available to householders on 12-month renewable tenancies. The formal allotment system in the UK developed from a myriad of informal land rental arrangements that existed between owners and non-owners of land. Although similar to other "home" or community garden arrangements in many countries worldwide (i.e. non-monetized activities of food growing, produce sharing, etc.), legislation from 1819 onwards specified provision of allotments, or "land to rent at a reasonable rate" to the poor.

The legislation to provide access to allotments was designed for a constellation of reasons. Widespread food and anti-enclosure protests had been seen in the UK since at least the Levellers movement in the 1600s, culminating in the "Captain Swing" riots during the 1830s (Bohstedt and Williams 1988; Moselle 1995; Archer 1997; Burchardt 1997; Fairlie 2009). These protests were concurrent with rising food prices, high levels of un-(der)-employment, and falling wages. The parallel processes of industrialization and rural-to-urban migration were accelerating, as was increasing trade of food out of its areas of production (Stevenson 1992). Proponents for allotments documented the benefits of food security and self-reliance as well as leisure, and it was evidenced that poor relief rates were much lower in parishes where land was made available (Way 2008). Intense national parliamentary debates took place over the social unrest as well as over the high demand for land to rent, which far exceeded the supply that estate-owners, farmers, and parishes were willing to make available (Burchardt 1997). Nationwide elections in 1880s were dubbed the "allotment elections", and the provision of allotments was finally accepted to be in the national interest (Chase 1988; Stevenson 1992; Way 2008; Boyle 2012). This recognition led to numerous acts of legislation throughout the nineteenth and twentieth centuries that required local authorities to provide allotments for their populations and gave protected status to many sites located throughout the UK in both rural and urban areas. Allotments ranging in size from an eighth to eight acres were rented to agricultural and industrial labourers, tradesmen, and craftsmen, as well as to some professionals as a result of this legislation (Burchardt 2002).

At the start of the twentieth century, during World Wars One and Two, allotments played a major role in helping to provide basic food supplies for the UK population, with the number of plots peaking at an estimated 1,400,000 in 1943 (MLNR 1969). However, post-war, available and affordable convenience food, together with increased levels of waged employment for women, greatly reduced demand for allotments and many sites became neglected. As UK cities expanded and in-filled, land speculation and values rose significantly and many allotment sites were sold for building development. A UK government review in the late 1960s suggested re-branding remaining sites along European lines, as leisure gardens (Thorpe 1975). However, from the 1970s onwards in the context of economic recession and increasing environmental and food quality concerns, there was a revival in demand for allotments fuelled by campaign groups (such as Friends of the Earth) and the media (for example, The Good Life, a TV series). A parliamentary committee in 1998 (DETR 1998) set up in response to concerns over a decline in allotment provision, called for their inclusion in public health strategies, pointed to their important role in local neighbourhood culture, as well as their alignment with other national policy objectives on food security and sustainability.

The themes of food security and autonomy (food sovereignty), community building and leisure opportunities (social cohesion), and "keeping the land in good heart" (sustainability), have been cited since the nineteenth century as grounds for provision of allotments (Chase 1988; Crouch and Ward 1997; Boyle 2012). Yet given the lack of official data on acreage or number of sites at a national level, the extent of the present-day contribution of allotments to health, culture, or environment is difficult to assess. Whilst the outcomes documented for newer urban food-related initiatives are largely the same as those long-recognized for allotments, clear distinctions also exist: local authorities have a statutory duty to provide urban land for allotment sites and legislation prohibits use of allotments for commercial purposes. The significance of these and other differences can be assessed with the aid of the conceptual frameworks used in this research.

4. Conceptualising diverse food networks

Households in the UK spent a total of £96bn on food and non-alcoholic drink for domestic consumption in 2016.[4] In a pattern similar to elsewhere in most of northern Europe and the US, food store multiples account for 98% of food expenditure for domestic consumption (source: Kantar World Panel 2017). Thus, despite their documented growth, the marketized share of the diverse food initiatives described above (Table 7.1) in the UK food system can only amount to an unknown fraction of the 2% "other expenditure". Nevertheless, as documented by national level statistics,[5] non-marketized activities can comprise a large part of household and community informal economies. As Gibson-Graham's (2002, 2003, 2008) seminal work on diverse economies indicates, there is a pressing need to make visible the non-monetized nature of much economic activity, so that it can be acknowledged, valued, and/or accounted for in analyses (see e.g. Allen and Sachs 2007; McIntyre and Rondeau 2011). To this end, Gibson-Graham (2008) have categorized the many diverse forms of economic relations as market, alternative market, and non-market. This has the effect also of enabling discussions to move beyond the concept of "conventional" as global and large and "alternative" as small and local, through recognising the ubiquitous nature worldwide of unpaid housework, including cooking and domestic food production (see also Massey 2007). For the purpose of this chapter then, the term "diverse food networks" (DFNs) is used experimentally to encompass the range of "other than" conventional food networks. The differences may be relational, spatial, and/or scalar, whether involving supermarket shelf space for local and ethical produce, guerrilla gardening, or a community garden.

Despite the diversity of activities encompassed in analyses of new food initiatives, evaluation of their requirements and outcomes can be also furthered through the capital-assets framework as used widely in development literature on sustainable livelihoods (Bebbington 1999; Scoones 2009), and more recently applied to local food initiatives in the US (Pigg *et al.* 2013; Schmit *et al.* 2017). This framework evolved from the work of Chambers and Conway (1992) which in turn was based on Sen's (1984, 1986) concepts of entitlements and capabilities. Derived from the WHO European Office for Investment for Health Development, the definition used by Morgan and Ziglio (2007) of an asset is

> any factor (or resource), which enhances the ability of individuals, groups, communities, populations, social systems and/or institutions to maintain and sustain health and well-being and to help to reduce health inequities.

Morgan and Ziglio (*ibid.*) further suggest that assets can protect and provide a buffer against "life's stresses". The concept of different dimensions of "capital" had also been proposed earlier by Bourdieu (1986: 24), albeit privileging economic capital over other forms:

> it has to be posited simultaneously that economic capital is at the root of all the other types of capital and that these transformed, disguised forms of

economic capital, never entirely reducible to that definition, produce their most specific effects only to the extent that they conceal (not least from their possessors) the fact that economic capital is at the root . . . of their effects.

However, in considering sustainability, and specifically that of food systems, the dimension of ecological, environmental, or natural capital-assets can also be seen as "at the root"; a trifold scheme of social, economic, and environmental is often used in debates on sustainability and resilience (see e.g. Basiago 1998; Pearson 2010; Zasada 2011; Wilson 2013). The livelihoods approach (Bebbington 1999; Scoones 2009) used a framing of four main assets or capitals: natural, economic/financial, human and social, "and others". Bourdieu (1989) discussed other categories such as intellectual, cultural, symbolic, and political capital in his analyses of education. More recently the Community Capitals Framework (CCF) used in the US separates economic capital into financial and built (see Emery and Flora 2006). The formulation used here aims to incorporate understandings from all of these fields and groups capital-assets into six categories: (i) human; (ii) social; (iii) economic; (iv) natural; (v) cultural; and (vi) political, as depicted in Figure 7.1.

These categories and short descriptions are largely self-explanatory but their application to allotments and diverse food networks are grounded in the discussion of the empirical material below. The formulation closely follows Crouch and Ward's (1997) classic analysis of UK allotments, which uses the terms of: security and refuge (human); sustainability (natural); place/earth connections and skills

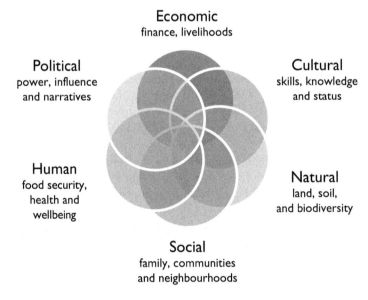

Figure 7.1 The capital-assets framework used in this research

Source: author

(cultural); new values (economic/social); and new groups of people (political). Inevitably any categorization can be critiqued, modified, and re-shaped. Further, critics of the concept of social capital contend that it has a "seductive simplicity" (Mohan and Mohan 2002: 191–193) and that it "has come to be privileged over material inequalities (between people and places) in a way which may be both analytically weak and practically disabling" (*ibid*: 204). The inclusion of political capital within a framework of multi-dimensional assets is in response to these concerns. This framing allows for analysis of urban food activities both in terms of their contingent requirements, for example of urban space (Lefebvre [1974] 1991), and of their existing and potential impacts.

Analyses that draw on distinctive categories soon also come up against the problem of blurred and overlapping boundaries. This does not imply the need to abandon the categories, but rather perhaps to acknowledge their inter-linkages, and even the ability for substitution between categories, or fungibility, in this case between the different capital-assets. A more detailed exploration of the capital-assets framework as applied to urban food initiatives is provided in this research by a temporal and spatial "snapshot", in this case, the city of Plymouth, SW England, in the present day.

5. Research methods

The empirical research into the food networks in Plymouth on which this chapter is based was undertaken during 2010–2013. It involved ethnographic work on allotments and with other food initiatives, ranging from participant observation to observing-participant (Jorgensen 1989). The nature of involvement included gardening, helping at events (e.g. making tea, pressing apples), and contributing to discussions, as speaker, researcher, note-taker, and audience member. As well as numerous conversations with allotment tenants over the period of the research,[6] over 60 interviews, ranging from formal to "conversations with a purpose" were carried out with key stakeholders in the area and region. These included allotment and local authority officers, food project managers, workers and volunteers. Extensive use was also made of existing sources of data and visual materials (archive documents, government datasets, minutes, reports, web pages, event flyers, etc.). The primary focus was on allotments, tracing their development through time and their functioning in the present day, providing comparisons to other food initiatives on the parameters of the capital-assets discussed above.

6. Diverse urban food activities in Plymouth and surrounding region

(a) The study area

Plymouth in SW England is now a city of 256,000 people, having developed over the centuries as a trading and naval port with national significance. As with other cities, sharp differentials exist across the city between areas of prosperity and deprivation, with life expectancies varying by 13 years. In common with other cities also, is the sourcing of the vast majority of food for residents through the major supermarkets, with only a very few remaining independent retailers (of fresh fruit and vegetables, fish, wholefoods and ethnic foods). In the recent past however, Plymouth has become recognized for its newer urban food initiatives, through its Food Charter, one of the first in the country, drawn up by the multi-sectoral partnership of Food Plymouth (see www.foodplymouth.org), and as a founder member of the Sustainable Food Cities Network (see sustainablefoodcities.org).

(b) Diverse food activities in Plymouth

Urban food activities in Plymouth can be grouped according to the scheme in Table 7.1. Although space precludes detailed descriptions of all of these, some examples are given in illustration of how the concepts of diverse economies and capital-assets can help clarify discussions. Apart from a couple of small private farms within the city boundaries, there are no other commercial food growing activities in Plymouth such as the urban agriculture or CSAs as described for other cities (DeLind 2003; Charles 2011; Colasanti *et al.* 2012). However, marketized exchange activities include several vegetable box schemes supplying into the city (e.g. Riverford, Keveral Farm, and Tamar Grow Local), whose customers are able to spend more on quality food than those who rely on discounted supermarkets. A farmers' market proved unpopular with large retailers who complained that it was damaging their trade, and that they paid business rates yearlong while stallholders only had to pay a small cost for a fortnightly stall. The market was discontinued in light of these objections despite protests from the market's customers.

As in other cities, there has been a steep rise in numbers seeking assistance from the existing Plymouth Foodbank[7] and another initiative (Devon and Cornwall Food Association) was more recently set up which distributes unsold food from supermarkets to charities throughout the city, enrolling volunteers to manage the scheme. Several community gardens, mostly located on allotment sites, and ten or more school gardens exist throughout the city. These also rely on voluntary labour together with project funding, for example, from the Big Lottery (Diggin' It), the UK Building Communities Initiative (Grow Efford), and neighbourhood regeneration funding (East End Community Allotments). These non-market community projects have common aims of building social cohesion and capital through their events and activities, providing opportunities to learn skills of growing and cooking, improve health through the exercise involved, and with outcomes of good food at little or no cost. However, the survival of projects beyond the grant, as reported for elsewhere in literature (McGlone *et al.* 1999; Cameron and Gibson 2005), has relied on the continuing commitment and motivation of a few individuals, much of which again is on a voluntary basis. Apart from funded projects, there have been several instances of sporadic guerrilla gardening in the city, but the two (one being Occupy!) that have involved "reclaiming land" through squatting have been evicted.

During the time of this research, the cross-sector city-wide partnership, Food Plymouth, brought together people from profit and non-profit sectors. All were involved in some aspect of food provision and with a desire to impact some or all of the different capital-assets outlined above. For example, participants included commercial wholesalers looking to supply produce into the city, academics and public health workers seeking to address health inequalities, and community development practitioners involved in regeneration projects. Thanks to funding from key partners, a part-time coordinator seconded from the Soil Association, and voluntary time commitments from committee members, a Plymouth Food Charter and accompanying action plan was developed, and the network consolidated into a community interest company (CIC). Although the Food Plymouth partnership developed a business case and plan for a local food outlet in the city centre, the rental for retail space combined with business rates was prohibitive and the plan floundered. To date the network has achieved minimal additional allocation of resources for food-related activities in the city, but it has brought "the new food agenda" into the policy view of many city decision-makers (Food Plymouth 2014).

(c) Plymouth's allotments

As in other UK cities, allotments in Plymouth were part of the pattern of urban development. During wartimes in the twentieth century, the city's allotment sites became central to producing food for its residents, as well as for crews of ships in its port. Yet official records from the war years show reluctance by the local authority to allocate urban space to food production despite requests from the national government to release more land in the national interest.[8] Post-war, in line with national trends, allotments became under-occupied and some sites were sold for building development. However, again in line with national trends, there has been a steep increase in demand for allotment plots since the 1980s, and more especially since the financial crisis of 2008. As at October 2012, there were around 1,300 individual plots on 32 sites throughout the city. At the same time there were around 1,000 people waiting for an allotment plot, or nearly as many again as the existing tenants.

The range of food and non-food production activities involved in allotment cultivation is discussed below in terms of requirements of and impacts on the different dimensions of capital-assets, illustrated by conversations and interviews with allotment tenants.[9] It touches on the similarities and differences with other urban food ventures, explored further in the subsequent sections of the chapter.

The human capital attained through cultivation of plots, in terms of food supplies, health, and well-being, was unsurprisingly a major reason for the time spent by tenants on their allotments. Attaining supplies of quality food was a key aspect for many:

> I don't trust stuff in the shops, you never really know what they've done to them.
>
> (F07)

Even from the veg box, they look great, and they're definitely organic, but they've still probably been sitting around for at least a few days. You know what they say, you need to run from the garden to the kitchen to get the best taste.

(F29)

However, actual levels of food supplies were not cited as a key concern by many of the tenants spoken to, indeed, there was a sense of surplus and bounty:

I know I could buy potatoes by the sackful quite cheaply, but there's nothing like the taste of ones just dug up from the allotment.

(F23)

I can't be doing with all that freezing and preserving lark. I'd rather just have my fill of whatever is in season and then move onto what's new.

(M27)

Even so, recognition of the costs of quality food was frequently referred to:

increasingly I think as I go round the supermarkets I'm looking at how expensive for example soft fruit is, I know there that I make a fortune because I grow so much soft fruit . . . I get tons of it and freeze it.

(F03)

Other tenants appreciated more the physical and mental health benefits of gardening and the "restorative value" of being in the natural environment:

What better way to spend a few hours relaxing than gardening; there's always something new, and always something interesting. I can just do my own thing, and listen to the birds, fiddle about, sit down a bit then go and do a bit of digging.

(M03)

The contribution to mental health through stress reduction was also underlined by the DETR 1998 report (para 14) such that "The mental health benefits for all plot holders should not be underestimated". However, motivations and impacts on the different dimensions of capital-assets were often conflated or difficult to separate out:

I do it more for the pleasure than I do to save money . . . I think there's absolutely nothing better than picking something and having it on your plate within the hour. . . . I do like the idea that there isn't a great distance between the plot and the plate and I like that it hasn't been tampered with.

(F01)

The above statements illustrate how different aspects of human capital are valued by plot holders, and how levels of inputs (contingent factors) such as physical health for digging, and outputs (outcomes) such as quantities of fresh food vary between individuals. Further, although supplies of quality food were frequently a key motivating factor, the valuation of these was interlinked both with the level of economic capital available to participants, as well as cultural capital in terms of growing and culinary skills.

Allotments have long been recognized to provide social and community opportunities and reduce social isolation especially for those not in paid employment (Crouch and Ward 1997; DETR 1998; Hope and Ellis 2009). This is not always the case though:

> I can mix with all the people I want outside [the site]; it's the chance to just "be" that I really enjoy here.
>
> (M03)

As also documented by Wiltshire and Geoghegan (2012), some tenants valued their allotment as a place "to get away from it all", including other people. Nevertheless, a ubiquitous feature is the gifting of surplus produce to fellow allotment tenants, wider families, and neighbours, as well as others they have links with, whether work, neighbourhood, or community associations. A classic example of social capital was described by one tenant:

> I take all my surplus to the bowling club, and they sell them, they're always trying to raise funds for this and that.
>
> (M29)

As well as gifting produce, time helping other tenants in cultivation was appreciated both by recipients and those giving.

> I like being able to help, it's hard when you're just starting.
>
> (M28)

> It really inspired me to try and produce bigger crops when [Mxx] told me the potatoes I gave him were the best he'd ever tasted.
>
> (F23)

Tenants' statements illustrated the enhanced skills and status involved, indicating building of social and cultural capital. They also confirm the central role in allotment culture of reciprocity and non-monetized exchange as frequently highlighted in literature (Crouch and Ward 1997; Buckingham 2005; Platten 2011).

Another longstanding recognition of allotments was their contribution to "keeping the land in good heart" (Chase 1988). On present day allotment sites in Plymouth, the "value" of natural capital or biodiversity varies greatly according to individual methods of cultivation, with attitudes towards different species ranging widely:

> I like to leave a corner wild; and really hope that a hedgehog or two might make their home there.
>
> (F17)

> Why bother to do the work if you're just going to let the slugs have it all.
>
> (M10)

These different perspectives are illustrated by corners and edges which are left uncultivated as well as in more designed wildlife spaces such as construction of "bug hotels", and in attempts to reduce competitors for food supplies.

This divergence in approach to ecological production, or natural capital, tended to be split by age and gender, with younger, female tenants more "eco-friendly". However, this was also dependent on how highly the supplies of food were valued and so in turn on levels of income.

The opportunity for self-reliance in provisioning of household food supplies through renting allotment gardens is limited by availability of vacant plots. During this research, people reported waiting over three years to be offered an allotment tenancy, a similar situation as reported for other cities in the UK in the present day. A city-wide Allotment User Forum exists for allotment tenants to raise issues such as cost of piped water, or fencing repairs needed, but has no political influence to gain access to urban space for food growing. Only some individuals demonstrated confidence in dealing with the local authority, by having phoned at regular intervals to check their status on the waiting list, indicating a certain political capital gained through social or cultural capital. However, local authority officials responsible for allotment sites in the city reported the need to continually justify the allocation of urban land to colleagues in other departments.

In essence, these multi-dimensional aspects of activities on Plymouth illustrate how the different capital-assets are often interlinked, and have diverse contingent factors and outcomes. The similarities and differences with other DFN activities are explored further in the discussion below.

7. Discussion: different strokes for different folks with different assets

This section compares the contingent factors and outcomes on the different dimensions of capital-assets for allotments and other DFN activities. It highlights the diverse forms of often non-monetized economic relations involved but also the fundamental requirements for natural capital in its most basic form, of urban land, together with certain levels of economic capital and/or political capital, albeit with a level of substitutability, or fungibility, between these latter two.

Allotments and other DFN activities in Plymouth demonstrate contributions to human capital in terms of food security, nutritional intakes, physical and mental health and well-being more generally, as documented in literature. For example, participants in community gardens are more likely to attain recommended levels of portions of fresh fruit and vegetables (Alaimo *et al.* 2008; Twiss *et al.* 2011) and attaining supplies of quality food is a key aspect of food gardening (Kortright and Wakefield 2011). However, the extent of impact on human capital for allotment tenants, or domestic and community gardeners, is also dependent on inputs of natural capital in the form of urban land available for cultivation but not necessarily significant levels of income. In contrast, gaining nutritional food supplies through a vegetable box does not require significant areas of urban land but does require an adequate income.

Allotment sites and community gardens in Plymouth demonstrate the building of social capital, as long documented for place-based initiatives (e.g. Shuman 1998), and indeed the aspect of socially-acceptable ways of spending leisure time was a key rationale for setting up the allotment system (Chase 1988; Way 2008). Building of social capital, or social cohesion, is also well-documented as a rationale and outcome for many DFN activities (e.g. Dowler *et al.* 2010; Milbourne 2012). Whilst other urban projects that involve food production provide the same opportunities for non-monetized exchange to a certain extent, these are usually in a more socially-structured environment, and often coordinated by an "expert" or paid professional grower. In comparison, on allotments, there is a distinctively "self-organising" nature to such exchanges and asset-building, supporting suggestions that a key common characteristic amongst allotment tenants is a desire for greater self-reliance (Crouch and Ward 1997). Such self-reliance was another key rationale for setting up the allotment system in the light of falling levels of wages and employment and the desire to cut the costs of poverty relief rates (Way 2008). In contrast, food banks provide "survival" rations for those with basic needs, though the quality of the food is reportedly often poor, and they are reliant on volunteers and charitable giving. Again, the inter-linkages between assets are clear: building social capital through DFNs requires inputs of natural, economic, and political capital-assets, whether to gain sites for allotments or community gardens or, as described above for Plymouth, to set up a retail outlet for local food or a farmers' market.

The potential exclusionary nature of DFNs has been a recurring theme in literature (e.g. Winter 2003; Goodman 2004; DuPuis and Goodman 2005; Born and Purcell 2006, Alkon and McCullen 2011), yet allotments and many other DFN activities provide opportunities to build social networks and contribute towards neighbourhood culture. The building of cultural capital demonstrated in DFN activities, of knowledge and skills (in growing or cooking) is also acknowledged; Pudup (2008) documents the enhanced status and skills gained by offenders involved in gardening projects, and cases of finding employment subsequent to volunteering in community projects were documented during this research. It is clear that food growing at any scale relieves strains on the food budget of the households and communities involved, whether monetized or not (Bakker *et al.* 2001), and so enhances economic capital. The potential of even a 250m² allotment plot to further provide a source of monetary income has also been long documented (Crouch and Ward 1997), and was referenced by participants in this research. Several CSA schemes in the Plymouth hinterland are alleviating household food budgets and providing a source of income for some participants. At the larger scales seen in some US cities and mainly peri-urban regions in the UK, livelihoods can be earned or jobs supported (Charles 2011; Choo 2011; Saltmarsh *et al.* 2011). However, the land required for income-earning opportunities to be realized through DFN ventures, whether through private or informal arrangement, is a key limiting factor in UK urban regions, despite often large areas remaining unused, designated "brownfield", and/or in local authority control.

As highlighted by the DETR (1998) investigation, it can be argued that release of land for food-related ventures would help to meet national and local authority policy objectives. The widely documented outcomes of DFN activities, as long-acknowledged for allotments, have potential to enhance mental and physical health and increase food security, and in doing so take the pressure off adult social services budgets and welfare benefit demands. Further, as Seyfang (2006) and others (Armstrong 2000; Wakefield *et al.* 2007; Kirwan *et al.* 2013; Lockie 2009), document, the skills and knowledge gained from participating in diverse urban food activities create informed citizens and consumers, contribute to social cohesion, and so contribute to the multi-dimensional capital-assets and goals of sustainability.

Environmental impacts of food provisioning, such as reduced levels of agrochemical pollution, packaging and food waste, and increased levels of recycling or composting, have been documented elsewhere for DFN activities (Pearson 2010; Connelly *et al.* 2011). Divergence in approaches to natural capital seen on Plymouth allotments compares to other newer urban food initiatives, whose participants more frequently referred to a concern for sustainability, as found elsewhere (Seyfang 2006). This may be due to the fact that allotments tenants in this research were from diverse socio-economic profiles and all age groups, albeit with the majority of 50 years of age or older. It may also be that desire and capacity for producing food supplies are greater amongst allotment tenants than, for example, amongst community garden participants.

Secondary data sources can be marshalled to provide assessments at national level (see Pretty *et al.* 2005), yet as with the differences in cultivation methods seen on Plymouth allotments, evidence for the contribution of urban food projects to sustainability is contested in relation to both local and translocal environments. Opposing views suggest either that provisioning food from local sources reduces the "food miles" that a household "consumes" in their diets (Footprint Consulting 2008) or that carbon emissions are lower from provisioning food through supermarkets than through farmers' markets (Coley *et al.* 2009). Apart from carbon emissions, the other key parameter of sustainability required by international agreement as a policy objective for local authorities and national governments is of biodiversity protection. The UK government's assessment of food security (DEFRA 2010) and Rockstrom *et al.*'s (2009) assessment of planetary boundaries also indicate that loss of biodiversity is a key challenge to sustainability of ecosystems and food supplies. A comprehensive biodiversity survey is clearly unattainable (too expensive) for most urban food projects and contestation over the wider environmental impacts of "conventional versus alternative" food production is ongoing (see e.g. Forssell and Lankoski 2015). To move beyond an impasse in debates over sustainability often focused on the sole parameter of carbon emissions, as illustrated here, the impacts of DFNs on natural capital in terms of biodiversity can be usefully assessed by cultivation methods used in food production. This can be simply determined by the extent of "landspare" or "landshare" techniques, whereby landspare involves a "set-aside" of areas for wildlife, and landshare involves ecological food production cultivation techniques; both of these approaches can be seen within the varied DFN activities in Plymouth and elsewhere.

The extent of impact of DFNs on natural capital in the form of biodiversity and sustainability more widely is again dependent on the scale and extent of their activities. Literature on food justice movements (Wekerle 2004; Levkoe 2006; Agyeman and McEntee 2014; Tornaghi 2017; Darly and McClintock 2017) suggests that diverse food projects in urban areas represent a reclaiming of urban space and a challenge to existing inequalities, and yet at the same time can enable continuing broader injustices. The precarity of the political capital involved was exemplified in this research by the speedy eviction of squatter groups from the "interstitial spaces" of the city, demonstrating the limitations of urban food growing initiatives given prevailing legal, institutionalized, and economic land use patterns. Allotment tenants in the UK in the present day have some security of tenure due to the political pressure that resulted in legislation in the nineteenth century, whilst community gardens are dependent on grant funding and goodwill of local authorities, and farmers' markets or vegetable box schemes are dependent on participants having adequate incomes: these contingencies illustrate how the potential for enhancing social or environmental justice is limited by initial inputs of key assets.

8. Conclusion

The above discussion explored the linkages and certain substitutability, or fungibility, between the different capitals and the parameters on which food ventures can be assessed. It touched on the requirements of and impacts on the different capital-assets involved in allotment gardening, illustrating both similarities and differences with other newer urban food initiatives. It has long been claimed that tenants of the UK allotment system benefit on all these different dimensions of capital. However, as for newer urban food initiatives and with a few exceptions (e.g. Crouch and Parker 2003; Wiltshire and Azuma 2000), there has been little literature on the contingent factors for these outcomes to be experienced.

The potential of allotments and other DFN ventures to meet the policy objectives of reducing health inequalities, enhancing social cohesion, and local sustainability has been illustrated, with different activities attracting different "actors". This research found that most allotment tenants are not motivated to participate in any politicized, radical, or even community gardening, but are motivated to spend often significant hours of time in cultivating their allotment, with varying degrees of informal social interaction. As also reported in literature (e.g. Platten 2011), allotments contribute non-marketized food supplies to wider family, friends, neighbours, work colleagues, or other associations, and so help to reduce food poverty or inequality amongst wider urban populations. Rather than through the largely one-way gifting involved in food banks, there is a sense of bounty and surplus with exchange of skills (between producers and, e.g. jam-makers) to maximize benefit from produce. Whilst being non-monetized, allotment gardening can nevertheless enhance human and economic capital, although is contingent on other forms of assets (e.g. cultivation skills). Allotments also provide a reservoir of natural capital in terms of biodiversity through plant material, seeds, and development of varieties which are suited to local ecosystems (landraces) (Platten 2011). Whilst many of these asset-building potentials exist in other DFN activities, allotments provide distinctive opportunities for those with low initial base levels of assets to achieve greater self-reliance, without inputs of grant funding, or charitable giving, albeit dependent on the high levels of political capital in the past. The complex inter-linkages of the different dimensions of capital-assets to lead to inclusive or exclusionary outcomes for DFNs could be contended to be not economic assets at root (cf Bourdieu (1986) but natural assets, in the most basic form of land (Shoard 1987). It can be deemed remarkable that so little academic attention has been given to this contingent factor and its key enabling conditions, viz. the economic, social, and political capital needed to enrol land into urban food networks (Steel 2008). Perhaps seen most clearly in analyses of allotments, the same constrictions and restrictions of access to urban land either facilitate or inhibit other DFN activities.

This research has proposed the usefulness of analysing DFN activities through the capital-assets framework and informed by understandings of diverse economies, as a way of evaluating the effects on social or environmental justice. The focus here has been on the differential contingent factors (capitals) to reduce inequalities. Discussion of the initiatives above illustrates the dearth of political capital within allotments or other DFNs in the present day and the resulting lack of natural capital in terms of urban land for their activities. Howard's Garden City concept, with which all planners are familiar, was a design of 1,000 acres of built land to 5,000 acres of farmland for a population of 32,000, or 64.6 hectares of open space per thousand population (Livesey 2011); today's allocation of "green space" in cities is around 1 hectare per thousand population, and targets for allotment provision for cities are at around 0.1 hectare per thousand population. The income to a local authority of around £500 per year per acre for allotments can be compared to potential income of around £1,165,000 per hectare for city land with permission for residential development (GVA 2011; DCLG 2015). Given these relative returns, it is unsurprising that those proposing further allocation of city land for allotments, or even maintaining the existing sites, need to continually justify such suggestions. Allotments are now seen as a subsidy for a small percentage of the urban population, as described by two local authority officers during this research.

Assets are interlinked and not always fungible, as with the prime example of natural capital in the form of land area. The UK-wide National Allotment Society works to protect sites from disposal,[10] but despite originating in strong articulation of issues of spatial justice, the allotment movement in the present day holds little sway over urban land resource allocations. Nevertheless, the newer urban food initiatives are adding to evidence of benefits to the different dimensions of capital-assets, and small areas of land in urban areas are being made available for food projects albeit on temporary leases.[11] Yet spatial inequalities are likely to prevail unless the newer groups involved in community and guerrilla gardening, and in (trans)national social movements such as The Land is Ours, Via Campesina, or other landless people's movements (see e.g. Caldeira 2008) can bring the focus of food justice to revive the more radical roots of the UK allotment system which at its height determined the outcome of national elections. The alternative scenario is a continued rise in charitable giving of generally poor quality food through food banks in the context of withdrawal of welfare benefits, or precarious instances of guerrilla gardening.

Historically, the legislation to make land available "at reasonable rent" was enacted in light of fears of continuing food riots as well as evidence of reduced poor relief rates in parishes where allotments existed (Chase 1988; Way 2008). The shortage of land to rent was addressed by reference to a "national interest". Current national policy objectives could also be marshalled to the support of allotment and DFN activities, as recommended by the UK government committee at the end of the twentieth century (DETR 1998): increased levels of physical activity, reduced levels of obesity, higher nutritional intake from fruit and vegetables, reduced health inequalities, cohesive neighbourhoods, improved local (and global) environments. The capital-assets framework and concept of diverse economies can be employed to provide evidence for their outcomes, not necessarily monetized but visible. Yet although allotments, and other urban food-related activities, may again come to be seen as in the national interest, it remains questionable how prevailing economic and political interests will acknowledge these as a valid use of (peri-)urban land. The take-home message is that to achieve greater social and environmental justice, the contingent factors (initial starting conditions) on all dimensions of capital-assets need to be recognized and accounted for in analyses so that they feature more highly on policy agendas.

Through a retrieval of the narratives of self-reliance, and a re-positioning of (scaling down of) nineteenth-century campaign messages,[12] a combination of new and old "food movements" may yet provide a force for reducing inequalities. Further work is sorely needed to move beyond the often mired debates (Tregear 2011) on "alternative", "local", or "diverse" food networks and their impacts on the multi-dimensional human, cultural, social, economic, political, and natural capital-assets. The discussions above indicate that research could usefully explore in more depth the relative importance of different capital-assets as contingent factors for diverse food ventures to flourish. Notable amongst this programme of work would be to develop the heterodox valuations that raise the visibility on political agendas (cf Moe 2005) of food, social, and environmental justice, in which issues of land allocation are central.

Notes

1 Dixon, R., 2007, Do farmers' markets really work? https://www.theguardian.com/life andstyle/wordofmouth/2007/may/24/ivebeenafarmersmarket [last accessed 21 May 2018].
2 Federation of City Farms and Community Gardens, 2018, Growing Communities: get inspired. www.farmgarden.co.uk/bit-history [last accessed 21 May 2018].
3 The National Allotment Society, 2018, What we do. https://www.nsalg.org.uk/about-us/our-history/ [last accessed 21 Mary 2018].
4 Statistica, 2018, Consumer spending on food and non-alcoholic drinks in the United Kingdom from 2005 to 2017* (in million GBP). www.statista.com/statistics/281938/ expenditure-on-food-and-drinks-in-the-united-kingdom-uk-since-2005/ [last accessed 21 May 2018].
5 OECD, 2018, Balancing paid work, unpaid work and leisure. www.oecd.org/gender/ data/balancingpaidworkunpaidworkandleisure.htm [last accessed 21 May 2018].
6 Identified in statements below solely as M male or F female.
7 The Trusswell Trust, 21018, End of Year Stats. www.trusselltrust.org/news-and-blog/ latest-stats/end-year-stats/ [last accessed 21 May 2018].
8 Plymouth and West Devon Records Office 1648/146, 3 February 1911.
9 Statements are from recorded interviews and as written in research log after site visits. F indicates female, M, male.
10 National Allotment Society, 2018, Protect Your Plots. www.nsalg.org.uk/news-events-campaigns/protect-your-plots/ [last accessed 21 May 2018].
11 Royal Horticultural Society, 2018, Get Involved. https://www.rhs.org.uk/get-involved [last accessed 21 May 2018].
12 The National Agricultural Union's campaign of "Three acres and a cow" appears off the radar for even the most radical land redistribution campaigns in the present day.

References

Agyeman, J. and McEntee, J., 2014, Moving the field of food justice forward through the lens of urban political ecology, *Geography Compass* 8(3): 211–220.

Alaimo, K. *et al.*, 2008, Fruit and vegetable intake among urban community gardeners, *Journal of Nutrition and Education Behavior* 40: 94–101.

Alkon, A.H. and McCullen, C.G., 2011, Whiteness and farmers markets: Performances, perpetuations . . . contestations?, *Antipode* 43(4): 937–959.

Allen, P. and Sachs, C., 2007, Women and food chains: The gendered politics of food, *International Journal of Sociology and Agriculture* 15(1): 1–23.

Archer, J.E., 1997, The nineteenth-century allotment: Half an acre and a row, *Economic History Review* 50(1): 21–36.

Armstrong, D., 2000, A survey of community gardens in upstate New York: Implications for health promotion and community development, *Health and Place* 6: 319–327.

Bakker, N. *et al.* (eds.), 2001, *Growing Cities, Growing Food: Urban Agriculture on the Policy Agenda*, Feldafing: DSE.

Basiago, A.D., 1998, Economic, social, and environmental sustainability in development theory and urban planning practice, *Environmentalist* 19(2): 145–161.

Bebbington, A., 1999, Capitals and capabilities: A framework for analyzing peasant viability, rural livelihoods and poverty, *World Development* 27(12): 2021–2044.

Blay-Palmer, A., Sonnino, R. and Custot, A., 2016, Food politics of the possible? Growing sustainable food systems through networks of knowledge, *Journal of Agriculture and Human Values* 33: 27. https://doi.org/10.1007/s10460-015-9592-0

Bohstedt, J. and Williams, D.E., 1988, The diffusion of riots: The patterns of 1766, 1795 and 1801 in Devonshire, *Journal of Interdisicplinary History* 19(1): 1–2.

Born, B. and Purcell, M., 2006, Avoiding the local trap: scale and food systems in planning research, *Journal of Planning Education and Research* 26: 195–207.

Bourdieu, P., 1986, The forms of capital, Ch. 9 in Richardson, J. (ed.), *Handbook of Theory and Research for the Sociology of Education*, Westport, CT: Greenwood.

Bourdieu, P., 1989, Social space and symbolic power, *Sociological Theory* 7(1): 14–25.

Boyle, D., 2012, *On the Eighth Day God Created Allotments*, London: Real Press.

Buck, D., 2016, *Gardens and Health: Implications for Policy and Practice*, London: The Kings Fund.

Buckingham, S., 2005, Women (re)construct the plot: The regen(d)eration of urban food growing, *Area* 37(2): 171–179.

Burchardt, J., 1997, *The Allotment Movement in England 1793–1873*, PhD thesis, Reading: University of Reading Department of History.

Burchardt, J., 2002, *The Allotment Movement in England 1793–1873*, Rochester, NY: Royal Historical Society.

Caldeira, R., 2008, 'My land, your social transformation': Conflicts within the landless people movement (MST), Rio de Janeiro, Brazil, *Journal of Rural Studies* 24: 150–160.

Cameron, J. and Gibson, K., 2005, Alternative pathways to community and economic development: The Latrobe Valley Community Partnering Project, *Geographical Research* 43(3): 274–285.

Chambers, R. and Conway, G., 1992, *Sustainable Rural Livelihoods: Practical Concepts for the 21st Century*, IDS Discussion Paper 296, Brighton: IDS.

Charles, L., 2011, Animating community supported agriculture in North East England: Striving for a 'caring practice', *Journal of Rural Studies* 27(4): 362–371.

Chase, M., 1988, *The People's Farm: English Radical Agrarianism 1775–1840*, Oxford: Clarendon Press.

Choo, K., 2011, Plowing over: Can urban farming save Detroit and other declining cities? Will the law allow it? *ABA Journal* 97: 43, August.

Clair, R. St, Hardman, M., Armitage, R.P. and Sherriff, G., 2017, The trouble with temporary: Impacts and pitfalls of a meanwhile community garden in Wythenshawe, South Manchester, *Renewable Agriculture and Food Systems*: 1–10.

Colasanti, K.J.A., Hamm, M.W. and Litjens, C.M., 2012, The city as an agricultural powerhouse? Perspectives on expanding urban agriculture from Detroit Michigan, *Urban Geography* 33(3): 348–369.

Coley, D., Howard, M. and Winter, M., 2009, Local food, food miles and carbon emissions: A comparison of farm shop and mass distribution approaches, *Food Policy* 34(2): 150–155.

Connelly, S., Markey, S. and Roseland, M., 2011, Bridging sustainability and the social economy: Achieving community transformation through local food initiatives, *Critical Social Policy* 31(2): 308–324.

Crouch, D. and Parker, G., 2003, 'Digginup' Utopia? Space, practice and land use heritage, *Geoforum* 34: 395–408.

Crouch, D. and Ward, C., 1997, *The Allotment: Its Landscape and Culture*, London: Five Leaves.

Darly, S. and McClintock, N., 2017, Introduction to urban agriculture in the neoliberal city: Critical European perspectives, *ACME: An International Journal for Critical Geographies* 16(2): 224–231.

DCLG, 2015, *Land Value Estimates for Policy Appraisal*, London: HMSO

DEFRA, 2010, *Food Security Assessment for the UK: Detailed Analysis*, London: HMSO.

DeLind, L.B., 2003, Considerably more than vegetables, a lot less than community: The dilemma of community supported agriculture, in Adams, J. (ed.), *Fighting for the Farm: Rural America Transformed*, 192–206, Philadelphia: University of Pennsylvania Press.

DETR (Department of Environment, Transport and Regional Affairs), 1998, *The Future for Allotments*, Fifth Report of the Select Committee on Environment, Transport and Regional Affairs, London: DETR.

Dixon, J., 2010, Diverse food economies, multivariant capitalism, and the community dynamic shaping contemporary food systems, *Community Development Journal* 46(suppl_1): i20–i35.

Dowler, E. *et al.*, 2010, 'Doing food differently': Reconnecting biological and social relationships through care for food, *The Sociological Review* 57: 200–221.

DuPuis, E.M. and Goodman, D., 2005, Should we go 'home' to eat? Toward a reflexive politics of localism, *Journal of Rural Studies* 21: 359–371.

Edwards-Jones, G. *et al.*, 2008, Testing the assertion that 'local food is best': The challenges of an evidence-based approach, *Trends in Food Science and Technology* 19: 265–274.

Ekers, M., Loftus, A. and Mann, G., 2009, Gramsci lives! *Geoforum* 40: 287–291.

Emery, M. and Flora, C., 2006, Spiraling-up: Mapping community transformation with community capitals framework, *Community Development* 37(1): 19–35.

Fairlie, S., 2009, A short history of enclosure in Britain, *The Land* 7: 16–31.

Food Plymouth, 2014, *Evidence Base for Plymouth Plan Food Theme Topic Paper*, unpublished.

Footprint Consulting, 2008, *The Social Return on Investment of Food for Life School Meals in East Ayrshire*, Edinburgh: Footprint Consulting.

Forssell, S. and Lankoski, L., 2015, The sustainability promise of alternative food networks: An examination through 'alternative' characteristics. *Agriculture and Human Values* 32(1): 63–75.

Gibson-Graham, J.K., 2002, Beyond global vs local: Economic politics outside the binary frame, Ch 1, in Herod, A. and Wright, M.W. (eds.), *Geographies of Power: Placing Scale*, Oxford: Blackwell's.

Gibson-Graham, J.K., 2003, Enabling ethical economies: Cooperativism and class, *Critical Sociology* 29(2): 123–161.

Gibson-Graham, J.K., 2008, Diverse economies: Performative practices for 'other worlds', *Progress in Human Geography* 32(5): 613–632.

Goodman, D., 2004. Rural Europe redux? Reflections on agro-food networks and paradigm change. *Sociologia Ruralis* 44: 3–116.

Goodman, D., DuPuis, M.E. and Goodman, M.K., 2012, *Alternative Food Networks: Knowledge, Practice and Politics*, Abingdon, UK: Routledge.

Goodman, D. and Goodman, M., 2009, Alternative food networks, entry, in Kitchin, R. and Thrift, N. (eds.), *International Encyclopaedia of Human Geography*, Oxford: Elsevier.

GVA, 2011, *Assumptions Report for CIL Charging Schedule*, Plymouth.

Harris, E., 2009, Neoliberal subjectivities or a politics of the possible? Reading for difference in alternative food networks, *Area* 41(1): 55–63.

Hawkes, F. and Acott, T., 2013, People, environment and place: The function and significance of human hybrid relationships at an allotment in South East England, *Local Environment* 18. Doi: 10.1080/13549839.2013.787590

Holland, L., 2004, Diversity and connections in community gardens: A contribution to local sustainability, *Local Environment* 9(3): 285–305.

Hope, N. and Ellis, V., 2009, *Can You Dig It? Meeting Community Demand for Allotments*, London: New Local Government Network.

Ilbery, B. and Kneafsey, M., 2000, Producer constructions of quality in regional speciality food production: A case study from South West England, *Journal of Rural Studies* 16(2): 217–230.

Jarosz, L., 2008, The city in the country: Growing alternative food networks in metropolitan areas, *Journal of Rural Studies* 24(3): 231–244.

Jorgensen, D.L., 1989, *Participant Observation: A Methodology for Human Studies*, Applied Social Research Methods Series Vol. 15, London: Sage.

Kingsley, J. and Townsend, M., 2006, 'Dig in' to social capital: Community gardens as mechanisms for growing urban social connectedness, *Urban Policy and Research* 24(4): 25–537.

Kirwan, J., Ilbery, B., Maye, D. and Carey, J., 2013, Grassroots social innovations and food localisation: An investigation of the Local Food programme in England, *Global Environmental Change* 23(5): 830–837.

Kirwan, J. and Maye, D., 2013, Food security framings within the UK and the integration of local food systems, *Journal of Rural Studies* 29: 91–100.

Kneafsey, M. *et al.*, 2008, *Reconnecting Consumers, Producers and Food: Exploring Alternatives*, Oxford: Berg.

Kortright, R. and Wakefield, S., 2011, Edible backyards: A qualitative study of household food growing and its contributions to food security, *Agriculture and Human Values* 28: 39–53.

Ladner, P., 2011, *The Urban Food Revolution: Changing the Way We Feed Cities*, Gabriola Island, British Columbia: New Society Publishers.

Lefebvre, H., [1974] 1991, *The Production of Space*, Oxford: Blackwell Publishers.

Leventon, J. and Laudan, J., 2017, Local food sovereignty for global food security? Highlighting interplay challenges, *Geoforum* 85: 23–26.

Levkoe, C.Z., 2006, Learning democracy through food justice movements, *Agriculture and Human Values* 23: 89–98.

Livesey, G., 2011, Assemblage theory, gardens and the legacy of the early Garden City movement, *Architectural Research Quarterly* 15(3): 271.

Lockie, S., 2009, Responsibility and agency within alternative food networks: Assembling the 'citizen consumer', *Agriculture and Human Values* 26(3): 193–201.

Marsden, T., 2010, Mobilizing the regional eco-economy: Evolving webs of agri-food and rural development in the UK, *Cambridge Journal of Regions, Economy and Society* 3: 225–244.

Massey, D., 2007, *World City*, Cambridge: Polity Press.

McClintock, N., 2014, Radical, reformist, and garden-variety neoliberal: Coming to terms with urban agriculture's contradictions, *Local Environment* 19(2): 147–171.

McGlone, P., Dobson, B., Dowler, E. and Nelson, M., 1999, *Food Projects and How They Work*, York: Joseph Rowntree Foundation.

McIntyre, L. and Rondeau, K., 2011, Individual consumer food localism: A review anchored in Canadian farmwomen's reflections, *Journal of Rural Studies* 27: 116–124.

Milbourne, P., 2012, Everyday (in)justices and ordinary environmentalisms: Community gardening in disadvantaged urban neighbourhoods, *Local Environment* 17(9): 943–957.

MLNR (Ministry of Land and Natural Resources), 1969, *The Thorpe Report: Departmental Committee of Inquiry into Allotments*, Cmnd 4166, London: HMSO.

Moe, T.M., 2005, Power and political institutions, *Perspectives on Politics* 3(2): 215–233.

Mohan, G. and Mohan, J., 2002, Placing social capital, *Progress in Human Geography* 26: 191–210.

Morgan, A. and Ziglio, E., 2007, Revitalizing the evidence base model for public health: An assets model, *IUHPE Promotion and Education Supplement* 2: 17–22.

Morgan, K. and Sonnino, R., 2010, The urban foodscape: World cities and the new food equation, *Cambridge Journal of Regions, Economy and Society* 3: 209–224.

Moselle, B., 1995, Allotments, enclosure and proletarianization in early Nineteenth-Century Southern England, *Economic History Review* 48(3): 482–500.

Mougeot, L.J.A. (ed.), 2005, *Agropolis: The Social, Political and Environmental Dimensions of Urban Agriculture*, London: Earthscan for IDRC.

Pearson, C.J., 2010, Challenging, multidimensional agriculture in cities (guest editorial), *International Journal of Agricultural Sustainability* 8(1–2): 3–4.

Perrons, D. and Skyers, S., 2003, Empowerment through participation: Conceptual explorations and a case study, *International Journal of Urban and Regional Research* 27(2): 265–285.

Pigg, K., Gasteyer, S. P., Martin, K. E., Keating, K. and Apaliyah, G. P., 2013, The community capitals framework: An empirical examination of internal relationships, *Community Development* 44(4): 492–502.

Platten, S., 2011, *Plant Exchange and Social Performance: Implications for Knowledge Transfer in British Allotments*, draft report from British Homegardens Project 2007–2010, unpublished.

Pothukuchi, K., 2004, Community food assessment: A first step in planning for community food security, *Journal of Planning Education and Research* 23: 356–377.

Pretty, J.N. *et al.*, 2005, Farm costs and food miles: An assessment of the full cost of the UK weekly food basket, *Food Policy* 30: 1–19.

Pudup, M., 2008, It takes a garden: Cultivating citizen-subjects in organized garden projects, *Geoforum* 39: 1228–1240.

Rockstrom, J. *et al.*, 2009, A safe operating space for humanity, *Nature* 461, 24 September: 472–475.

Sage, C., 2003, Social embeddedness and relations of regard: Alternative 'good food' networks in South-West Ireland, *Journal of Rural Studies* 19: 47–60.

Saltmarsh, N., Meldrum, J. and Longhurst, N., 2011, *The Impact of Community Supported Agriculture*, November, Bristol: Soil Association.

Schmit, T.M., Jablonski, B.B.R., Minner, J., Kay, D. and Christensen, L., 2017, Rural wealth creation of intellectual capital from urban local food system initiatives: Developing indicators to assess change, *Community Development*: 1–18.

Scoones, I., 2009, Livelihoods perspectives and rural development, *Journal of Peasant Studies* 36(1): 171–196.

Sen, A., 1984, Rights and capabilities, in Sen, A., *Resources, Values and Development*, 307–324, Oxford: Basil Blackwell.

Sen, A., 1986, *Food, Economics and Entitlements*, WIDER Working Paper No 1, World Institute for Development Economics Research, United Nations University.

Seyfang, G., 2006, Ecological citizenship and sustainable consumption: Examining local organic food networks, *Journal of Rural Studies* 22(4): 383–395.

Sherriff, G., 2009, Towards healthy local food: Issues in achieving Just Sustainability, *Local Environment* 14(1): 73–92.

Shoard, M., 1987, *This Land Is Our Land: The Struggle for Britain's Countryside*, London: Paladin.

Shuman, Michael, 1998, *Going Local: Creating Self-Reliant Communities in a Global Age*. New York, NY: Routledge.

Soja, E., 2008, *The City and Spatial Justice*, paper prepared for the conference Spatial Justice, Nanterre, Paris, 12–14 March.

Sonnino, R. and Marsden, T., 2006, Beyond the divide: Rethinking relationships between alternative and conventional food networks in Europe, *Journal of Economic Geography* 6(2): 181–199.

Steel, C., 2008, *Hungry City: How Food Shapes Our Lives*, London: Chatto and Windus.

Stevenson, J., 1992, *Popular Disturbances in England 1700–1832*, London: Longman.

Stocker, L. and Barnett, K., 1998, The significance and praxis of community-based sustainability projects: Community gardens in western Australia, *Local Environment* 3(2): 179–189.

Thorpe, H., 1975, The homely allotment: From rural dole to urban amenity: A neglected aspect of urban land use, *Geography* 268: 169–183.

Tornaghi, C., 2017, Urban agriculture in the food-disabling city: (Re) defining urban food justice, reimagining a politics of empowerment, *Antipode* 49(3): 781–801.

Tregear, A., 2011, Progressing knowledge in alternative and local food networks: Critical reflections and a research agenda, *Journal of Rural Studies* 27: 419–430.

Twiss, J., Dickinson, J., Duma, S., Kleinman, T., Paulsen, H. and Rilveria, L., 2011, Community gardens: Lessons learned from California healthy cities and communities, *American Journal of Public Health* 93(9): 1435–1438.

Venn, L. *et al.*, 2006, Researching European 'alternative' food networks: Some methodological considerations, *Area* 38(3): 248–258.

Wainwright, J., 2005, Politics of nature: A review of three recent works by Bruno Latour, *Capitalism Nature Socialism* 16(1): 115–127.

Wakefield, S et al., 2007, Growing urban health: community gardening in South-East Toronto, *Health Promotion International* 22(2): 92–101.

Way, T., 2008, *Allotments*, Oxford: Shire Publications.

Wekerle, G., 2004, Food justice movements, *Journal of Planning Education and Research* 23: 378–386.

Wilson, A.D.V., 2013, Beyond alternative: Exploring the potential for autonomous food spaces, *Antipode* 45(3): 719–737.

Wilson, G.A., 2013, Community resilience, policy corridors and the policy challenge, *Land Use Policy* (31): 298–310.

Wiltshire, R. and Azuma, R., 2000, Rewriting the plot: Sustaining allotments in the UK and Japan, *Local Environment* 5(2): 139–151.

Wiltshire, R. and Geoghegan, H., 2012, Growing alone, growing together, growing apart? Reflections on the social organisation of voluntary urban food production in Britain, Ch. 28 in Viljoen, A. and Wiskerke, J.S.C. (eds.), *Sustainable Food Planning: Evolving Theory and Practice*, Wageningen: Wageningen Academic Publishers.

Winter, M., 2003, Embeddedness, the new food economy and defensive localism, *Journal of Rural Studies* 19: 23–32.

Zasada, I., 2011, Multifunctional peri-urban agriculture: A review of societal demands and the provision of goods and services by farming, *Land Use Policy* 28: 639–648.

8 Contesting the politics of place

Urban gardening in Dublin and Belfast

Mary P. Corcoran and Patricia Healy Kettle

Introduction

Social exclusion and social polarization are characteristic of many cities where "urban space, while it is functionally and economically shared, is socially segregated and culturally differentiated" (Robins 1993, p. 313). Against this backdrop research shows that public and voluntary bodies operating in the civil society sphere can play a crucial role in fostering better social relations, integration, and social cohesion (Vertovec 2007). Recent literature suggests that a "shared politics of place" attained through joint activities which acknowledge difference and promote inclusion, foster social integration and provide people with a means to practice cooperation (Baumann 1996; Sanjek 1998; Sennett 2012). Such a shared politics of place is most likely to occur in the context of public space conceptualized broadly as "the setting for everyday spatial behaviour of individuals and communities, emphasizing ordinary activities of citizens" (Lownsbrough and Beunderman 2007, p. 8). In this chapter we investigate the extent to which a shared politics of place can be created and nurtured amongst the cultivating citizenry, and the implications of that for urban equity and sustainability.

Allotment gardening in both Dublin (Ireland) and Belfast (Northern Ireland) was originally provided for under British legislation which has ensured its provision, maintenance, and statutory legitimacy to the present day. The residualization of UA was a marked trend in both cities during the twentieth century. More recently, a renewal of interest in UA is evidenced in rising demand among the citizenry for plots, increased provision by municipalities and private landowners, and a growing public awareness of the value of growing your own. Our aim is to identify what role UA can play in fomenting a shared politics of place as a basis for social cohesion given both the general challenges faced by cities today, and the specific challenges faced by Dublin and Belfast. We argue that UA is not just an environmental or ecological intervention in urban space. Rather it is a social process that contributes to the tradition of nurturing inclusive and vibrant public space and public infrastructures in the contemporary city (Amin 2010). As such UA has a key role to play in advancing a more equitable and sustainable vision of the city.

Toward a shared politics of place

In this chapter we illuminate elements of the interactive order of everyday urban life focusing particularly on the cultivation practices of urban allotment holders. We are interested in the potential of urban allotments to help re-shape the politics of place at a time when cities are viewed as becoming ever more privatized, more polarized, and more exclusionary (Punch 2005; Sennett 2005; Sassen 2013). Lownsbrough and Beunderman (2007) while acknowledging these trends point to the emergence of new types of public space in cities and neighbourhoods: formal and informal, public and semi-public, deliberate or spontaneous. They identify eight main types of "spaces of potential": exchange, productive, service provision, activity, democratic/participative, staged, in-between, and virtual. These are not to be interpreted in a narrowly spatial sense: in practice many places will have elements that cut across more than one definition, since the category into which a space falls is dictated by the activity happening within it at different times. It is the central importance of trust and confidence from users in creating valuable public space that links these "spaces of potential". The elements of new public space include: capacity for multi-use, accessibility, legibility, clarity about the boundaries between public and private, local relevance, adaptability to people's diverse needs and desires, open-endedness, and safety. Madden (2010) counsels that we move the analysis of public space beyond questions of inclusion and exclusion, and "toward an empirical examination of the powers, practices, institutions and ideas which do the work of constituting the public" (2010, p. 191). We argue that the empirical investigation of allotment gardening in two urban contexts reveals the possibility of re-framing a local politics of place, to produce a more socially inclusive notion of the public. This is possible because participants' commitment to cultivation is premised on individual labour carried out in a common cause, observance of mutually agreed tacit rules of engagement, and tolerance of diversity. Thus, they fulfil an important role associated with public urban life (Sennett 2011). Moreover, allotment gardening, facilitated and supported by local municipalities, promotes a more public politics of place (open, accessible, and traversed by all) which stands in contradistinction to a more privatized politics of place (evidenced in shopping malls, gated communities, policed public thoroughfares, and so on). These themes are elucidated in more detail in the remainder of this chapter.

Researching urban gardening in Dublin and Belfast

Tornaghi, in a recent critical review of urban agriculture research, argues that we still lack a systematic analysis of "the geography of urban food cultivation and its relations with the politics of space" (2014, p. 3). She calls for an exploration of the meaning of UA initiatives in different urban contexts, and in particular, its role in addressing urban problems. This chapter addresses gaps in the literature by focusing on two cities in the Global North each of which has faced specific localized challenges – the financialization of urban space (Dublin) and the politicization of urban space (Belfast).

Dublin city flourished economically during the early years of the twenty-first century. Incomes and spending power rose in Ireland, generating high levels of consumer exuberance among large swathes of the populace. This was evidenced in the exorbitant prices paid for modest homes, an increase in international travel, and dramatic levels of consumer spending (dependent on credit rather than savings) generally. After the economic collapse of 2008 (largely attributed to a property bubble) came the IMF/EU bailout of 2010. The mandated imposition of austerity policies resulted in significant drops in income, higher unemployment levels, and a contraction in consumer spending (Rigney 2012). Crucially though, the availability of vacant space arising from the property crash created opportunities for UA (Corcoran et al. 2017). We have observed a demonstrable rise in UA practices in the city of Dublin, reliant on both public and private provision of allotments in the city and on its perimeter. Demand has been partially driven by a flourishing civil society sector committed to promoting sustainable forms of production, greater food awareness, better strategies for health and well-being, and food sovereignty.

Despite the political resolution of the conflict in Northern Ireland, Belfast remains a city divided along religious and ethno-national lines. The sectarian inscriptions on the landscape continually reinforce both the idea and the reality of a divided city. The physical environment of the city and its morphology – in terms, for instance, of the range and distribution of places of worship – demonstrates the continued salience of religion in everyday urban life (O'Dowd and McKnight 2013). Violent division is effectively inscribed in the cityscape, through periodic protests, riots, and paramilitary campaigns aimed at disrupting the normalization process underway in the wake of the political resolution of the conflict. O'Dowd and McKnight note that although there are examples of alternative forms of social solidarity and social mobilization that engage in bridge-building across the community divide in the city, these are less frequent, less visible, and are less embedded in either civil society or the state. To some degree the publicness of the city has been re-configured as a theatre of action in which two ethno-national traditions are publically performed and played out. This raises the question of what avenues may be available that can allow urban dwellers in Belfast to engage in a shared politics of place despite the history of sectarianism and residual ethno-national conflict. We argue that urban agriculture sites might be classified as non-contested space and as such have the potential to become shared-in-common places in the city. Given the significant policy and political commitments to social cohesion and social inclusion in both Ireland and Northern Ireland, there is, we argue, "a need for a more thorough analysis of the potential for different types of public space to support positive interactions between different social, economic and ethnic groups" (Lownsbrough and Beunderman 2007, p. 10).

The four Dublin municipal authorities currently provide 1,120 allotment sites across ten locations in the Greater Dublin area (many more allotments are provided by private landowners). The population of the Greater Dublin area is 1,325,700 (Census 2016). Belfast City Council serving a population of 339,000 (NISRA 2016) currently provides 278 sites across six locations. (In both cities there are long waiting lists to access sites). Our study employed multi-sited ethnographic methods using methods of triangulation (semi-structured interviews, participant observation, and visual analysis). Field work was conducted in two phases between 2009 and 2013, and involved photographing seven allotment sites in Dublin and six in Belfast. While some allotment gardens are sited close to the city centre, the majority tend to be located in the suburbs or on the urban perimeter. Both publicly and privately provisioned sites were included in the sample. Data was also gathered at a community garden in West Belfast, located in an interface area where Protestant and Catholic communities remain almost wholly segregated. Forty-eight interviews were carried out in Dublin and 27 interviews in Belfast. Interviewees were primarily drawn from the ranks of plot holders, with additional inputs from allotment activists, and relevant members of local municipalities. The case study based approach was adapted as an optimal means of elucidating the potential of UA to generate a shared politics of place on the ground in the contemporary city (for more details on methodology see Kettle 2014).

Access, sociality, and social levelling on allotment sites

There is a certain tension inherent in allotment gardening in terms of their legal, physical, and normative publicness/privateness. In terms of their spatial distribution allotments are frequently located in interstitial or peripheral places in the city. While nominally public in terms of location (generally provided on public lands), they exhibit tendencies towards privatization as evident in their weak visibility to the public-at-large, difficulties of access, and security concerns. Security is an issue on both Belfast and Dublin sites. Respondents in Belfast informed us that there are strict rules about sites being locked at all times to ensure everyone's safety. Sites have to be secured on entering because there is residual conflict in the city and tensions remain high. Similarly, in Dublin allotment holders are issued with keys to the sites and are expected to secure access point on entry and egress.

Municipal allotments are provided on public lands, or on private lands leased by the authorities. As such, they constitute a public good in which all tax payers and citizens have a stake. As a resource held in public trust they are potentially open to all. In terms of social practices, however, allotments are at least semi-privatized through gated access, boundary creation and maintenance, and formal tenant/landlord arrangements. They require payment of a fee, however nominal, which constitutes a further barrier to entry. Some are characterized by contingent status, but all limit security of tenure through an 11-month leasing system. Furthermore, waiting lists for allotments indicate that supply exceeds demand and that access is therefore limited for prospective plot holders. Newer allotment sites are being provided on private lands on the city perimeter, particularly in Dublin.

Here tenancy is also limited, and the cost of renting a plot is not subsidized but rather is set by market demand.

Once access is gained, allotments provide an arena for socializing and sociality. They enable individual and collective cultivation, exchange, and dissemination of knowledge. They are spaces that are conducive to lingering, and allow for plot holders to be individually busy and active, *and* to interact with one another. They are also sites of production and exchange which explicitly eschew a cash nexus. In that specific sense they constitute a productive space that exists between the market and the state. Allotment holders now constitute a diverse population. No longer dominated by older, working-class males, plots are tended by working-class and middle-class women and men, the unemployed, immigrants and community groups, and advocacy groups catering for clients with special needs. People join together in a common understanding, with a shared concern for cultivation in a designated space. They act in concert despite the fact that they bring with them "multiple geographies of affiliation" and may only have "fleeting encounters with strangers" on site (Amin 2010, p. 4):

> That is the huge potential of allotments, the sense of bringing people together. I really feel that. I have seen that countless times. Out there, there are no boundaries or no barriers. It is a great social mixing place. Now more people on neighbouring plots might get to know each other because there are no walls or fences like there are with gardens. Every plot almost merges into the next.
>
> (MF, DN, 082009)

One plot holder in Belfast explained that allotment space allows people to move beyond parochial understandings of their lives and the constraints of institutionalized sectarianism. His own efforts to promote allotment gardening, particularly for men, are intended to give people a sense of private ownership and control of a space *albeit* in the public realm:

> they could come in their own time, they could come in the evenings, you know, they could come on Sundays, whenever, and they had an ownership of it . . . so if they had one of these wee beds they could come up and own it, look after it, in their own time, and simply talk to people and break down barriers that were there for so long.
>
> (CH, BT 30052013)

Busy professionals who live relatively compartmentalized lives testify to the elective affinities that are generated purely as a result of cultivating an allotment alongside unknown others. As one female plot holder based in Belfast explains allotment cultivation is a total contrast to her scheduled and highly structured work life:

> this is like a free flowing and I like that. It's a social thing on one level, and I mean the man whose working here beside me, he's been working there since

the year I was born and his company has been very stimulating. He's really into this on a very deep level. I see him carrying his little plants and he sows like it's a sacrament . . . and then there's all the guys around here who are good *craic*.

(GX BT 082012)

The absence of physical boundaries, (walls), and the creativity associated with designing, managing, and maintaining one's plot, facilitates the construction of "a peopled-landscape" (Viljoen et al. 2012) which provides an opportunity to meet with and interact with others, and generates a sense of belonging. As noted earlier, allotment gardens are frequently located on the city perimeter, or if within the city boundaries, in interstitial places. They constitute terrain not at the centre, but on the edge. As Sennett has observed this very edge-like quality is precisely where "one community, one difference, meets another" (Sennett 2011, p. 396). In this context, allotment holders observe a form of presentation of self in which particularities are eschewed in favour of commonality focused purely on the activities associated with working the land. Allotments are perceived by those who frequent them as a *social leveller*. Plot holders eschew divisions based on class and status, and insist that social categorizations are left at the gate. As one woman on a Dublin allotment site explains:

We've got guards [police officers] here. . . . We've civil servants. You've bank managers. You've people unemployed. From all walks of life. And when you're up here in your wellies full of muck it doesn't matter who you are. You're the same. Everybody's the same. When we walk in that gate, we're all the same. . . . it gives you the excuse to come out and meet others without having to prove yourself, explain yourself, what you do for a living. It doesn't matter what car you drive, what kind of home you have, and what you do for a living. When you come in that gate, you're the same, we're all the same and everyone treats each other that way . . . it's a leveler that's what it is, and you can come up here and de-stress, lose yourself for hours and meet wonderful, wonderful people you wouldn't have ever met out on the street.

(DX DN 2013)

Another Dublin plot holder reiterates this point observing that symbolic markers of class and status are rendered irrelevant when people are engaged in the task of cultivation:

You're up there in your working clothes, there's no symbols of wealth as such. There are no suits. You know there's no people dressed in their good clobber. You're in there with your spade and your veg and it kind of . . . it's a neutralising environment where you wouldn't feel threatened by talking to another person.

(FN2, DN 2009)

Similarly, on the sites in Belfast there is also an explicit recognition that the allotments are not an exclusively working-class preserve. People recognize that they attract people from different social classes as well as different communities in the city. This is significant in the context of Belfast where so much of public space tends to be inscribed with ethno-national territorial claims, and as a consequence, is effectively proscribed for those who do not share those claims.

> there's people from both communities here, absolutely, and people from different social strata as well.
>
> (BX, BT 07062013)

> It [the allotment site] completely disregards your class, your religion. It's just about growing, that's what brings people here.
>
> (RX BT 062013)

> Well, there's all walks of life up here. That's what it's all about. There's men and women from all backgrounds and everyone mixes. . . . You've some Chinese people here too and we gave them a bit of a dig out and got a wee thing going, like to make them feel welcome and that you know.
>
> (GI BT, 062013)

On the allotment site the problem of how strangers express themselves to each other is solved through a focus on applying knowledge, skill, and physical labour. The terrain sets the boundaries to interaction. In both Dublin and Belfast respondents reported that in general the sociality they experience on site does not extend beyond the site. People who share this public space and engage in rites of cooperation and sociability with others, tend not to continue those social relations once off-site. Encounters with others are primarily about *civil interfacing*, rather than creating lasting or deep attachments. Sennett has written of how disparate groups might make use of theatrical language and role play as a basis for a common speech "which creates an 'as if' as though they are in the same realm" (2011, p. 395). Plot holders, intimately connected to the material practices of cultivation, privilege that version of themselves above all other as a means of creating a common ground with unknown others. It is all about *the doing*, the getting on with the practical task of cultivation. But this practice necessarily draws them into circuits of sociality as well as shared knowledge. These exchanges produce "vivacity" in the public space of the allotments.

Allotments facilitate the striking up of easy interactions between plot holders. They are places where strangers seem less strange:

> When I'm coming for four hours I'll always bring me flask and if someone was around I would say do you want a cup of tea, they might take it and they might not take it.
>
> (FN1 DN 2009)

There is a sense of fellowship connected to the joint project even if each plot holder is in effect engaged in an individual enterprise. A premium is placed on the willingness and capacity to share the place with others. In Belfast, one respondent fondly recalled the words of a longstanding plot holder:

> Old Colin used to say if you don't have time to sit down in the communal shed and have a cup of tea with your fellow allotment holders, then you shouldn't be here.
>
> (GI, BT 062013)

Activists in particular are keen to stress the potential of allotments as social levellers:

> Allotments should not be a refuge for retired males. I thought that families should have access to them, I thought that young couples should have access to them. They should be available to all . . . irrespective of employment status, age that families should have access, special groups-mental health groups should have access. I have been arguing for multi use.
>
> (MF, DN 092009)

For advocates the allotment landscape acts as an important resource in the city that facilitates social interaction. They see that UA can offer the contemporary urban dweller an opportunity to reconnect with the land but, crucially, to connect with other social actors. For plot holders, the spatial layout and in particular, the absence of physical boundaries facilitates, promotes, and enhances the construction of a sense of belonging to the place. As two women plot holders in Dublin note:

> Well I bought my apartment in the height of the boom and paid a fortune for it, and although I have a balcony, it's really not enough. I grew up here (in the area) and my parents had a large garden and I didn't realise how much I'd miss having a garden until I bought my own home. . . . I like coming here and a lot of the time I'd sit and read or potter around in the shed, tidy it up and do little odd jobs . . . oh I love the company here. I absolutely love it. There's x down there, and y here beside me and we're all great buddies.
>
> (KX DN 2013)

> Well I just had to have one. The minute I saw this [site] opening I was down in a shot. . . . you've no room in the new apartments and like you've the park there for a walk and that's ok if you've a dog and you'd go walking regularly, but it's pretty lonely going on your own all the time. I do go, and I love it but here, here I can have a chat, do a few bits and basically just enjoy the open air.
>
> (HX, DN 2013)

The physical reconfiguration of Dublin in the years of the economic boom created new modalities for living to which Dubliners continue to adjust. Apartment living is a relatively new phenomenon in the city and here we see how people respond to the challenges which this new kind of living engenders. A patch of land for cultivation re-grounds them, providing recreational access to the outdoors, an opportunity to grow food for consumption, and a version of shared public space that is not available in the context of privatized apartment living.

Moving beyond ethno-national divisions

We have already alluded to the problem of Belfast as a divided city. Ethno-national divisions are inscribed in the cityscape in very public ways. Remarkably, such demarcations are noticeably absent from the allotments spaces. Allotments offer a space where people can interact *without* having to be conscious of or adhere to prescribed ethno-national distinctions. What stands out is the neutrality of these spaces in a city with markers of identity at every turn and where interface barriers are designed to "police" divisions between the two main communities.

On allotment sites, manifestations of religious or political views are frowned upon. Significantly, politics are not generally discussed on Belfast sites. Most respondents were adamant that such subject matter was effectively out of bounds, not permitted under the tacit rules of engagement. Respondents maintain that religious views or political opinions are completely irrelevant in the context of shared cultivation of land:

> No, no. . . . they wouldn't talk about religion. No. You know, nobody really knows what religion you are . . . . it's a neutral kind of eh . . . there's never any question whether you're [coughs]. . . . the sole interest is the allotment, and our conversation revolves around that, and that's it. No, no one would ever speak of anything like religion . . . you're not interested in any of that carry-on in here.
>
> (JK, BT 062013)

> I know more people on this allotment in four weeks than I do living on my street for eight years. If you don't feel like being friendly you can just hide in your shed but you wouldn't do that. No one talks about any of that stuff in here . . . I've never been asked about my political opinions or that, and I do not think it's really anything people would bring up to be honest. I really don't think people would be bothered with that in here.
>
> (IC BT 062013)

In general, politics cannot be discussed on the site as there is a latent fear that one could all too easily antagonize people. One plot holder who had previously worked for the prison service observed that:

You don't discuss your background, and I certainly can't get into any conversations about that here, *with my background.*

(GG BT 2013) emphasis added

This capacity to bracket difference, even temporarily, is relatively novel in a divided city such as Belfast. Plot holders are entering a public space and discarding the particularities of their identities – class, gender, ethnicity, religion, political affiliation. In effect, the allotment site constitutes a public realm which enables plot holders to transcend distinction and difference and move beyond self-interest (Arendt 1958). They enter into "a community of equalization of speech in which self-reference is a violation of the norms of politics" (Sennett 2011, p. 396). Through the application of this tacit rule of engagement a new politics of place is thus opened on the allotments. The allotment space provides a level playing field enabling the dissolution of an ethno-national configuration and its replacement by a community of growers, whose *raison d'etre* derives from ground up cultivation:

> Well everyone is just all one, and we just all work together here. Everyone is all one, we all teach each other and share what we know. . . . there's none of that nonsense in here . . . everyone's all one in here. . . . . I've met people from different creeds and from different parts of Belfast and I never had trouble with any of them.
>
> (FX, BT 07062013)

A number of initiatives are underway in Belfast to create opportunities for disadvantaged young people and ex-prisoners to become involved in UA. This mirrors similar initiatives undertaken in Dublin, albeit that the context is much less politicized than in the North. It is noteworthy that some respondents in Belfast were hesitant about the rehabilitative possibilities that allotments might be required to sustain. For some, social mixing is all very well when people share the same broad class categories and hail from what they perceive as the law-abiding sections of the ethno-national communities. Such respondents who reject overt political violence have their doubts about integrating people who "had not kept their noses clean" i.e. people who had been involved in political or paramilitary activities. There is a fear that the presence of this "other" on the site might lead to a disengagement of existing plot holders. When asked about their openness to potential plot holders who "had a past" they were equivocal:

> It's hard to . . . I mean in the interest of, like I rarely come in here to the shed and I usually stay up on my own allotment, but I would certainly exchange the time of day with them, and I certainly wouldn't be antipathetic. Plus, I would be watching for a trend, to make sure that they kept their nose clean and that we didn't have unintended consequences.
>
> (GI BT 062013)

The legacy issue of the Troubles cannot be easily erased as another respondent observed:

> Oh well, I found that over a long, long time because if you live for maybe 30 or 40 years and your life depends on either keeping your mouth shut or keeping your head down or making sure you're in the right place, even though things have changed, there would be a residual wariness.
>
> (GI BT 062013)

While generally the majority of plot holders are deemed to leave their politics at the gate, there is concern about how making one's political views known, particularly if they were deemed to be antagonistic to one community or the other, could destabilize the tacit rules of engagement. Nevertheless, respondents are adamant that most plot holders conform to the social requirements:

> The vast majority of people are ordinary decent people who you could trust your life with, borrow their bits, could get advice, you'd get assistance and there'd be no hassle, and you'd be quite comfortable with, have a chat and go on ahead, and all would be well.
>
> (GI BT 062013)

But crucially, they observe that the kind of integration that occurs on the allotments is organic rather than prescribed. They believe that any forced attempt to, for instance, apply quotas to the numbers from different ethno-national communities in the allotment allocations policy would be doomed to failure. The beauty of the allotments is that the prime focus is on the love of the land for *its own sake*. The commitment to cultivation pushes all other identifying markers into the background, rendering them less salient and demonstrating through practice the possibility of integrating different communities. Several respondents recounted small acts of unforced kindness. A Catholic plot holder commented on the generosity of her neighbours when she had to leave her site in Belfast for several weeks while her sister was terminally ill in Dublin:

> They all got together and looked after it, and I choke up when I think of that. . . . so that I wouldn't lose it [the plot]. A couple who subsequently moved to the plot next to me, and a woman up there and another couple . . . I didn't know their names . . . and they were Protestants too, and I was very touched by that.
>
> (GX BT 082012)

An ex-paramilitary saw allotment gardening as a means of moving on from a past which had involved him in conflict and sectarian violence. The allotment constitutes a refuge, a place away from home that affords the prospect of low intensity sociability. He repeatedly spoke of it as a place which offers "peace of mind". His view is that:

The allotment helps the kids see a different way forward, away from all the sectarianism that's going on.

(TX BT 062013)

From this perspective, the ethno-national conflict sits firmly in the past, and the allotment provides a template for how to get on and grow together. Respondents accept that there are differences between people – political, religious, and cultural – but suggest that these differences can be transcended:

you have to tolerate that, we're all different here, and you just have to get along.

(TX BT 062013)

Well my attitude is that success in Northern Ireland is measured in small amounts, and you know it's been analyzed to death and this is why I can't be bothered with things like that and here I think the majority of people feel the same. . . . They're here to grow vegetables and socialize, regardless of where you are from. People just want to move on, so it's a measure of how well things have moved on.

(GG BT 2013)

Another respondent referred to the possibility of "softening" attitudes even among those older plot holders who held entrenched political views. This attitude softening might be the unintended consequence of working in harmony with others in a shared space with a defined, avowedly non-political, practical goal. The nature of agricultural productive work which requires both *individual* enterprise as well as *collective* responsibility creates a very visceral imperative "to get along".

Lownsbrough and Bunderman have documented the particular qualities associated with good public space. They argue that a constellation of "spaces of potential" have emerged in recent years with the potential to sustain and increase interaction in public space (2007, p. 19). This comparative study of allotment gardening in two cities – Dublin and Belfast – provides an opportunity to test whether UA can act as a "space of potential" wherein social or ethno-national cleavages might be managed, challenged, and/or transcended. We have demonstrated the extent to which UA as a practical activity can engender cooperative responsiveness to others on their own terms (Sennett 2012, p. 6). We argue therefore that the kind of civil dis-affiliation associated with privatization and marketization in the contemporary city is not inevitable. Contrary to what is often assumed urbanites (and suburbanites) may exhibit a strongly developed sense of place attachment and belonging, that overcomes – even if only temporarily – class and ethno-national differences. As we have demonstrated this is evidenced in the orientations and practices of plot holders in the context of allotment gardening in the cities of Dublin and Belfast. They overtly challenge those forces which may undermine a sense of shared public space: in Belfast, the heightened sensitivity about ethno-national territoriality and in Dublin the valorization of social class differences. Just as places may become non-places over time, it is also possible that non-places may be re-fashioned as places that are both meaningful and functional within the urban vernacular. We suggest that the urban allotment is a significant "space of potential" in the twenty-first century. Moreover, we have shown that allotments constitute a particular localized form of public space that can play a crucial role "in providing a focus for practical solutions that increase our sense of society and mutuality" (Lownsbrough and Beunderman 2007, p. 3). They have, therefore, a role to play in urban sustainability.

Urban gardening and sustainability

Interest in sustainability has broadened the terms of reference of analysts to the extent that a wider range of disciplines from within and outside of the traditional social sciences are now being called upon to contribute to a sustainability agenda. The EU Communication on Green Infrastructure explicitly links natural capital depletion to social capital depletion, if more emphasis is not placed on sustainability in planning futures (COM 249 2013, p. 2). This Communication (even if largely discursive rather than pragmatic) represents a significant advance at supra-national policy level in linking society and nature, affording them co-equal concern. Promoting the well-being of its citizens is a primary objective of the European Union (Article. 3 [1] of the Treaty), but how we define well-being has to be linked to wider social, political, and environmental contexts of sustainability. In practice, most cross-national comparisons have been based almost exclusively on economic variables such as GDP that are wedded to the concept of growth. However, a developing body of work (including the current volume) addressing the issue of sustainability is having an increasing impact on critical policy and research debates. The report by the Stiglitz-Sen-Fitoussi Commission (2009) represents a milestone in terms of the recommendations it made on developing a more comprehensive approach toward gauging human well-being. The goal of promoting urban sustainability through, for instance, fostering social cohesion and minimizing social polarization, is predicated on enhancing the capacity of people to participate fully in the life of their society, and this is central to quality of life. Socio-economic security and a sense of empowerment and personal capacity foment collective social capital and enhance the collective life world. Parra and Moulaert (2012) advocate a perspective in which "the social" is primarily seen as a socio-political process that dialogically reveals the essential multi-partner and multi-scalar nature of sustainable development and its governance process.

Pathways to urban sustainability, especially as articulated at policy level, are frequently aspirational with little practical guidance on substantive content or strategies for implementation. By focusing on real practices of urban sustainability such as those outlined in this chapter and in the wider volume, social scientists can make the connections between sustainability goals (articulated from above) and the life world of real citizens (articulated from below). Urban gardening as an intervention in urban space has grown in prominence in response to shrinking cities, "degrowth" agendas, and the failure of neoliberal develop- ment models. The significance of urban gardening has been amplified in the context of the recent global economic downturn. Whether in Dublin or Belfast or other cities across the Global North, the practice of urban gardening in its myriad manifestations is contributing to urban sustainability. However, we need to adapt urban sustainability policies appropriately to the growing diversity of urban populations, and develop more scepticism about the prevalent discourse on sustainability which especially reflects middle-class values (Bradley 2009). As the contributors to this volume demonstrate, social scientists have an important role to play in interrogating the grassroots experiences and practices of actors on the ground, and to mediate those to relevant policy makers.

Conclusion

This chapter set out to explore urban gardening as a particular and localized instance of a "shared politics of place". We demonstrated the potential of gar- dening activities to generate civic and social dividends for participants, thus contributing to urban sustainability. The chapter focused on the experiences of plot holders in the city of Dublin where daily life has been largely overshad- owed by austerity policies since 2008. Austerity succeeded a period of intense financialization of everyday life. We also focused on plot holders in post-peace process Belfast, a city still coming to terms with the ethno-national divisions that shaped its past. The chapter drew on extensive qualitative data gathered in both cities to demonstrate the centrality of allotment cultivation to the creation of shared-in-common places. Public space, far from being marginal space in the city, can be defined by its centrality to the city's life world. Ideally, individuals and communities create and sustain *civil interfaces* where barriers are dismantled, knowledge is exchanged, stereotypes are challenged, empathies are generated, and where people get on with the business of simply getting on with their lives. As we have demonstrated, this is how allotment gardening works in both con- texts, predicated on a willingness to disregard social and ethno-national catego- rizations once on site.

We argue that such a reshaping occurs through the process of social levelling on site. Key features of the allotment sites – their openness to all comers, their democratic structure and the low threshold of entry – position them closer to the public than the private realm. Furthermore, the kinds of social markers that have a taken-for-granted currency in everyday life are generally eschewed by plot holders. Identifying characteristics are parked at point of entry which allows for the creation of a different kind of politics of place. Class, status, and ethno-national identities are rendered less salient, as allotment holders invest their mental and physical labour in the care and cultivation of the land. The social levelling which results – albeit temporary and site specific – indicates that urban gardening facilities constitute an important "space of potential" in the city.

This is not to deny that such differences exist, and that they are salient beyond the allotment gates. However, in the cultivation practices that prevail on the allotments sites a degree of cooperation and civil integration is generated in the sense that plot holders become engaged in "the acquisition and routinization of everyday practices for getting on with others in the inherently fleeting encounters that comprise city life" (Vertovec 2007, p. 4). UA in the city has the potential to reinvigorate sites that are unused or underutilized, to green brown fields, to create sustainable models of growth and development, *and* to revive the public realm at the heart of the city.

O'Dowd and Komovara report that it is easier to secure a measure of cross-community agreement in Belfast on issues that involve making decisions about space with less determinate boundaries (2009, p. 6). Allotments are relatively open spaces that proffer the opportunity to engage in a politics of shared place. This is relatively novel in the context of Belfast, and also to some extent in Dublin, a city that is highly socially segregated in terms of social class. According to Sennett (2012) living with difference – racially, ethnically, religiously, or economically – is the most urgent challenge facing civil society today. Sennett argues that it is imperative that we move beyond tribalism in the modern city, and take up the challenge of evolving cooperative relations with unknown others. But this task is made all the more difficult because modern society has been de-skilling people in the practice of cooperation. The practical activity of land cultivation which links us back to the rural past and addresses some of the equity and sustainability challenges of the present, offers a template for reform. Working the land, not just as individuals but as cooperating partners with unknown others points the way ahead toward a new "geography of acceptance" (Massey 1995, p. 74) in cities of the Global North.

References

Amin, A., 2010. *Living with Diversity: For a Politics of Hope without Fear: A Manifesto for Another Europe*. Barcelona: Forum of Concerned Citizens of Europe.

Arendt, H., 1958. *The Human Condition*. Chicago and London: University of Chicago.

Baumann, G., 1996. *Contesting Culture: Discourses of Identity in Multi-ethnic London*. Cambridge: Cambridge University Press.

Bradley, K., 2009. Planning for eco-friendly living in diverse societies. *Local Environment: The International Journal of Justice and Sustainability*, Vol. 14, No. 4, 347–363.

COM, 2013. 249 final Communication from the Commission to the European Parliament, the Council, the European Economic and Social Committee and the Committee of the Regions: Green infrastructure (GI)-Enhancing Europe's Natural Capital. Brussels: European Commission 6.5.2013.

Commission on the Measurement of Economic Performance and Social Progress, 2009. *Also Known as the Stiglitz-Sen-Fitoussi Commission*. Paris, France: Government of France.

Corcoran, M. P., Kettle, P. and O'Callaghan, C., 2017. Green shots in vacant plots: Urban agriculture and austerity in post-crash Ireland. *ACME: An International Journal for Critical Geographies*, forthcoming.

CSO, 2016. *Central Statistics Office: Population Trends*. Dublin: CSO.

Kettle, P., 2014. Motivations for investing in allotment gardening in Dublin: A sociological analysis. *Irish Journal of Sociology*, Vol. 2, No. 2, 30–63.

Lownsbrough, H. and Beunderman, J., 2007. *Equally Spaced? Public Space and Interaction between Diverse Communities*. London: Demos.

Madden, D., 2010. Revisiting the end of public space: Assembling the public in an urban park. *City and Community*, Vol. 9, No. 2, June, 187–207.

Massey, D., 1995. The conceptualization of place. In P. Jess and D. Massey, eds. *A Place in the World? Places, Cultures and Globalization*. Oxford and New York: Oxford University Press and Open University, 45–86.

NISRA, 2016. *Northern Ireland Statistical Research Agency: Population Trends*. Belfast: NISRA.

O'Dowd, L. and Komavara, M., 2009. Regeneration in a contested city: A Belfast case study. *Divided Cities/Contested States*, Working Paper No. 10, 1–30. www.conflictincities.org

O'Dowd, L. and McKnight, M., 2013. Urban intersections: Religion and violence in Belfast. *Space and Polity*, Vol. 17, No. 3, 357–376, DOI: 10.1080/13562576.2013.850823

Parra, C. and Moulaert, F., 2012. "The governance of the nature-culture nexus: Literature and lessons to learn from the San Pedro de Atacama case", *Paper presented at the International Workshop Beyond Utopia: Crisis, values and the socialities of nature*, University of California Santa Barbara, USA.

Punch, M., 2005. Problem drug use in the political economy of urban restructuring: Heroin, class and governance in Dublin. *Antipode*, Vol. 37, No. 4, 754–774.

Rigney, P., 2012. *The Impact of Anti-Crisis Measures and the Social and Employment Situation: Ireland*. Dublin: Irish Congress of Trade Unions.

Robins, K., 1993. Prisoners of the city. In E. Carter, J. Donald and J. Squires, eds. *Space and Place: Theories of Identity and Location*. London: Lawrence and Wishart, 303–330.

Sanjek, R., 1998. *The Future of Us All: Race & Neighbourhood Policies in New York City*. Ithaca: Cornell University Press.

Sassen, S., 2013. "Expulsions: The fifth circle of hell", *Public Lecture*, Sociology UCD-TCD Lecture Series, Trinity College Dublin, January 13.

Sennett, R., 2005. Civility. *Urban Age Bulletin*, Vol. 1, Summer.

Sennett, R., 2011. Reflections on the public realm. In G. Bridge and S. Watson, eds. *The New Blackwell Companion to the City*. Somerset, NJ: John Wiley and Sons, 391–397.

Sennett, R., 2012. *Together: The Rituals, Pleasures and Politics of Cooperation*. London, UK: Allen Lane.

Tornaghi, C., 2014. Critical geography of urban agriculture. *Progress in Human Geography*, Vol. 38, No. 4, 551–567.

Vertovec, S., 2007. *New Complexities of Cohesion in Britain: Super-Diversity, Transnationalism and Civil Integration*. Commission of Integration & Cohesion. West Yorkshire: Communities and Local Government Publications.

Viljoen, A. et al., 2012. *Sustainable Food Planning: Evolving Theory and Practice*. Netherlands: Wageningen.

9 Exploring guerrilla gardening
Gauging public views on the grassroots activity

Michael Hardman, Peter J. Larkham, and David Adams

Introduction

There is a noteworthy gap in recent research on the growing activity of guerrilla gardening. The purpose of this chapter is to provide a voice to those who dwell or work close to sites which have been colonized by guerrilla gardeners. It explores personal research-led interactions with "guerrillas", a term often used to refer to a group of guerrilla gardeners. We begin by arguing that much of the existing commentary on guerrilla gardening is one-dimensional, deriving from those practicing the activity who fail to look relationally, including Reynolds (2008) and Tracey (2007, 2011) and various other writers and informal bloggers (see, for example, D.C. Guerrilla Gardeners, 2012; Glasgow Guerrillas, 2012; Pothole Gardener, 2012). This chapter provides a perspective from recent interactions with guerrilla gardeners and offers a more personalized approach than previous studies in this area. We call for this more personal approach to research in this field to be used more widely, liaising with not only the guerrillas but the wider community.

At its most simple, guerrilla gardening is "the illegal cultivation of someone else's land" (Reynolds, 2008: 16). Guerrilla gardeners are volunteers who, without permission, target spaces of neglect: they transform the environment without the landowner's consent, and thus could be deemed to be acting unlawfully (Flores, 2006; Hou, 2010). Whilst there is a nascent literature base exploring the guerrilla gardener as an "actor", there is little discussion and focus on those who are potentially affected by guerrilla gardening; the communities, workers, and other individuals who live, work, and play near to the sites transformed through guerrilla practices. This chapter focuses principally on exploring their perceptions of this transformation; however, we also review our experiences with guerrilla gardeners over a two-year period, reflecting on the ethnographic journey with, and core objectives of, three guerrilla groups in the Midlands area of the UK.

Defining "guerrilla gardening"

The prefix "guerrilla" has a military connotation, often being used to describe rebels who are in conflict with an oppressive dominant power (McKay, 2011).

Richard Reynolds, the self-proclaimed general of the guerrilla gardening movement, emphasizes this and plays on the similarities: declaring that "fighting and gardening really are quite natural human pastimes, so combining the two offers no great contortion" (Reynolds, 2008: 28). But there are important differences in their motives: whilst battle-driven guerrillas aim to topple a government or combat an invading army, guerrilla gardeners are generally portrayed as attempting to beautify neighbourhoods and increase biodiversity in areas which generally suffer from neglect (Cobb, 2011; Flores, 2006; Lewis, 2012).

As Reynolds mentions, guerrilla gardening is portrayed as an illegal activity, with actors altering land without the knowledge or permission of the relevant authority. Thompson and Sturgis (2006) for example, encountered the wrath of authority when they attempted to plant trees without permission. On this occasion, they were lectured at great length about "insurance culpability" (Thompson and Sturgis, 2006: 17). In a similar manner, Reynolds has often faced situations where authorities, from police to the local council, have attempted to quash his guerrilla antics (Reynolds, 2008). Effectively, the actions of guerrillas could potentially constitute criminal damage or theft, depending on the context; if for instance, a group of guerrilla gardeners removed existing vegetation "roots and all", in the UK this would result in the activity being deemed illegal.

Guerrilla gardeners tend to occupy space that is either "stalled" or underused (Hou, 2010; Metcalf and Widener, 2011; Thompson and Sturgis, 2006). These spaces present the perfect playgrounds for various types of urban explorers (guerrilla gardeners, graffiti artists, gangs, and so forth) to engage in activities that would be forbidden elsewhere (DeSilvey and Edensor, 2013; Edensor, 2005; Qviström, 2007). By practicing in such spaces, these actors are challenging the way in which these areas were meant to be seen and used, as perceived by the designers (Lefebvre, 1991). Dual carriageway central reservations, intended to prevent cars colliding with pedestrians, can become sites of beauty (Adams and Hardman, 2014), whilst existing railway stations and other public amenities are transformed for agricultural activity (Flores, 2006).

There is evidence to suggest that guerrilla gardening has been practiced for centuries (Flores, 2006; McKay, 2011; Reynolds, 2008), although the origin of "modern" guerrilla gardening is virtually impossible to determine. Richard Reynolds argues that the term was first coined in New York City (guerrillagardening.org, undated). In 1973 the "Green Guerillas" (*sic*) formed a grassroots movement in NYC, initially using seed-filled condoms to beautify inaccessible abandoned spaces (Paul, 2009). Today the "Green Guerillas" have rebranded themselves; now more mainstream and less covert, they aim to educate residents about the benefits of community gardening (Green Guerillas, undated). More recently, Pudup describes the conflict between New York City gardening activists and the Giuliani administration's plans in the early 1990s to privatize public use land, maximize property values, claiming that "gardening in such collective settings is an unalloyed act of resistance" (Pudup, 2008: 1232). McKay (2011) suggests that, although small sporadic outbreaks of urban guerrilla gardening occurred throughout the late-twentieth century in the Global North, one of the first large-scale, media-featured "resistive" guerrilla actions occurred in 1996 during the "Reclaim the Streets Movement". Specifically, some activists used large umbrella-like skirts to hide saplings that were intended to be planted into the tarmac of Britain's shortest motorway – the M41 – as a way of opposing both the overbearing and controlling corporate forces of capitalism, and the car as the dominant mode of transport (Jordan, 1998).

The activity has inevitably received large amounts of media interest (see for example BBC News, 2009; CBC, 2012; Fox News, 2008; Sky News, 2009); awareness of and interest in guerrilla gardening has reached a new level, with entertainment series and documentaries following groups on the ground. An example of this is the Australian prime time show 'Guerrilla Gardeners': "the show's narrative revolves around a group of six rather attractive young people with horticultural and build-ing expertise, who aim to beautify various ugly spaces in peri-urban and suburban Sydney" (Lewis, 2012: 319). Perhaps most relevant to this research is how this series portrays these guerrillas as young, "hip" individuals making a positive impact on cities and rebelling against an oppressive authority (Network Ten, 2010). The show's producers use a variety of catchy headings to lure the viewers in: "wearing hard hats and safety vests as a disguise, they perform their unique raids right under the nose of police, council workers and government rangers" (Network Ten, 2010), playing on the danger and illegality associated with the act (Lewis, 2012).

Despite the growth of interest in guerrilla gardening, in tandem with Rich-ard Reynolds' influential web-based forum (www.guerrillagardening.org), other forms of social media, and a burgeoning literature surrounding guerrilla garden-ing, the majority of accounts present a distanced, over-celebratory, and "heroic" representation of guerrilla action, with authors failing to interact with troops "on the ground" (Adams and Hardman, 2014). Guerrilla gardeners are often viewed exclusively as positive enablers who transform space, for the better, without authority involvement (Johnson, 2011; Lewis, 2012; Tracey, 2007, 2011). Tak-ing this even further, Metcalf and Widener (2011) argue that guerrilla gardening should be encouraged to transform neglected spaces; possibly even adding value to areas which have suffered due to excessive amounts of abandoned land: they can make significant impacts on forgotten landscapes.

Attempts to study guerrilla gardening

Research into guerrilla gardening derives from a host of disciplines: from Tor-naghi's (2012) planning-orientated exploration to McKay's (2011) focus on the sociological aspects of the movement, or the many guides on how to encourage new guerrillas into the practice (Johnson, 2011; Reynolds, 2008; Tracey, 2007, 2011). Several previous accounts have described the act of guerrilla gardening as being intrinsically resistant because of the way its practitioners run against dom-inant planning and architectural codes that are inscribed into particular spaces (for example, Douglas, 2011; Merker, 2010; Reynolds, 2008; Tracey, 2007).

Crane (2011: 6) claims that "there is a lack of in-depth analysis, or academic work" on guerrilla gardening; while Milbourne (2011) points out the different types of space that the guerrillas seek to occupy and/or transform, and suggests that while much academic attention has tended to focus on the guerrilla activity which re-appropriates "stalled" space (Edensor, 2005) – i.e. land that has been identified for regeneration – much less has been written on how (and why) "underused" mundane public space (grass verges, parkland, playing fields) is being appropriated (see Adams and Hardman, 2014). Perhaps the most recent study, and closest to this research, is Crane *et al.*'s (2012) subsequent paper. Crane and her co-authors adopt a more directly participant role to explore guerrilla gardening in Ontario, Canada; she *is* a guerrilla gardener: the leader of a troop. This creates an uneasy dichotomy, with the author acting as both a research subject and researcher, actively participating in what could be deemed an illegal activity (McKay, 2011; Reynolds, 2008).

Crane *et al.* provide an overview of guerrilla gardeners growing food in the city; revealing feelings towards this form of action from community members and other key actors. Crucially, they identify how the semi-illegal nature of guerrilla gardening is often an attraction for thrill seekers (Adams and Hardman, 2014). Crane *et al.*'s (2012: 14) study of her troop in Ontario indicates how these individuals thrived on the "creativity and autonomy" associated with the activity. Reynolds (2008); McKay (2011); and Tracey (2007, 2011) and others suggest that a significant draw to guerrilla gardening is this escape from reality and the opportunity to break rules. Whilst guerrilla gardening is often viewed as a small-scale activity, Milbourne (2011) demonstrates how the practice can initiate and eventually deliver large, legitimized projects: starting community gardens and other established spaces on land originally claimed through the guerrilla activity. Apart from Crane *et al.*'s study, few reflections on guerrilla practice are drawn from empirical research, perhaps due to the difficulties associated with locating and interacting with these groups in a research-led context.

The majority of other accounts of guerrilla gardening appear to originate from student texts (see for example Crane, 2011; Harrison, 2010; Zanetti, 2007). A recent PhD thesis, for instance, investigated the act of guerrilla gardening in relation to other grass-root movements, adopting an approach which mainly involved reviewing secondary sources (Harrison, 2010). Harrison relies heavily on ideas from Reynolds and Tracey to frame her argument, which concentrates specifically on how guerrillas operate, before comparing it with other forms of grassroots activity. Zanetti (2007) demonstrates one of the first attempts of an author to engage in guerrilla gardening, with the intention of attempting to understand how actors use public space: using participant observation to interact with the guerrilla gardeners in the closest possible manner.

Ultimately we argue that those who investigate the activity are mostly "disconnected": commentaries on guerrilla gardening are often romanticized, and since the majority of academics rely on these accounts, it provides only one side of the activity. Several authors view guerrillas either through this remote perspective from secondary sources (see Cobb, 2011; Harrison, 2010; Johnson, 2011 and others) or, when a more personal approach is adopted, they use techniques which allow only the activists' views to be expressed (see Crane, 2011; Crane *et al.*, 2012; Zanetti, 2007). We were consciously explicit about our intent and provided a balanced account of our research to the would-be subjects. Before venturing into the field with the guerrilla gardeners, we understood that a position had to be adopted which would ensure the safety of not only ourselves, but the research subjects and the institution which we represented. Ethnography influenced large parts of this study, particularly participant observation, with the field researcher adopting a purely observational stance during the data collection.

The technique has been employed before in guerrilla gardening (see for instance Crane, 2011; Crane *et al.*, 2012; Zanetti, 2007), yet we argue that it has been used in a way which potentially situates the researcher and their institution in a problematic position, through direct involvement in an activity which could be considered unlawful. We suggest that whilst an approach intimately connected with the activity is required, a passive participant (or equivalent) position could be adopted: enabling researchers to view the activity, but distancing the academic sufficiently from the action. In our research, this position provided sufficient distance from the action whilst simultaneously enabling the research to comply with university procedures and other relevant guidance, for instance, those of the British Sociological Association (BSA, 2002).

Although guerrilla gardening is often described as an illegal activity – with members liable to criminal prosecution if discovered (McKay, 2011; Zanetti, 2007) – in reality guerrilla gardening projects rarely cross this line: instead contravening planning policies or civil legislation (Hardman et al., 2017). Radywyl and Biggs (2013) claim that guerrilla gardening is a form of tactical urbanism which involves slightly altering the city through low-risk intervention: informally changing the landscape without permission or formal support. On occasion a guerrilla troop may trespass or cause damage to urban furniture, but this is strongly discouraged (Reynolds, 2008). Thus whilst it may seem drastic to urge future researchers to adopt a more passive approach, this will of course all depend on the context in question: troops differ with their actions, with some more radical in their activities than others.

With this in mind, we were aware that an appropriate research approach was needed: one which did not involve the researcher too much in the action, but which was sufficient to detail the guerrilla gardeners' actions. Hardman, the field researcher, acted as a passive observer with the three guerrilla gardening groups; informal interviewing was conducted at the sites, with the more formal semi-structured interviews occurring at a later date. These interviews were positioned at strategic points throughout the research process. Several interview stages promoted in-depth discussion and interesting revelations could be followed up; liaising with those who resided near to the guerrilla sites in an informal (during observations) and more formal (following the observations) manner.

Crucially, this study did not merely interact with the guerrilla gardeners, but liaised with those who resided close to the spaces which were transformed. Interviews were conducted with individuals who worked, lived near, and interacted with the guerrilla sites. Discussions occurred in pubs, on the street, and with neighbours in order to gauge their views on the area: whether they noticed any transformation, how involved they were, and their responses to the change. Few studies have gathered feedback from the local population (see Crane *et al.*, 2012), and there is still a lack of focus on those who could be affected by this form of action, thus this approach ensured that those affected by the activity were engaged by the research process.

The guerrilla gardeners

Between 2010 and 2017 we followed multiple guerrilla gardeners across the world, from the UK to South Africa and beyond. In this piece we focus explicitly on a research study into guerrilla gardening practices in the Midlands region of England, much of which was undertaken in 2010. This study, part of a PhD by Hardman, captured the activities of three "types" of guerrilla gardeners: from F Troop, a group of local authority employees who colonized land next to an inner city dual carriageway, to a solo guerrilla gardener who occupied a network of alleyways, to a group of women who started an unpermitted community garden on authority land.

These guerrillas were tracked through a combination of Reynolds' forum, social media, and personal networks. Figure 9.1 shows the three sites and demonstrates the different scales of action surveyed, from a 0.3ha community garden, to the small corridors of land colonized by F Troop and the solo guerrilla. In each case, observations and interviews occurred with the groups; revealing their motivations, practices, structures, and ambitions for future activities.

The three groups with which we interacted during our research demonstrates the diversity of actors involved in guerrilla gardening: from the middle-class, well-educated F Troop and solo guerrilla, to the women's group, which mainly consisted of individuals who relied on state benefits. The three groups also practiced in distinctly different areas, from a dual carriageway barrier, to an alleyway and a community centre's land: a connecting theme emerged around how all three occupied abandoned land and transformed the space to accommodate vegetation. We became interested in these groups due to their express ambition to embed the concept of urban agriculture within their locales; guerrilla gardeners "tend to fall into two groups: those who are driven to beautify space and those who seek to grow crops in it" (Reynolds, 2008: 28), and we were interested in the latter activity.

The three groups investigated held a common core reason for pursuing this form of action: their disagreement with government rhetoric. All three groups shared a feeling that working with officials would render them liable to be incorporated into the often neoliberal agendas of authorities. This clash correlates with the narratives provided by Holland (2004); Milbourne (2010, 2011); and Pudup (2008) and others, who demonstrate the reluctance, in many cases, of gardening activists to engage with authorities pursuing these agendas. In the case of F Troop, members were wary of new political concepts, such as the "Big Society",[1] which they felt would jeopardize the activity if a legal route was adopted. The same distaste for this agenda was shared by the solo guerrilla gardener who refused to be labelled as part of this official scheme.

It must be noted again that perception of authority, and current political rhetoric, played only a part in the three groups' reasons for adopting guerrilla gardening; each had their own micro-motives for pursuing the activity. For instance, to a large extent the pursuit of the "thrill" element drives F Troop's action. The need for this thrill again aligns F Troop and the solo guerrilla gardener with other urban practices which disobey authority and use the environment for pleasure (Adams and Hardman, 2014). In stark contrast, the women pursued this course of action due to their perception that a formal route would take too long: obtaining planning permission for a legitimate site conversion was an uncertain and time-consuming route.

Figure 9.1 The three guerrilla gardening sites, from left to right: F Troop, the solo guerrilla, and the women's group

Source: authors

On the ground with the guerrillas

Prior to exploring the views of those who surrounding the guerrilla gardening sites, we wish to provide an overview of the observations and interviews with the groups. Observations began in 2010 and continued through to 2012, although this varied according to the activities of the guerrilla group. With F Troop, Figure 9.2 shows that Hardman embedded himself within the group: these guerrilla gardeners had five "digs" in total, which brought together a variety of individuals, from businessmen to friends and family. Their goal was to regenerate the neglected patches of land next to the dual carriageway barrier and cultivate parts of it; pursuing the idea of urban agriculture.

We argue that, of the three explored in this paper, F Troop most closely matches the "traditional" guerrilla idea: the group met through guerrillagardening.org and used Reynolds's (2008) text as a guide on how to cultivate the land. The following extract, from Hardman's initial encounter with the troop, shows how they came equipped and ready to tackle the neglected piece of land:

> I'm initially greeted by three individuals, two females and one male. The group wait for late arrivals, which soon turn up (albeit 10 minutes later

Figure 9.2 Hardman and F Troop in action

Source: authors

than the planned time). The new arrivals (one female and one male) come equipped with spades, rakes and extra plants. It's immediately apparent that some group members have thought about what they want to do. They've already 'scouted' the site; creating a basic diagram of where it lies. We set off to the phase one dig site which is located near to a set of busy traffic lights.

(Dig 1 field diary entry)

This was a common theme throughout the five digs conducted by F Troop, with members creating the plan away from the site without involvement from the community or those who regularly interacted with the space. The troop would perform the same process over and over again:

1 Break ground.
2 Turn soil.
3 Organize arrangement by putting pots on intended planting spot.
4 Plant.
5 Clean up and head to a pub.

(Dig 2 field diary entry)

As the digs progressed, F Troop became more confident and began to experiment with vegetables on the space:

The leader of the troop has brought peas and spinach to experiment on the land. Other members have brought plants to rejuvenate the area. Nasturtiums also make an appearance again, with one particular member also bringing several bags of seeds. The leader suggested before the dig that troop members bring bulbs as opposed to seeds, this call was obviously ignored.

(Dig 3 field diary entry)

In terms of the other two guerrilla gardeners explored, unlike F Troop who built up to the idea of planting vegetables, the women's group and solo guerrilla gardener held food growing at the heart of their activities from the beginning. The women's group consisted of a community worker and several members drawn from parts of the surrounding areas. They wished to enable greater access to food through creating a community garden, although initially the leader sought to gain permission for an allotment space:

I actually contacted the allotments planning person to begin with, I wished I hadn't. Then I said to him 'oh forget it, we're not going to do an allotment', and we're not. We're not an allotment, we are a community garden.

(women's group leader)

With the failure to obtain permission, the women's group embarked on a quest to change a patch of land to accommodate a community garden. This process was completed in 2009 without permission from the local authority or those who surrounded the space; the women were consciously colonising land and thus, we argue, can be deemed to be acting as guerrilla gardeners. Observations primarily focussed on the users of the space and how the produce was used, particularly if there were sufficient amounts to supplement local diets.

Interactions with the last of the three guerrilla gardeners observed – the solo guerrilla – were less intensive. These were due to conditions placed upon the field researcher: this guerrilla gardener only wished for a minimal amount of interaction, due to personal issues. Nevertheless, it was still important to reflect on her practices and observe how a guerrilla gardener can "go it alone". The solo guerrilla operated from 2009 to the present day, cultivating an alleyway adjacent to her home. Unlike the other two guerrilla groups in this chapter, her dig site was extremely close to her home, enabling her to practice on a regular basis.

The solo guerrilla had previous experience colonising other patches of land around the city, but now, due to old age, she wished to remain closer to home. She transformed a local authority-owned alleyway into a haven for urban agriculture: using old tyres and other furniture found in the space to provide a home for the beans, tomatoes and other vegetables now grown there. The solo guerrilla stated how she had attempted to engage with the neighbours about the idea of cultivating the space, but few were interested.

Consulting the public: views on guerrilla gardening

Whilst the section above provides a brief introduction to our work with the guerrilla gardeners, we now wish to focus explicitly on the impact of their action. Literature on guerrilla gardening has often failed to include the nearby community and their views: it is frequently "guerrilla-centric". These communities are usually neglected and do not play any part in either academic, activist, or media reports; hence there is a severe lack of exploration into the direct local impact of guerrilla gardening. In this section we review some of the comments about guerrilla gardening obtained from those near to the areas transformed.

In each group setting, we sought to liaise with not only with the guerrilla gardeners, but those who surrounded the sites; this was not possible with the solo guerrilla due to tensions in the area,[2] but indirect feedback was obtained through her own experiences. Those consulted at each site ranged from residents, workers, passers-by, and the occasional pub patron: questions focussed on how frequently they used the area and whether they were aware of any change. The following provides an overview of the data collected, including the community interviews at each site:

Table 9.1 A basic overview of the data collected across the sites

Case Study	Observations	Interviews (group members)	Interviews (community)	Total
F Troop	5 phases	3 interviews	10 interviews (pub patrons; car park attendants; other actors)	18
Women's group	20 digs/events	8 interviews	9 interviews (residents; youths; community organizations)	37
Solo guerrilla	Sporadic/ around 3 digs	1 interview	N/A	4
				59

Source: authors

The following sections provide a summary of feedback from those who reside near to the three sites we investigated. As Table 9.1 shows, nearby residents and users were consulted; casual passers-by were not the main target for this feedback, since many may not have held an intimate relationship with the landscape. Rather, we focussed explicitly on individuals who spent a considerable amount of time near the guerrilla sites.

Perceptions of the three sites

In all three contexts, we gathered positive feedback about the guerrilla action; this ranged from comments regarding the functionality, with some sites producing large amounts of food, to comments suggesting that the area was regenerated through the action:

> Well it's nice to have a bit of colour as you can see. I've got my hanging baskets out and everything and I think it add a nice bit of colour, bit of flowers and that. You need it as much greenery in the city centre as you can get.
> (Pub Landlady, F Troop site)

> They've done ever so well you know, she's really good, made an effort. She's done ever so well here you know, and everyone seems to like the food she's done. You know, she gets all the stuff from the garden.
> (Resident, women's site)

> One lady brought around a box of brownies she'd baked and said it was for doing the lane because she really liked it and she found out who was doing it. So that was lovely, she was a young person who travels a lot so she sort of bobs back up and around again to see how nice it looked.
> (Solo guerrilla gardener)

Despite all three groups experimenting with the idea of urban agriculture, the core of the positive comments focussed on the guerrilla gardeners' efforts on improving the spaces: "It's a lot cleaner than it has been, there's not as much rubbish about" (Male, F Troop site); "well, it's nice to look at, better than looking at just a plain piece of grass" (Female, women's site); "people do come back and throw bottles and that has really stopped a lot" (Solo guerrilla gardener). The majority of those surrounding the sites found the aesthetic improvements welcome and encouraged more activities to improve spaces across the area.

Whilst there was a substantial amount of positive feedback regarding each site, there were some issues aired by those who resided nearby. In relation to F Troop for instance, it became apparent through the regular interactions how the guerrilla troop did not interact with the community in the first two digs (in the space of a year): "patrons from the local pub seem interested in the dig and approach the site a few times; keeping to themselves rather than interacting with the group" (Hardman's diary entry). Further reinforcing this notion that F Troop failed to interact with those who surrounded the site were interviews conducted in 2011. It appeared that during their first year of operation, the guerrillas did not speak with any community members, at first excluding the pub's staff and patrons from being included in their action: "No we just stood there watching them do it. As far as I'm concerned there was no conversation with me, to them. If they'd have spoke to me, I'd have spoke to them" (Male near F Troop site).

This counters the almost romantic, rogue notion of F Troop's action. In this instance, the troop is shown as a set of "outsiders" who enter an area with which they have little connection; transforming the zone according to their own values, and not consulting the local populace. Comments from other patrons repeat this feeling of isolation, neglect, and confusion over the action:

> Well just before spring, noticed [them] under-cover of darkness planting stuff down that end. They didn't say hi or owt.
>
> (Male, F Troop site)

> [The landlady] was talking about the secret gardeners or something. Something about them doing stuff on their own without the council.
>
> (Female, F Troop site)

> It's all right, if it makes a difference, but after they've done it, its gone wild again . . . it looked nice afterwards, but as I say, couple of days later it was just like a bloody dustbin.
>
> (Male, F Troop site)

A similar story emerged with regards to the solo guerrilla gardener, who suggested that conflict had arisen over her approach to altering the alleyway. This confrontation almost became physical on one occasion, with a neighbour furious that the guerrilla gardener had planted at the rear of his property: "he felt that because his house backed onto the lane, it was somehow threatening to him for me to plant things" (Solo guerrilla gardener). Whilst conflict has previously been witnessed during guerrilla activity,[3] clashes with the public are rare. Nevertheless, this incident demonstrates the potential danger associated with the activity, with a resident almost physically assaulting a guerrilla gardener: angered by the guerrilla colonizing land without his permission and changing property close to him without his direct input (although he did not own the land in question).

The women's group slightly differs from the other two; the locals were unaware of the guerrilla nature of the group's actions. Rather, comments focussed on the accessibility of the site; which, although portrayed as an asset for locals, functioned more as an allotment site:

> we call it a community garden, because if you call it an allotment you've got to have all sorts of permits and it just opens a can of worms.
>
> (women's group leader)

> Well we are not allowed to call it our allotment, as it's not politically correct, so we just call it our community garden.
>
> (Female member 1)

> Some of us call it the allotment, some of us call it the community garden.
>
> (Female member 2)

> We can't call it an allotment because we'll have to pay for the land, so that's why it's called a community garden.
>
> (Female member 3)

> I just call it our garden or an allotment.
>
> (Female member 4)

> the women's group have some of the goods out of the garden or the allotment.
>
> (Female member 5)

> I see it as kind of a mini allotment.
>
> (Female member 6)

This questions the notion of the community garden, as clearly the grow space was not intended for the local residents. An allotment is typically a portion of land, restricted in dimensions and leased from the local authority, for the private production of food (Groundwork, 2011). Indeed, the modern idea of an allotment has not altered from the original nineteenth-century concept: "his Lordship, we believe, had the honour of being the first individual who let out small portions of land upon the plan which is now universally known by the name of the Field Garden or Allotment system" (quoted in Burchardt, 2002: 242). In essence an allotment is a controlled space, and one which is in short supply, but high demand, in many UK cities (Milbourne, 2012; WRO, 2012). The operational style of the garden was noticed by some residents, who called for more access to the produce: "I'd like to see more access" (Homeless male), "more access would be good" (Elderly male resident).

Whilst it is not unusual for spaces in community gardens to be personalized by those who use or operate them (see for instance Milbourne, 2010), in this instance the restriction on access resulted in the garden becoming inaccessible and colonized by the women: the design was personal and did not include any input from the wider community. In a similar manner to F Troop and the solo guerrilla gardener, the women adopted tactics which completely excluded those near to the space. Nevertheless, unlike their counterparts, the women's attempts to introduce relatively large-scale agricultural activity into the landscape is accepted by the majority of the community; it is a less drastic example when compared to F Troop or the solo guerrilla, who bring edible plants into spaces with which they would not normally be associated.

Evaluating guerrilla practice

A recurring practice in guerrilla gardening appears to be this attempt to swoop into locations and transform the space without permission of not only the authority, but the local population; several examples demonstrate how guerrilla gardeners prefer to act in isolation, usually arriving in the dead of night or without the knowledge of the locals, altering spaces without speaking or involving those who live nearby (McKay, 2011; Reynolds, 2008; Winnie, 2010). This was most apparent in the case of F Troop, generating several comments which suggested that the process of making changes went unnoticed:

> No I haven't actually because obviously I'm working on this side but never really noticed anything no. Until you said that, I was clueless about it to be honest.
>
> (Car park attendant)

> Outside the front door? Only the grass is mown, that's about all . . . Where the bushes are and the weeds? Ahhh its just crap you know.
>
> (Pub patron)

> More cigarette ends. . . . More cigs yeah, gets filthier by the day. . . . No [change] not that I can see anyways.
>
> (Pub patron)

When the site is noticed, the anger with guerrilla practice is most explicitly expressed in the F Troop and solo guerrilla contexts, with some residents perplexed by the actions of the guerrilla gardeners. The former generated comments regarding their lack of support for the transformed space, with the area relapsing into a state of disrepair a few days following the changes. The latter was accused of changing a neighbour's space without permission: an alteration which almost brought about a physical response from this specific individual. In the context of the women's group, a few residents were disgruntled about the lack of access to the site, a space once open to the public but which had since been fenced off following the creation of the community garden.

The views collected demonstrate a mixture of responses surrounding guerrilla gardening: whilst the majority are positive, several core negative issues are raised:

1   The lack of communication/input from communities
2   Unsustainable practices
3   Issues with ownership

Whilst the above provide a broad overview of the main issues arising during our investigation, we merely wish to raise the notion that guerrilla practice has a darker side. The ideas that guerrilla gardeners should communicate with the local population and think in a more long-term manner could be seen as ridiculous and unachievable by some, since the practice aims to do the complete opposite: the buzz is partly achieved by colonizing space for the short term without anyone's knowledge (Crane *et al.*, 2012; Milbourne, 2010). An approach could be adopted in a similar manner to F Troop in which informal discussions enable community buy-in to the growing scheme. We understand that guerrilla gardeners would not have the resources (or desire) to undertake a formal consultation, but some inter-action with locals may prevent criminal damage and ensure the sustainability of the site.

There is also an issue here regarding the unregulated nature of the concept. The above already demonstrates the lack of consultation and discussion with local actors, but alongside this guerrilla gardening avoids other obstacles which formal sites must scale. For example, there is no soil testing at any of the sites despite the majority growing directly into the soil; this is an issue due to potential contamination, with many sites having a previous industrial use prior to growing. One may argue that regulation would contravene the very principles of guerrilla gardening and the desire of its community to carry out activities without a rigid system in place. Nevertheless, we argue that guidelines for potential guerrillas need to be more specific and detailed regarding consultation and soil testing, although the latter may not be possible due to a lack of funds, raised beds and other tools can be used to mitigate against such challenges.

The emergence of a "guerrilla trap"

In this chapter we have outlined how the existing coverage from academics, the media, and others regarding guerrilla gardening is overwhelmingly positive: commentary on the activity is frequently guerrilla-centric. Fundamentally, we challenge the prevailing notion that guerrilla gardening should be automatically encouraged and viewed in a purely positive light. Prominent, well-cited, guerrilla gardening literature, such as that by Flores (2006); Hou (2010); McKay (2011); Reynolds (2008); and Tracey (2007), fails to identify and account for the negative aspect of the activity. These accounts are frequently used by other authors in an attempt to reinforce the idea that guerrilla gardening should be encouraged, to promote concepts such as urban agriculture and the greening of cities (see, for example, Astyk and Newton, 2009; Elliot, 2010; Lewis, 2012; Pudup, 2008; Winnie, 2010).

This chapter has revealed evidence which urges future research to provide a more distanced picture of guerrilla gardening: there is a need to step back and assess the extent to which guerrilla gardening impacts on the nearby environment, and how the majority of guerrilla gardeners colonize and transform space changing the area according to their own views and interpretations. In a similar manner to Purcell's (2005) "local trap", which argues that academics automatically view the local scale as desirable, a "guerrilla trap" emerges here; with academics and non-academics alike unquestioningly promoting guerrilla gardening. Whilst the three guerrilla projects depicted in this chapter may visually improve the spaces in which they were situated, in all three instances the guerrillas fundamentally colonized land without prior notification: consultation was nonexistent and their practices excluded those who interacted with the areas on a frequent basis.

Conclusion

Unlike previous accounts on guerrilla gardening, this chapter calls for future studies to explore guerrilla gardeners' actions, their motivations, and their interactions with local residents and/or community members. Rather than focusing ostensibly on the guerrilla perspective through the use of interviews and questionnaires, or observation techniques, this research highlights the potential harm, both to the environment and surrounding community, which guerrillas can unknowingly (or knowingly) inflict.

Fundamentally, this work challenges the often celebratory depiction of this grassroots movement and brings to the surface some dangers of unregulated action. This research is crucial here, since some claim that the activity is growing, with the movement expanding rapidly across the world, primarily due to the popularity of social networks (Harutyunyan *et al.*, 2009; Reynolds, 2008). If this is true, then perhaps more unsustainable and intrusive practices could be happening under the noses not just of authority, but also the communities which surround these informal sites.

Whilst we present a darker side of guerrilla gardening, it must also be noted that the overwhelming majority of responses provided evidence to suggest that the change was welcome. Indeed, guerrilla gardening does much for urban sustainability, with spaces beautified and produce grown in the most exotic of locations; projects such as the Incredible Edible network would not be here if guerrilla gardening was restricted. This chapter aimed to highlight that a more rounded account of the action is required and that consulting with those who surround the sites is a useful strategy for researchers and even for guerrillas themselves. Furthermore, this research demonstrates how guerrilla gardening can be considered illegal in some contexts, with groups encountering issues with police and other authority members (see, for instance, Reynolds, 2008); a suitable approach should be adopted to account for this and other difficulties which researchers may encounter.

There are many different angles for future research projects, particularly if one takes forward some of the revelations identified during this research: from testing the soil at unregulated guerrilla sites and evaluating the edibility of the produce, to further investigating the roles of the guerrilla gardeners (for example in terms of geographies of gender) or focussing specifically on the deprived communities in which they act (see, for instance, Milbourne's, 2011) work on gardening in less affluent communities). In each case we call for researchers to carefully adopt an ethical approach which will protect the guerrillas, themselves and their institutions. This is a priority since exposure, or incorrect research practice, could have serious implications for those involved. One must remember that interacting with guerrilla gardeners will require large sacrifices and long amounts of time in the field: embedding researchers with the troop to fully reveal and understand their actions. In addition, accessing guerrilla troops is even more difficult: with the uptake of popular social media, guerrillas are moving away from Reynolds's forum and other central communication hubs where action was previously predominantly organized; Facebook, for instance, allows closed groups, which guerrillas occasionally use to communicate through, instead of an open platform. This presents an obstacle for interaction, with private groups and other barriers preventing researchers from initially interacting with these individuals. Future research should prepare to encounter such issues and consider searching popular social media to find guerrilla action in their areas.

Notes

1 A concept promoted by the UK Coalition Government, which involved community members taking over local authority services on a voluntary basis.
2 It was made explicitly clear that this individual did not wish for anyone, including the researcher, to speak with those who lived in the adjacent properties.
3 See for instance a video of Richard Reynolds clashing with Police www.youtube.com/watch?v=L8WTlqiwYdQ

References

Adams, D. and Hardman, M. 2014 Observing Guerrillas in the Wild: Reinterpreting Practices of Informal Gardening *Urban Studies* 51 (6), 1103–1119.

Astyk, S. and Newton, A. 2009 *A Nation of Farmers: Defeating the Food Crisis on American Soil* New Society Publishers, Gabriola Island.

BBC News 2009 *Guerrilla Gardening* http://www.bbc.co.uk/devon/content/articles/2009/04/22/guerrilla_gardener_feature.shtml Accessed 5 May 2018.

BSA 2002 *Statement of Ethical Practice for the British Sociological Association* (www.britsoc.co.uk/about/equality/statement-of-ethical-practice.aspx) Accessed 3 June 2013.

Burchardt, J. 2002 *The Allotment Movement in England, 1793–1873*, The Boydell Press, Rochester.

CBC 2012 *Guerrilla Gardening Projects Aims to Give Food for All* http://www.cbc.ca/hamil ton/news/story/2012/06/27/hamilton-guerrilla-gardening.html Accessed 14 April 2018.

Cobb, T. D. 2011 *Reclaiming Our Food: How the Grassroots Food Movement Is Changing the Way We Eat* Storey Publishing, North Adams.

Crane, A. 2011 'Intervening with Agriculture: A Participatory Action Case Study of Guerrilla Gardening in Kingston, Ontario' Unpublished Masters Dissertation Queen's University, Canada.

Crane, A., Viswanathan, L. and Whitelaw, G. 2012 Sustainability through Intervention: A Case Study of Guerrilla Gardening in Kingston *Ontario Local Environment: The International Journal of Justice and Sustainability* 18 (1), 1–20.

D.C. Guerrilla Gardeners 2012 *About D.C. Guerrilla Gardeners* (http://dcguerillagarden ers.blogspot.co.uk/) Accessed 22 March 2013.

DeSilvey, C. and Edensor, T. 2013 Reckoning with Ruins Progress in Human *Geography* 37 (4), 465–485.

Douglas, G. 2011 Do-It-Yourself Urban Design Paper presented to the Regular Session on Popular Culture at the American Sociological Association annual conference in Las Vegas, August 21st 2011 (http://home.uchicago.edu/~gdouglas/GCCDouglas_DIYUr banDesign-ASA2011.pdf).

Edensor, T. 2005 *Industrial Ruins: Spaces, Aesthetics and Materiality* Berg, Oxford.

Elliot, B. 2010 *Constructing Community: Configurations of the Social in Contemporary Philosophy and Urbanism* Lexington Books, Plymouth.

Flores, C. H. 2006 *Food Not Lawns: How to Turn Your Garden and Neighbourhood into a Community* Chelsea Green, White River Junction.

Fox News 2008 *Guerrilla Gardening in Los Angeles* (http://www.foxnews.com/wires/2008Ju l04/0,4670,GuerrillaGardening,00.html) Accessed 5 April 2018.

Glasgow Guerrillas 2012 *The Glasgow Guerrilla Gardeners* (http://glasgowguerrillagarden ing.blogspot.co.uk/) Accessed 22 March 2013.

Green Guerrillas Undated *It's Your City, Dig It* (www.greenguerillas.org/) Accessed 4 June 2013.

Groundwork 2011 *Community Spaces* http://www.community-spaces.org.uk/default.aspx? page=4 Accessed 23 August 2013.

Guerrillagardening.org Undated *Guerrilla Gardener Forum* (www.guerrillagardening.org/ community/index.php) Accessed 23 May 2013.

Hardman, M., Chipungu, L., Hangwelani, M., Larkham, P.J., Scott, A.J. and Armitage, R.P. (2017) Guerrilla Gardening and Green Activism: Rethinking the Informal Urban Growing Movement, *Landscape and Urban Planning*, 170: 6–14.

Harrison, C. E. 2010 'Rethinking the Divide: Beyond the Politics of Demand versus the Politics of the Act Debate' Unpublished PhD thesis University of Exeter, Exeter.

Harutyunyan, A., Horschelmann, K. and Miles, M. 2009 *Public Spheres After Socialism* The University of Chicago Press, Chicago.

Holland, L. 2004 Diversity and Connections in Community Gardens: A Contribution to Local Sustainability, *Local Environment: The International Journal of Justice and Sustainability*, 9 (3): 285–305.

Hou, J. 2010 *Insurgent Public Space: Guerrilla Urbanism and the Remaking of Contemporary Cities* Taylor and Francis, New York.

Johnson, L. 2011 *City Farmer: Adventures in Growing Urban Food* Greystone Books, Vancouver.

Jordan, J. 1998 'Anti-Road Protests and Reclaim the Streets' in Mckay, G. ed. *DiY Culture*, Verso, London.

Lefebvre, H. 1991 *The Production of Space*, Blackwell, Oxford.

Lewis, T. 2012 There Grows the Neighbourhood: Green Citizenship, Creativity and Life Politics on Eco-TV *International Journal of Cultural Studies* 15 (3), 315–326.

McKay, G. 2011 *Radical Gardening: Politics, Idealism and Rebellion in the Garden* Frances Lincoln, London.

Merker, B. 2010 Taking Place, in Hou, J. ed. *Insurgent Public Space: Guerrilla Urbanism and the Remaking of Contemporary Cities* Taylor and Francis, London.

Metcalf, S. S. and Widener, M. J. 2011 Growing Buffalo's Capital for Local Food: A System's Framework for Sustainable Agriculture *Applied Geography* 31 (4), 1242–1251.

Milbourne, P. 2010 Growing Places: Community Gardening, Ordinary Creativities and Place-Based Regeneration in a Northern English City, in Edensor, T., Leslie, D., Millington, M. and Rantisi, N. eds. *Spaces of Vernacular Creativity: Reconsidering the Creative Class and Creative Clusters* Routledge, London, 236–258.

Milbourne, P. 2011 Everyday (In)Justices and Ordinary Environmentalisms: Community Gardening in Disadvantaged Urban Neighbourhoods *Local Environment: The International Journal of Justice and Sustainability* 17 (9), 1–15.

Milbourne, P. 2012 The Spaces of Community Gardening: Complexities, Hybridities and Creativities. Paper presented at: Association of American Geographers, New York City.

Moss, G. G. 2010 *Gardening and Violence* Free Range Enterprises, Aotearoa.

Network Ten 2010 *Guerrilla Gardeners* http://ten.com.au/guerrilla-gardeners-about-the-show.htm Accessed 21 July 2017.

Pothole Gardener 2012 *An Olympic Series of Pothole Gardens* [Online] (http://thepothole gardener.com/) Accessed: 22 August 2017.

Paul, A. 2009 *No Need for Green Aids Here*, Alberta: City Life.

Pudup, M. B. 2008 It Takes a Garden: Cultivating Citizen-Subjects in Organized Garden Projects *GeoForum* 39 (3), 1228–1240.

Purcell, M. 2005 Urban Democracy and the Local Trap *Urban Studies* 43 (11), 1921–1941.

Qviström, M. 2007 Landscapes Out of Order: Studying the Inner Urban Fringe Beyond the Rural-Urban Divide *Geografiska Annaler* 89 (3), 269–282.

Radywyl, N. and Biggs, C. 2013. Reclaiming the commons for urban transformation *Journal of Cleaner Production*, 50, 159–170.

Reynolds, R. 2008 *On Guerrilla Gardening: A Handbook for Gardening without Permission* Bloomsbury, London.

Sky News 2009 *Shrub Man on Mission to Root Out Evil Weeds* http://news.sky.com/skynews/ Home/UK-News/Human-Shrub-Replanting-Tubs-InColchester-With-Flowers-After-They-Became-Overgrown-With-Weeds/Article/200907215332291 Accessed 5 January 2014.

Thompson, E. and Sturgis, J. 2006 *The London Gardener: Guide and Sourcebook* Francis Lincoln, London.

Tornaghi, C. 2012 Public Space, Urban Agriculture and the Grassroots Creation of New Commons in Viljoen, A. and Wiskerke, J. S. C. eds. *Sustainable Food Planning: Evolving Theory and Practice* Wageningen Academic Publishers, Wageningen, 349–365.

Tracey, D. 2007 *Guerrilla Gardening: A Manifesto* New Society Publishers, Gabriola Island.

Tracey, D. 2011 *Urban Agriculture: Ideas and Designs for the New Food Revolution* New Society Publishers, Gabriola Island.

Winnie, M. 2010 *Food Rebels, Guerrilla Gardeners, and Smart-Cookin' Mamas: Fighting Back in an Age of Industrial Agriculture* Beacon Press, Boston.

WRO 2012 *Community Food Grown in Wales* Welsh Government, Cardiff.

Zanetti, O. 2007 'Guerrilla Gardening: Geographers and Gardeners, Actors and Networks: Reconsidering Urban Public Space' Unpublished MA dissertation' Queen Mary, University of London, London.

10 The making of a strategizing platform

From politicizing the food movement in urban contexts to political urban agroecology

Barbara Van Dyck, Chiara Tornaghi, Severin Halder, Ella von der Haide, and Emma Saunders

In different cities and in diverse ways, we – the authors of this chapter – are connected to gardens, to building the urban commons and to knowledge creation. We met at the International Conference of Critical Geography "Precarious Radicalism on Shifting Grounds: Towards a Politics of Possibility" in Ramallah (Palestine) in July 2015. The organizers of the conference wanted to create a space where scholars, activists, artists and others interested in critical socio-spatial praxis could discuss how "the rise on authoritarianisms, revanchists' responses, encroachment of fundamental rights, precarity of subsistence, social relations, employment, or the consolidation of populist right wing and fundamentalist movements, [eclipses and undermines] the political space and fundamental work of individuals, communities and movements around the world". The conference wanted to be an opportunity to share thoughts on how to transform these times into "a moment of political possibility by reconsidering and/ or expanding existing paradigms as well as by reconnecting solidarities and struggles".[1] The letter conversation that is reproduced below was written part in preparation and part at the aftermath of this stimulating conference. We found that the "letter" was a form of communication that reflected well the type of connection and relationships we were trying to build, and at the same time suitable to look at the future while creating an "active memory" of the process, emotions, and exchanges we were living. In these letters we discuss our experiences of being embedded in often contradictory green urban activities, while also being scholars theorizing about those developments. We share our doubts, motivations, and ways of contributing to (urban food) movements from this double position, what questions arise, and how to deal with them.

***

Dear all,

At present we (primarily) live, do research, and garden in Belgium and the UK respectively. We share great frustration over dogmas of good governance and "solutionism" coming from a new Green Revolution, which coupled with neoliberal economic policies and austerity, lead civil society organizations and researchers alike to set priorities by criteria of survival and adaptation in a time of growing precarity. In the midst of these transformations, urban food movements are characterized by a strong focus on strategies of gender-, class- and race-blind individual behavioural change, universalism, and consumer oriented awareness-raising campaigns. Public debate and urban struggles that radically question root causes (such as the private and exclusive ownership of land and food commons) or that challenge strategies and incompatible choices in food systems are often marginalized. This is reflected in the weak imaginaries in large parts of the urban food movements (see Alkon and Agyeman, 2011; McClintock, 2014; Tornaghi, 2014) on the necessity and possibility of social transformation.

Questions on the post-political condition (e.g., Swyngedouw, 2009), the evacuation of the political from the urban, and the retraction of the political with regard to urban food movements (e.g., Guthman, 2008; Holt-Giménez and Altieri, 2013) are very present in our thoughts. We are sure that we are not alone with these analysis and frustrations. Therefore we want to reach out to you to explore ways of strengthening the politicizing power of urban food movements.

If this speaks to you, we invite you to come to our "strategizing platform on politicizing the food movements in urban contexts", which will take place at the International Conference of Critical Geographers in Ramallah, Palestine, in July 2015. We would like to share experiences of food skill sharing, collective learning, collectivized direct action, growing experiences, popular education, power decentralization, movement building, and food scholar activism.

Looking forward hearing from you,

Barbara and Chiara

***

Dear fellow-thinkers and do-ers,

You responded to the call for contributions to a strategizing platform on politicizing urban food movements. It is truly exciting to know that we will soon be meeting in person in Ramallah. But why wait until summer to start thinking together about strategies and methods of action research in the food movement?

Let me start by presenting myself. My energy, curiosity, indignation about injustice, and belief in social transformation drive my research as much as my social engagement. Within the Belgian food movement, I feel connected to the values and strategies of what we started to refer to as "patatistas". The term patatista encompasses the idea of working together to gain control over our lives by transforming food systems. We seek to work in solidarity with peasant farmers, dream of nutritious and culturally adapted food as a right, internationally reach out to the Nyéleni food sovereignty movement, and connect with struggles against what is referred to as "large useless infrastructures" such as highway or airport expansions, new prisons, and more. Without eschewing political lobbying to demand policies that support the conditions for thriving peasant farming and fair food systems, our strategies focus on increased autonomy through access to land for food growers, seed sovereignty, cutting out middle-men to build strong and short food chains, fighting genetically engineered crops, and strengthening knowledge and skill sharing.

On several occasions, I learnt that voicing indignation about injustice and environmental destruction that drives much of my doing and thinking mainly helps me to strengthen the reputation of being a troublemaker, and definitely not that of a proper scientist. A good researcher after all, so I was told, is not only curious, but also able to work objectively and detached from the context of which (s)he is a part. At other moments, I would rather have hidden scholarly institutional affiliations. It raises suspicion. Most probably I am "out there" to make a career out of studying "them", so it is presumed. And rightly so is the suspicion. Have we [scholars] not made careers out of studying farmers, social movements, *avant gardistes*? Have we not been trained to adopt a position of superiority in knowing? And yet, the more patatista I became, the more important it seemed to claim researcher as part of my identity.

In 2014, in an act of civil disobedience, a few hundred people planted potatoes on *de facto* farm and parkland on the fringes of the city of Brussels. A few years earlier, the land had been bought by the Belgian State with the intention of building a prison with a capacity to imprison up to 1,190 men and women. The new prison was proclaimed to do away with the ongoing dehumanizing conditions in the overpopulated Belgian prisons where mostly poor (wo)men and people of colour are detained. Through a variety of tactics, ranging from political lobbying, over public awareness campaigns, to direct action, people have organized against the construction of this maxi-prison since 2012. The "illegal" potato planting in 2014 reinforced the ongoing opposition. The event not only gave increased visibility to the struggle by drawing attention to questions of access to land and choices of urban development trajectories, it equally opened up reflections on the interrelatedness of the enclosure of land and the locking up of people.

Experiencing the mutual reinforcement of struggles, strategies, and tactics in opposing the building of a maxi-prison in Brussels has been important in my own reflections on how food scholarship could engage with the evasion of politics from the urban food movement. That question is finally crucial in what will bring us together in Ramallah. The coalition against prison building showed me the strength of the food movement in reinforcing broader struggles. The act of occupying public land through potato planting can be understood as social movement building around food and agriculture, and has little to do with "food movement building". Democratizing and regaining control of the food system are not goals as such, but a means of reclaiming the future. This awareness seems crucial to me if, through activist scholarship, we do not want to contribute to reinforcing food movements devoid of any political awareness and transformative capacities.

This brings me to a second patatista experience. In May 2011, more than 400 people showed up to perform or support the uprooting of genetically engineered (GE) potatoes during the liberation of a public field. At that time, a field trial with GE potatoes was set up by a consortium of Flemish public research institutes in cooperation with the chemical multinational BASF. The Big Potato Swap, or the uprooting of GE potatoes with the intention of replacing them with organic ones, was a means for us to, on our own terms, participate in the collective experiment with GE crops. The action transformed a supposedly technical question, the development of GE crops, into a political one about the future of farming, eating, and democratization of the sciences. The Big Potato Swap was indeed the start of a highly polemic controversy on the use of genetic engineering in agriculture and the privatization of life through gene patenting, but went way beyond that. The role, financing, and functioning of universities made it into headlines. Questions such as "public research in whose interest?" or "what are the consequences of turning universities into enterprises?" became highly disputed items of public debate in Flanders.

So what do these experiences mean for action research in the domain of urban agro-food issues? Whether it was about illegally planting or harvesting potatoes, in both cases patatistas brought important difficult and marginalized questions into the public domain. Activist scholarship has a role to play in mobilizing skills, knowledge, experiences, and privileges to make the inconvenient questions on the finality and consequences of technocratic approaches that urban activists where predisposed to ask (!), as important as they are. The contrast with the more common (political) role of scientists to blindly promote new technologies, and often stuck in the idea that more information on the technicalities of genetic engineering or other silver bullet solutions will bring wider public acceptance, could not be bigger.

And this brings me to the last point of this letter. Activist scholars are often part of the same establishments that employ small groups of scientists who, in cooperation with the (agro-)industry, work hard to define what our collective future will look like. Geo-engineering to combat climate change, modern prisons to maintain social order, highly centralized energy networks based on nuclear power, industrialized food production to feed the cities, you name it. Scholarly activism, I believe, can reinforce social movements in their efforts to empower people (including scientists, students, and politicians) to no longer accept techno-phantasies of progress. By making visible the pathways of choice in innovation trajectories as well as their respective implications (see Stirling, 2010), activist scholarships can contribute to foster critical enquiry, credibility, and legitimacy to what are presented as realistic, or on the contrary unrealistic, ways forward. Societal change towards just and ecologically sustainable food systems (and societies) is not a technical endeavour but first and foremost one of shifting paradigms and transforming power relations (cfr Meadows, 1999).

Social movements function as de-intoxicators from the prevailing idea that there are no alternatives to industrial agro-food futures in neoliberal cities. They fuel new initiatives, shared visions, and agendas to be born. In that regard, we need first movers, people, action, initiatives instilled with an understanding of the need to challenge and transform power relations that inspire and invite to come along. For me, activist scholarship lives up to its aspirations when it finds ways of stretching peoples' imagination and so pushes the boundaries of the possible. In particular, I believe that we ought to use our social positions as researchers to oppose the instrumentalization of the sciences to the benefit of concentrating corporate power, by critically interfering in questions and arenas (whether or not we are invited to do so). Debunking the idea of dis-interested food research, knowing that working in the interest of the agro-industry is more likely to attract funding, being published in top journals, and so on is no easy task. We are made to believe that certain types of knowledge, devoid of their context, become the norm, are neutral and therefore incontestable. Let this not stop us from asking simple, inconvenient questions that bring the underlying values, issues, and assumptions that underpin food research strategies and policies to the surface.

Seeking to challenge hegemonic positions of science-in-society that are based on the idea of superiority and neutrality of technical expertise from within universities is not new. Berkeley, Sorbonne, and many other universities in the late 60s and 70s were central loci to contest the militarization of research, its massification and orientation towards the primacy of the technosciences underpinning modernist development strategies. Today, I see a lot of frustration among colleagues about the way increasingly corporatized universities work. Activist scholarship can build on that frustration to invite students and colleagues to make choices. Controversies such as the potato-ones referred to in this letter, are moments that help to take sides. We can learn from our work in the movements in combination with the privileges that come with (university) jobs, to channel frustration and anger among fellow urbanites, peasants, researchers, and students into the creation of the social-ecological fabric that sustains alternatives. I truly hope that the building of a strategizing platform will contribute in such ways to opening up spaces that support the kind of ideas we are promoting.

In solidarity,

Barbara

***

Dear scholar activists and garden mates,

Inspired by the wonderful call for contributions, we want to present to you our struggles to support the creation of an urban garden movement from within – and between – activism and academia. We are both urban garden activists who are doing action research, living in Berlin and Munich but inspired by political struggles from all over the world, especially Latin America where we have both been involved with grassroots projects and urban agriculture. That's where we first encountered militant research, popular education, and agroecology. We are working in different projects, cities, and universities, but we have been supporting each other for almost ten years now through listening, reflection, and collaborations.

All over Germany, there are tens of thousands of urban gardens such as school gardens and allotment gardens, some of which have been creating roots for over 100 years. The spread of a new type of "Intercultural Urban Community Gardens", with a strong focus on the participation of migrants and refugees, began in Germany 20 years ago. In Göttingen a group of migrants founded the first garden of that kind (Interkulturelle Gärten Göttingen) in 1996; soon many others followed their positive experiences, and a national network of Intercultural Community Gardens was created. In 2009, another type of young urban artistic and stylish community garden emerged and became well-known. Since then, more than 400 (intercultural) community gardens have been founded. While most of the community gardens are flourishing, some have been evicted and many have been co-opted by public politics or advertisement. So we ask ourselves, what can be done to support the growth of a radical garden movement, and what are the challenges that we face?

First of all, we observe that these new urban community gardens do not have common aims. These gardens often function as a platform for a variety of issues, such as public space, migration, commons, community building, therapy, and education. Food and agriculture is often just one aspect among a range of issues: they lack a collective identity and common ideas for urban transformation. We especially observe a growing divide between the older and the new intercultural community gardens, although the urban gardeners themselves rarely reflect on these differences.

Second, we are trapped in our own fame! The creation of hundreds of community gardens led to heavy media and scientific attention; this attention produced a positive image and led to the creation of more community gardens. However, we are also confronted with the co-option of these images in advertisements for cars, cigarettes, and furniture. This makes us fear the transformation of these initiatives into meaningless green washing objects and a tool for neoliberal urban development, especially because the most famous German community garden pushed the concept of mobile gardening and made the projects useful tools for neoliberal urban developers.

Third, damn it, we are "sustainable"! Community gardens have received financial and institutional support and acceptance in recent years. As one result of this support, the gardens have become part of the dominant environmental discourse of sustainability. A collective discussion about the struggles of urban farmers historically rooted in the "environmentalism of the poor" (cf. Martinez-Alier, 2002) and strengthening their ties with political struggles, such as Right To The City or De-Growth, have been developed in some gardens. Unfortunately, numerous urban gardens have been appropriated by mainstream discussions and transformed into a part of the emerging dominant urban "green" capitalism development practices and discourses.

The political implications of urban garden activities were often removed from media coverage, and soon pictures and narratives of urban gardens were seized by city marketing, investors, the food industry, and the advertising industry. Therefore, urban gardens run the risk of being turned into stylish middle-class recreational gardening or inner city agribusiness production (for example, ECF – efficient city farm systems project in Berlin), losing their potential for a different socio-ecological urban metabolism.

By facing these obstacles we are searching for answers, which we would like to discuss with you: how can we build, feed, and strengthen a radical urban community garden movement?

We will present two examples as responses to the aforementioned challenges. One essential part of both attempts is the idea of finding a fruitful way of combining activism and research to organize and collectively politicize the urban garden movement.

The urban gardening manifesto – a collective writing process to locate the political in urban gardens

Facing co-option, the unstable temporary in-between-use access to land, and the lack of a collective identity within urban community gardens, a group of activists from different gardens and institutions decided in 2012 to collectively start writing a manifesto with the purpose of expressing the political localization of the urban garden movement.

Already existing networks enabled a partly centralized editorial working group consisting of scientists, (scholar-)activists, journalists – and some local collective writing and editing processes. Over 100 gardeners participated in the process. The authors of the manifesto aspired to create a discourse on the importance of community gardens. The urban gardening manifesto rejects co-option for the neoliberal city. In its statement, it refers to the importance of free access to public space, opposing its increasing privatization and commercialization. Further, the urban gardening movement positioned itself politically in alignment with the "Right to the City" movement, highlighting the importance of urban green for "*buen vivir*", commons, collectively used public space through neighbourly collaboration as well as social and ecological diversity, food sovereignty, and seed preservation. The manifesto puts it this way:

> We summon the politicians and urban planners to recognize the importance of community gardens, strengthen their position, integrate them in the construction and planning law and initiate a paradigm shift towards a garden-friendly city. [. . .] We want our gardens to take root here. The city is our garden.
>
> (urbangardeningmanifest.de)

By 2016, over 130 urban gardens and other initiatives had signed the manifesto and it has been translated into English, Turkish, Arabic, and Polish. The manifesto initiated a process of self-reflection and fostered political discussions within the gardens. It pushed the idea of a "movement" and the feeling of a collective identity. Local garden initiatives were supported in their struggles and articulation of their aims in communication with officials. The manifesto changed the external perception of urban gardens into a more political phenomenon and helped build alliances to other political struggles. However, the process has been almost completely ignored by the media and the public, while commercial co-option of community gardens is ongoing. In addition, the manifesto did not explicitly mention the intercultural aspects of urban gardens, and somehow deepened the divide between the old and the new community gardens. Undoubtedly the manifesto was just a first step to discussing the political sphere of community gardens and needs to be continued.

The "Allmende-Kontor" – pushing the urban garden movement from within

The Allmende-Kontor (Commons-Office) started as a network of community gardens and urban agriculture in Berlin. The most visible result of the process is the Allmende-Kontor community garden, founded in April 2011 on the grounds of the former airport Tempelhof. The Squat Tempelhof Demonstrations in 2009, the opening of the field for public use in 2010, and the invitation of temporary projects to the field in 2011 (that developed their own political agendas), strengthened the process of claiming the airfield publicly. These processes resulted in a city-wide referendum in 2014, which rejected the mayor's plan to develop the former airport into a modern "park landscape" with apartments, commercial spaces, a gigantic public library, and maybe some hidden place for community gardens. This can be seen as a success of the All-mende-Kontor's fight for public space, urban ecology, commons, and community gardens.

The Allmende-Kontor network, however, with its focus on supporting, organizing, and politicizing the Berlin garden movement, is less visible. The size of Berlin, and the quantity and diversity of the over one hundred gardens in the network, makes it difficult to organize an urban garden movement on a city-wide level: despite the existence of some personal links between Berlin garden activists, no real organizational structure or collective identity has been achieved.[2]

Nonetheless, small steps to organize and visualize the diversity of the urban garden movement were made through meetings, maps, and online platforms, made available through access to academic resources and strong interaction between academia and garden activists.

It became clear that fruitful scholar–activist collaborations are possible, when they are based on solidarity and mutual understanding for needs and possibilities. This culture of cooperation was achieved by, for example, valorizing the collective creation process and not just the product. In the process, it was crucial to push academics to think outside of the box to come up with creative and accessible proposals. The meaningful and practical project results that were achieved were accompanied by a lack of clarity regarding the limits of participatory projects and their hidden power relationships. This situation, together with the uneven distribution of the projects' economic resources, generated small conflicts. Reflective moments within the scholar activism working group of Allmende-Kontor helped to deal with these tensions. While this academia-movement collaboration was crucial for the Allmende-Kontor network, an exhausting double pressure pressed the scholar–activists acting in between the two spheres. This was the starting point for a learning process that demonstrated to us that scholar activism requires a lot of time and patience, and needs to be accompanied by a struggle for acceptance within academia and for understanding within activism (cfr Halder 2018; cfr Halder et al. 2017).

As you can imagine, we have many more questions and doubts rooted in our lucky and messy situation as scholar–activists; therefore we feel the need for more exchange with mates like you!

We are looking forward to meeting you soon

Severin & Ella

***

Dear Barbara, Ella, Emma, and Severin,

I am on my way back from a gathering of the UK Food Sovereignty movement in Hebden Bridge, here in the UK, and I have so many thoughts bubbling in my head that I feel it's time to write you again. It has been a while since we all came back from our panel in Ramallah. Over these months I felt that the exchange we had at the conference was not only energizing, but also truly cathartic: understanding how many of you could completely understand my pain has allowed me to get over much frustration, to stop blaming myself for how things had turned out, to find the positive energy needed to move on and to engage in new projects. Yet, in this process of elaboration, the questions and critical issues look as if they have been distilled: they seem now sharper, defined and still relevant, and urge me to go back to nurture our strategizing platform.

I came to Ramallah at a precise turning point of my life. I had just left the city where I lived, worked, and have been actively engaged for the past seven years, to take on a new exciting academic post in another city and institution. This has meant also taking the decision to leave a project and a group to which I have contributed to build over a long while. It has been a difficult and painful decision, which, however, I should have taken much earlier, when value dissonance and conflicts reached a peak. However, I was not prepared to give up being part of a group of people that I had considered a mix of "fellow activists and friends" in a broad sense, and built through an intermingling of action research and active citizenship. Instead, I spent months consuming my energies bundled into attempts to keep nurturing those projects and dreams that were still in buds, witnessing hijacking, experiencing sexism and manipulation, being speechless at friends' un-sidedness, and yet trying to keep building constructive relationships between the group and the outside. I just simply couldn't believe how frustrating it was all becoming. We had come such a long way together . . . from digging the grassy soil of a park and claiming the food should be for all, to holding meetings in the council hall and winning political consensus to start a participatory food policy making. More was at stake and the more the value-clashes became evident, then self-interest came to the fore, the battles turned nastier. A change of geography helped me to leave this project, but not without a sense of failure.

My motivation to co-organize the panel at the Ramallah conference partially came from the need to reflect with others on the ambivalence I felt around my experience of action research interwoven into scholar activism and active citizenship, and partially due to the desire to look ahead. While in our discussion in Ramallah I have been more focussed on listening to your trajectories and sharing the emotional side of struggles and contradictions of my own experience within the urban food movement, I feel I can now see much more clearly the methodological nodes that generated them. If at first the experience let me doubt whether it was worth and whether I had the skills and inclination to work in such a politically and ethically heterogeneous environment, the change in life and work circumstances have also helped me to rediscover where my activist efforts tend to go. I am embracing once again the challenge of outside (or perhaps, "across") "the radical" movement. In rediscovering myself as the activist-scholar who knocks at the door of the "power chamber", I have seen more clearly the methodological nodes that appear over and over again. So perhaps it is time I come to terms with them and reflect on what needs to be on the agenda for our future discussion.

Reporting and funding system

The turning of universities into neoliberal institutions that are more and more engaged into metrics and accounting procedures to assess research "impact" and bring research income, has greatly impacted on some actions I have taken during my research experience as a scholar-activist. Rushed decisions, rigid timeframes, pressures to enumerate and describe tangible "outcomes": they have all constrained organic processes of learning, empowerment, partnering building, summing up, handing over. In my bitter experience, they have surely affected how things have turned out. I also felt that the cycles of research-funded "action research" don't often overlap with the messier trajectories of movements and scholar activism. Yet, we often depend on grants to create the resources and time to be activist scholars. So my questions are: what strategies can we put in place to overcome these constraints and be able to nurture our activist trajectories? What compromises/limits can and cannot we accept, and how do we challenge and steer this system towards a more virtuous one? Can we develop a policy of resistance in the spirit of the one developed by the Great Lake Feminist Collective for a slow scholarship[3] (Mountz et al. 2015)?

Values and justice

Awareness of positionality is obviously a core and recurrent issue in our trajectories. As activist scholars we engage in action research with a very open approach to locating and sharing our own values and ideas of justice. At the same time, as action-researchers, we engage in processes of group building and new solidarity formation that put us in contexts where we build or redefine our identities as group members. The enthusiasm and sense of commonality that emerge around specific projects and actions can sometimes prevent us from seeing the deeper values that underlie the people around us. However, deep discrepancies between visions of justice can emerge, and, when they do, it is more likely to be during critical moments when the group is required to take a specific position on a matter of concern or contention. In these circumstances, deep-rooted value systems might emerge, revealing all those sharp differences that our enthusiasm and the mingling of our own individual contradicting multiple identities have helped to conceal.

In my own experience, for example, a confrontational episode has put me in the position of having to choose between being true to my own values and positionality on food justice, or serving the needs of the group (at the time involved in a particularly fragile political negotiation), and speaking in the name of a far less positioned ensemble of people I was representing on that particular occasion. Conflicts emerging as a consequence of differing value positions can be very divisive, jeopardizing years of work. At the same time, however, these can also be opportunities for the "uncertain" to take sides, and for a periodic "values-check" within a group, reassessing the motivation and values that drive each member.

The urban food movement – growing fast, fed by a mix of new enthusiasts, gardeners, urban farmers, old activists, and emerging green-washers – is a context particularly prone to extremely divergent values and visions. What I have learnt from my – at times frustrating – experience in this matter is the need to be more reflexive on this diversity and decide where to stand. This might mean being kinder to myself and accepting when the time to leave a group has come, as well as to push for more value-checks more regularly, and ultimately to question the relationship between action research and politics more actively.

Contexts – urban

In Ramallah we have started to discuss how "a school" is something that might bring us to work together. One of the difficulties I felt we had during that early play with imagination was in finding unity about who are we imagining to speak and walk with. The farmers? The urban-based activists? The food planners? Having just returned from another gathering (the UK Food Sovereignty Movement) – I feel more strongly that more needs to be done to understand the specificities of the "urban" in our work, and more in general in all that concerns struggles for agroecology and food sovereignty. What struck me at the recent gathering was to perceive a substantial silence around the urban. I felt surrounded largely by urban-based activists imagining and fighting for a rural, peasant/farmers-led revolution, but what about the urban one? In times in which the co-optation of food initiatives is at its peak, and the urban food movement seems to embrace the narrative and ideals of food sovereignty, it is perhaps the moment to question what would a liberation from the food regime mean for an urban setting, moving away from simplistic ideas that farmers' revolutions and urban agriculture will solve our problems. We need much deeper and interwoven changes that affect not only food production elsewhere and food consumption locally, but a whole range of processes related to the way we use, share, and reproduce natural resources. We have to shift from re-politicizing "the food movement" to building an "urban agroecology". I feel it is time to ask – and ask again! – how does the urban condition constrain and qualify our struggles for agroecology and food sovereignty? What is the meaning of "urban" in "urban agroecology"? If we are not just simply shifting ideas and food practices from a rural/agrarian context into an urban one, but rather challenging neoliberal urbanism and re-thinking the "urban" as a common, what imaginaries do we mobilize for our urban agroecology perspective? What are its specific challenges? And how would a geography-sensitive strategizing platform address them?

There is a geography conference coming up in London at the end of the summer (2016). What about organizing a panel there to take our discussions from Ramallah further? Perhaps Barbara and I could plan a call?

Chiara

***

Dear all,

It is nice to take the time to write, and re-read your thoughts, stories, questions alongside the ones that I formulated or not in the process of thinking about activist-research, the urban food movement and "what is to be done" [to wink at our political inclinations].

I'm currently on the recovery from a bike accident, which has provided its harvest of following complications. My bed and the sky as horizons for the last days have brought my rushed life to a standstill. I almost hear the chants of the protests in Paris over the proposed labour law as I reflect over the discussions we have had. A good lesson of patience and of the need to reflect even as prescient struggles call.

Throughout our interactions, I have felt both inspired, excited, and on a parallel plane with our group. I'm no longer involved in urban gardening and right-to-water movements but I felt excited by a group who questioned our institutions, the research process imposed on us, and our role as people secured (and exploited!) by institutional locations in fostering change. As activist–researchers, our topic of coalescence as of now is different since I am rooted in community organizing groups in France and the UK, tenants' activism and international unionism, rather than in a garden, but I believe we share the same fight.

Preparing my presentation for Ramallah, I had written:

Chiara and Barbara have challenged us to seek ways to continue to politicize the Urban Food Movement. Whilst it would seem ambitious to redefine what is politics in 30min interventions, here are a few thoughts I'd like to share, which bring together both food and water:

- Remembering that one should not disconnect emotions and bodies, anger and joy from politics. When someone cannot access water there is a "raw" anger that builds on one of the primary emotions that I believe is political, that of: "this is unjust". One crosses a fundamental line (e.g., the water movement in Ireland) that expresses what many (Ranciere in Grelet et al. 2009; Swyngedouw 2010, but also earlier on Marcuse) identify as the fundamental refusal of the current partition of the sensible/reality. In the simple sentence, we find the rock-bottom and widely shared sense of what is justice, and what is injustice. I believe it is that raw, "bodily", almost irrational sense of justice that the Urban Food Movement should awaken if wanting to remain political. [words such as "fair" work too, although I do find that they have been quite depoliticized . . .]

- Thinking about which scale of participation/demand we want to engage in: protecting individuals, neighbourhoods, cities, a movement?
- Thinking of what are our demands and our targets: a company, a municipality, a state. . . . Which levers of power do they have and do we have against them? Within which discourse are they embedded (consumer, citizenship, administrative, public/private law . . .?)

I question on an ongoing basis the role of a scholar–activist, or an activist doing research or a scholar doing activism. The boundaries are delicate, be that in terms of identities, missions, tasks, outputs, loyalty (the "bottom line"), goals, and visions. We endorse various roles throughout the day. Yet, it is one thing to do activism outside of one's working hours and another to re-conceptualize our work as activism, especially when our work is to be divided between research and teaching. When working with a movement/activist group already constituted, I find myself asking myself precisely which role am I playing, and try to develop different typologies to clarify my tasks and my relationship with the group:

- Is it a "presential" role? *helping out with everyday tasks, *helping write grant applications?
- Is it an observing role? *documenting (ethnography, interviews, etc.) what is happening, *highlighting key issues and demands?
- Is it a role of helping movements to reflect on: *their external strategies; *internal practices; *success/failures
- Is it a training role? *methods? *wider stories/history of the movement? *capacity and knowledge building?
- Is it a data collection role of the public with whom the movement is working: *interviews, *surveys
- Is it a strategic role: *specific knowledge (e.g., legal situations, histories), *networking, *delivering evidence for policy changes . . .
- . . . Ongoing!

I'm still grappling with these thoughts, of justice, scale, targets, and roles. I'm still making mistakes and learning. I met people in Ramallah who, I felt, had turned their emotions [anger, desire, sadness] into questions, actions, and hopes. I felt we similarly held both a grounding in action and had learnt to ask simply: is this normal? Is this just? Is this violent? Who bears that violence? How to fight to change the situation? How to light up people's desire for change? Can the concepts of "food", "water" or just generally "the commons" mobilize? If so when, how, where? No answers today, but I hope a conversation.

I remain rooted in the concept of justice. I believe much of a movement's strength comes from speaking of commons that should not be commoditized.

When fighting for tenant's rights, for labour rights, against land-grabbing, or for publicly supplied water, I respond to political and geographical conjunctures that, suddenly, have ignited a sense of this isn't just and this needs to change. I believe our role is to be attentive to these conjunctures, and sometimes allow ourselves to be pragmatic regarding which are the best angles of attack. I take on a flexible, rather than principled politics, although the base remains the same: justice and equality in situated encounters. I wonder what you think about this. Do we agree to disagree on these tactical stances?

Scale refers to this ongoing struggle of finding commonality in diversity. Severin and Ella highlighted some of these issues when articulating the tension between existing gardens, new sprouting commercial ones, and a hesitant national network. Smith (1992), and many others, discuss the need for people and movements to learn to jump scale, just as capital and states have learnt. What does jumping scale in theory and in practice mean when part of our activism (organizing or gardening) is so grounded? What are tools, values, imaginaries, and demands that could build a common story from located and diverse hotspots (see Anderson 2015)? Is it through personal links, institutional structures, or temporary getting together to work together?

I believe our conversation highlights common lessons as well: the need to start with everyday issues, to build small victories, to dare to prompt the conversation in public speech and action, and to think of the sphere of production and consumption as dialectically related, political and powerful. I believe we should continue to link our various identities as workers, citizens, members of communities, and consumers to reclaim our commons. Another question I stumble upon: how to be normative without being judgmental when working in broad alliances for change?

Listening to our small group's experiences, I am trying to cultivate both this normative sense of justice tied to emotions and an ongoing curiosity for others. I'm trying to take my stance in my academic community, in my activist life and yet listen with kindness and curiosity to students, people, colleagues. I strive to fight without judging, and fight with and alongside political communities for a while.

I hope we can continue this conversation by letters, in and through events and practice.

Speak soon, more, and elsewhere,
Kind thoughts,

Emma

***

Dear Barbara, Chiara, Emma,

I'm quite shocked to see how long it has taken me to reconnect to our "strategizing platform" started in Ramallah. I have been quite occupied by playing my part in local struggles, supporting our community gardens to invite their new refugee neighbours, promoting counter-mappings, fostering transatlantic urban agroecology knowledge exchange, and writing my PhD thesis. All of these fill me with joy, work, and ideas. I feel in the present, but as I am doing all this stuff, a "platform of collective education and action" also becomes more relevant.

So I'm happy to continue dreaming about the "political urban agroecology school" we started imagining in Ramallah. I believe we have to continue to talk about "the political" in urban agroecology, especially in these times when agroecology is starting to be co-opted by dominant discourses and actors, or is primarily discussed with a focus on ecological issues (urban.agroeco.org), while urban gardens are turning even more into a mainstream green urban development tool, and their co-option is reaching new heights (cf. mind grabbing and aesthetic gentrification through a commercial mural at Prinzessinnengarten in Berlin Kreuzberg or the Berlin wide green washing campaign "Pflanzt was!" by Vattenfall based on a "fake" community garden).

But what will we learn in our school of political urban agroecology?

First that it is essential to bring in radical thoughts on the social, cultural and political aspects of urban agriculture by discussing urban political ecology, environmental justice, and food sovereignty. This way we can "denaturalize" the uneven impacts of political and economic forces within the production of urbanized environments from the point of view of marginalized groups. Thus, we will be able to analyse the role that urban agriculture plays in shaping and changing socio-natural relations in cities.

Our political urban agroecology school should re-politicize urban food and green space production by combining visions of agroecology (cf. Altieri 2012) with militant research (cf. Colectivo Situaciones 2008) and popular education (cf. Freire 2007). Agroecology is teaching us how we can bring together science with traditional agriculture and social movements. When we translate this idea into an urban context, we have to create connections to peri-urban small-scale farmers on the one hand and to urban social movements, which may not necessarily (already) be directly linked to agrarian struggles on the other. Militant research will help us to create space for an alternative to traditional academia as well as to traditional activism. It shows us ways of supporting those fighting on the ground by combining fruitfully critical theory and radical practice. Popular education will hand over the tools for empowerment and collective knowledge production by enabling dialogue between gardeners, peasants, earthworms, seeds, and scholar activists.

So our school will obviously subvert the traditional school paradigm. I'm dreaming of places of mutual exchange, where we are all farmers, students, teachers, researchers, and militants at the same time, enabling creative and collective education outside the narrowness of classrooms, working in the fields, gardens, and streets by fostering local struggles. A school where we will develop through collective practice a common language for the radical socio-ecological visions of urban farmers, activists, and scholars. A school that is locally rooted and at the same time aiming towards an international scholar-activist meshwork, new kinds of self-organized, decentralized, and non-hierarchical alliances and networks

(Harcourt and Escobar 2005: 14). Learning by digging! Teaching by struggling! Resisting by planting!

To materialize our ideas I would prefer to meet in a less academic and more activist context next time. Maybe we can organize a workshop together? We could slowly prepare it and start a critical brainstorming process right now, perhaps by collectively writing a letter of reflections for the Urban Green Commons Book (Kumnig et al. 2017)?[4]

Viva, viva, viva Agroecologia!

Severin

P.s. Garden-Greetings from Ella! We are already concretizing some ideas step-by-step and are planning the first scholar-activist workshop at the Neighbourhood Academy in Berlin in August (2016)[5] to discuss the contradictions of urban agriculture. We hope to see you there.

***

Dear Severin, Ella, and Emma,

We enjoyed reading your letters and writing our own. Another letter that surely inspired us a few years ago when we started to unpack and write about our own questions and doubts on how to reconcile research and activism (Tornaghi and Van Dyck 2015) is Laura Pulido's (2008) open letter to scholar activists.[6] Meanwhile, we have understood far better how we were trapped in dichotomies of action and research, the researcher and the researched, politics and knowledge. Transgressing these dichotomies makes us today less concerned about reconciling one with the other and more focused on deconstructing research approaches and finding ways of using our research skills to the best in our political work. Be it through public writing, fleshing out some issues, joint reflexive, or strategic work (cfr Emma's letter).

Rereading our letters, and with the pair of glasses of researchers – which after all we love to wear – we started to reflect on how exactly the strategizing platform (or "action research exchange space"?) is, contributing to our own *reflexivity*, to our *tools* in bringing forward urban political agroecology; and what did we learn from the *process* of platform-making that we believe it is worth sharing here.

Reflecting on *the process*, we have understood that the making of a strategizing platform is a non-linear trajectory made of experimenting with multiple places and formats for interaction. This contemplates going backwards and re-planning, giving ourselves time to think, to leave, to reconnect at different speeds and in different places; it is a process driven by following intuitions and letting ourselves be inspired and excited by our questioning nature, and above all by openly sharing our emotions – our deep pain about injustice – and nurturing the dream of fighting it together.

Reflecting on how the platform helps our own *reflexivity* reveals a strong focus on, and at times uncomfortable feelings about, the ambiguities/ambivalences/problematics of our roles as activist scholars, both within the movement and within academia. It has helped us to share commonalities on the constraints that funders and employers load on our roles as academic researchers, and on the importance of re-stating our positionalities remaining true to our roots in the concept of justice and humbleness. It has also spelled out clearly our need to keep our politics connected with our bodies, emotions, anger, and joy.

As for the sharing of *tools and tactics*, the platform has already so far been a place to share success and absences: using manifesto building for political positioning, organizing debates and actions to push people into taking sides, the need for regular value checks, the need to reinsert imaginaries of social change, building movement by reconnecting urban struggles. These tactics have revealed important in our work, but at the same time we have been dreaming of moving forward. We have started to shift from a desire to strengthen the urban food movement, to a desire to substantiate a political urban agroecology.

In some ways the exchanges in this process closely resemble conventional interactions among peers in academic disciplinary fields: they challenge researchers intellectually in their analysis and observations as a mechanism to sharpen analysis and knowledge claims. The loose platform unpacks our conceptualizations of urban agriculture, politicization, urban food movements, and scholar activism. While thinking together is crucial, the role of care taking, creating space for emotions and human chemistry, sharing practical suggestions on how to navigate neoliberal universities, and giving tactical or strategic feedback is not considered academic work but, as we experience it, it is fundamental to scholar activism. This also explains why we decided to withdraw the panel on political urban agroecology that we had planned in the geography conference later this year as a way to take forward the strategizing platform.

We decided that our call for contributions was not only too vague, but also because, as Severin rightly pointed out, the format of a conference is not fit for the type of exchanges we want to create and nurture. The platform after all is still taking shape in its nest and so far has not become a stage for the public expression of ideas.

While we love this process of pushing reflection, sharing strategies, building an active memory of experiences (Vercauteren 2003), caring and inspiring, we are eager to meet again to find ways of how to forge dialogue and strategic alliances with soil bacteria, earthworms, nutrients, food waste, school kids, and peasants. This reminds us of a passage in Michael Newman's (2006: 174) *Teaching Defiance*:

> it is no accident that people travel long distances to attend meetings. Problems can cease to exist as the result of a touch on the elbow, the linking of an arm, a handshake or an embrace. [. . .] at these moments the 'talk' is through physical presence. Words take second place. Sometimes we need to foreground the talk, but the talk itself and not the substance will be important.

Spending time together, getting to know each other's smells, fears, tastes, voices, and ways of interacting generates the energy and trust for meaningful talking, political strategizing, and thinking together.

Barbara and Chiara

Notes

1 https://iccg2015.org
2 In 2017 a new community garden network emerged in Berlin. They organized a series of meetings and a demonstration to defend urban green spaces from eviction.
3 The collective is composed of a number of academic women who have developed a strategy to resist the pressures of neoliberalism on teaching, research, and publication targets, by preserving spaces for intellectual freedom and creativity, protecting their mental health, and preserving a work-life balance. Is it possible to develop something similar, focused on the nexus/friction between (action) research and activism?
4 The book mentioned here is where this collection of letter (the Ramallah letters) was first published, in German, in 2017. The present contribution in English is the original version, which was translated in German and published with the title "Der Aufbau einer Strategieplattform: vom Politisieren urbaner Ernährungsbewegungen zu urbaner politischer Agrarökologie" and published in the book by Kumnig, Sarah; Rosol, Marit; Exner, Andrea*s (Eds. 2017) *Umkämpftes Grün – Zwischen neoliberaler Stadtentwicklung Zwischen neoliberaler Stadtentwicklung und Stadtgestaltung von unten*. Bielefeld: transcript, pp. 81–108.
5 http://www.nachbarschaftsakademie.org/en/about/.
6 In "Frequently Asked Questions on Being a Scholar/Activist" (2008). Laura Pulido draws on her own experiences to write an open letter to (potential) scholar activists. In this letter she deals with frequently asked and unasked questions of students and young scholars by passing on what she learnt from her own "organic-praxis". We found such initiative particularly helpful and inspiring when, in on our own trajectories, we were confronted with many of the issues she raised.

Bibliography

Alkon, Alison H. and Agyeman, Julian (Eds.) (2011): *Cultivating Food Justice: Race, Class and Sustainability*. Cambridge: MIT Press.

Altieri, Miguel (2012): *Agroecologia – bases científicas para uma agricultura sustentável*. São Paulo: Expressão Popular – ASPTA.

Anderson, Jeremy (2015): Towards Resonant Places: Reflections on the Organizing Strategy of the International Transport Workers' Federation. *Space and Polity*, Vol. 19, No. 1, pp. 47–61.

Colectivo Situaciones (2008): Something More on Research Militancy: Footnotes on Procedures and (in) Decisions. In: Graeber, David (Ed.): *Constituent Imagination: Militant Investigations, Collective Theorization*. Oakland: AK Press, pp. 73–93.

Freire, Paulo (2007/1970): *Pedagogy of the Oppressed*. New York: Continuum.

Grelet, Stany et al. (2009): Insistances démocratiques Entretien avec Miguel Abensour, Jean-Luc Nancy et Jacques Rancière. *Vacarme*, Vol. 48, No. 3, pp. 8–17.

Guthman, Julie (2008): "If They Only Knew": Color Blindness and Universalism in California Alternative Food Institutions. *The Professional Geographer*, Vol. 60, No. 3, pp. 387–397.

Halder, Severin; von der Haide, Ella; Artola, Miren; and Martens, Dörte (2017): Aktivismus trifft Forschung in Gemeinschaftsgärten – Praktische Erfahrungen mit einer fruchtbaren Beziehung. In Kumnig, Sarah; Rosol, Marit; and Exner, Andrea's (Eds.): *Umkämpftes Grün. Zwischen neoliberaler Stadtentwicklung und Stadtgestaltung von unten*. Bielefeld: [transcript] UrbanStudies, pp. 109–138.

Halder, Severin (2018): Gemeinsam die Hände dreckig machen – Aktionsforschungen im aktivistischen Kontext urbaner Gärten und kollektiver Kartierungen. Bielefeld: transcript.

Harcourt, Wendy and Escobar, Arturo (2005): *Women and the Politics of Place*. Oxfordshire: Taylor & Francis.

Holt-Giménez, Eric and Altieri, Miguel A. (2013): Agroecology, Food Sovereignty, and the New Green Revolution. *Agroecology and Sustainable Food Systems*, Vol. 37, No. 1, pp. 90–102.

Guterres, Ivani (2006): *Agroecologia militante – Contribuições de Enio Guterres*. São Paulo: Expressão popular.

Kumnig, Sarah; Rosol, Marit; and Exner, Andrea's (Eds.) (2017): *Umkämpftes Grün – Zwischen neoliberaler Stadtentwicklung und Stadtgestaltung von unten*. Bielefeld: [transcript] UrbanStudies.

Martinez-Alier, Joan (2002): *The Environmentalism of the Poor: A Study of Ecological Conflicts and Valuation*. Cheltenham: Edward Elgar Publishing.

McClintock, Nathan (2014): Radical, Reformist, and Garden-Variety Neoliberal: Coming to Terms with Urban Agriculture's Contradictions. *Local Environment: The International Journal of Justice and Sustainability*, Vol. 19, No. 2, pp. 147–171.

Meadows, Donella (1999): *Leverage Points: Places to Intervene in a System*. Hartland Vermont: The Sustainability Institute.

Mountz, Alison; Bonds, Anne; Mansfield, Becky; Loyd, Jenna; Hyndman, Jennifer; Margaret, Walton-Roberts; Basu, Ranu; Risa, Whitson; Hawkins, Roberta; Hamilton, Trina; and Curran, Winifred (2015): For Slow Scholarship: A Feminist Politics of Resistance through Collective Action in the Neoliberal University. *Acme: An International Journal for Critical Geographies*, Vol. 14, No. 4, pp. 1235–1259.

Newman, Michael (2006): *Teaching Defiance: Stories and Strategies for Activist Educators*. 1st edition. San Francisco: Jossy-Bass A Wiley Imprint.

Pulido, Laura (2008): FAQs: Frequently Asked Questions on Being a Scholar/Activist. In Hale, Charles R. (Ed.): *Engaging Contradictions: Theory, Politics and Methods of Activist Scholarship*. Berkeley: University of California Press, pp. 341–366.

Smith, Neil (1992): Contours of a Spatialized Politics: Homeless Vehicles and the Production of Geographical Scale. *Social Text*, Vol. 33, pp. 54–81.

Stirling, Andy (2010): From Enlightenment to Enablement: Opening Up Choices for Innovation. In: López-Claros, Augusto (Ed.): *The Innovation for Development Report: 2009–10*. London: Palgrave Macmillan, pp. 199–210. ISBN 9780230239661.

Swyngedouw, Erik (2009): The Antinomies of the Postpolitical City: In Search of a Democratic Politics of Environmental Production. *International Journal of Urban and Regional Research*, Vol. 33, No. 3, pp. 601–620.

Swyngedouw, Erik (2010): *Post Democratic Cities: For Whom and for What?* Paper presented in Concluding Session Regional Studies Association Annual Conference. www.scribd.com/document/366271792/Swyngedouw-Post-Democratic-Cities-For-Whom-and-for-What

Tornaghi, Chiara (2014): Critical Geography of Urban Agriculture. *Progress in Human Geography*, Vol. 38, No. 4, pp. 551–567.

Tornaghi, Chiara and Van Dyck, Barbara (2015): Research Informed Gardening Activism: Steering the Public Food and Land Agenda. *Local Environment: The International Journal of Justice and Sustainability*, Vol. 20, No. 10, pp. 1247–1264.

Vercauteren, David (2011/2003): *Micropolitiques des groupes. pour une écologie des pratiques collectives*. Paris: Les prairies ordinaires.

11 Contesting neoliberal urbanism in Glasgow's community gardens

The practice of DIY citizenship

John Crossan, Andrew Cumbers,
Robert McMaster, and Deirdre Shaw

Introduction

In this chapter we use a case study of Glasgow's community gardens to highlight the potential for alternative forms of "Do-It-Yourself" (DIY) Citizenship (Hartley 1999; Ratto and Boler 2014). Our argument is that Glasgow's community gardens promote an equality-of-participation in place and community making. This is fundamentally different from the neoliberal construction of citizenship, which aims to produce an atomized citizen subject independent of any broader social responsibility or embeddedness. As such, we argue that community garden work can be generative of progressive forms of political practice that offer us glimpses of a radical future for the urban citizenry.

Glasgow is an archetypical post-industrial city that has undergone both deindustrialization and various attempts at regenerating and reimagining the city over the past three decades (Cumbers et al. 2010; Helms and Cumbers 2006; MacLeod 2002). While elements of the city council are keen to pursue a more "green" agenda, in the context of a broader UK politics of austerity and state retrenchment, a more dominant neoliberal agenda of property-led accumulation has framed Glasgow's approach (Gray and Porter 2014). Despite these unpromising political and economic circumstances, as we demonstrate, community gardening activities do offer scope for different kinds of citizenship and politics.

We have two central and interrelated aims in this chapter. First, we aim to counter the over-arching Marxian and other claims about capitalism as the dominant urban logic that subsumes all alternative non-capitalist urban practices. We do this by adopting an attitude of "tentative non-judgment"[1] towards Glasgow's community gardens. Rather than adjudicate any particular project as a neoliberal induced "flanking mechanism" (Jessop 2002) or an actually existing space of "neoliberal governmentality" (Pudup 2008) we prefer to further theorize the radical possibilities nascent within the gardens. Second, we aim to illustrate the wider progressive potential of community gardens by invoking the concept of DIY Citizenship. While we are not the first to use this term (see Hartley 1999; Ratto and Boler 2014), we wish to advance the idea by spatially and materially embedding it in Glasgow's community garden network. Our argument is that there is much emancipatory potential in this type of citizenship formation, which is nascent within much of the collaborative organizational processes and intentional place-making practices that take form in the setting of community gardens.

We begin the chapter by critiquing a growing literature that views community gardening as "garden-variety neoliberalism" (McClintock 2014:154). Subsequently we draw upon literature concerned with neoliberal citizenship, contrasting this condition with the concept of the DIY Citizen to understand the possibilities of a counter-hegemonic and autonomous community politics evolving from community garden work. We then explore these themes through the experiences of Glasgow's community gardeners, highlighting the generative potential of the gardens as places that produce counter-hegemonic forms of political citizenship and identity.

Community gardening, neoliberalism, and political agency

In her work on community gardening in Berlin, Marit Rosol (2011:249) refers to these grassroots "enterprises" as "private activity in the public realm". Political acceptance and support for community gardens, she contends, is an expression of "roll-out neoliberalism" (see Peck and Tickell 2002) and attendant changes in the form and function of urban governance (Rosol 2011). Taking a similar position, Rina Ghose and Margaret Pettigrove (2014:1095) argue that citizens practicing community gardening, and other forms of community development, "can become complicit in the construction of neoliberal hegemony". Writing in a North American context, they argue that such hegemony is maintained through the day-to-day work of neoliberal citizen–subjects (i.e. community gardeners), which "alleviates the state from service provision". In their study of Milwaukee's Harembee community gardens, Ghose and Pettigrove (2014:1104) suggest that some community groups are further impoverished as a result of their volunteerism, which "requires extracting material and labour resources from already resource-poor citizens". Adding more weight to these claims that community garden work produces a citizen complicit in neoliberal urban practices, Mary Beth Pudup (2008:1230) writes:

> The agents of neoliberal roll-out gardening technologies . . . are less neighbourhoods rising up to reclaim their communities and resist their marginalization and rather more a variety of non-state and quasi-state actors who deliberately organize gardens to achieve a desired transformation of individuals in place of collective resistance and/or mobilization.

Certainly, there are aspects to community gardening that fit within broader neoliberal urban governance agendas, in terms of increasingly severe welfare regimes, which erode employee rights, social rights, and benefits, and simultaneously heighten precariousness and fear (Wrenn 2014), and in the sense of shifting discourses away from state provision to a more disciplinary regime of both enforcement and "faux" volunteerism. However, there is also a danger here that neoliberalism is portrayed as a "hegemonic story" (Larner 2003:509) that serves to subjugate all alternatives: "an analytic category [blinding] academic commentary and critique . . . to new political opportunities" (Harris 2009:61). From this perspective the voluntary work of a community group regenerating a derelict site in their neighbourhood is categorized alongside the type of "enforced" volunteerism that is increasingly part of neoliberal workfare regimes. Conflating the nuances of volunteerism in this way omits key differences concerning the physicality and location of the work, and the motivations and identities articulated through the work.

Ghose and Pettigrove (2014); Pudup (2008); and Rosol (2011) acknowledge the work of more progressive and transformative political subjectivities in the gardens, but there is the implication here that these more progressive actors, although well intentioned, are duped by state and powerful others, whose interests lie with the neoliberal project (see also Alkon and Mares 2012; Allen and Guthman 2006; Holt-Gimenez and Wang 2011). Such an impression assigns authorship of terms like "self-help", "mutual aid", and even "community" to neoliberal protagonists. There is a tendency to recognize the autonomous agency that is present in community gardens but see this as spatially and politically marginal within broader processes of urban development. For example, of the Harambee community gardens in Milwaukee, which have a predominantly African-American volunteer base, Ghose and Pettigrove (2014:1096) write:

> The gardens function as spaces of citizenship practice in which participants transform space according to their own interests, claim rights to space, engage in leadership and decision-making activities, contest material deprivation, and articulate collective identities. The residents of this neighbourhood have always struggled to be incorporated politically and to meet material needs, caused by the effects of racial politics and deindustrialization. . . . Community gardens represent a spatial strategy by which residents navigate these forms of marginalization.[2]

The authors separate "spatial strategy" from political strategy and in doing so undermine the transformative political potential of this spatially transformative work, essentially going on to present it as self-defeating. We suggest that the spatial form of "citizenship practice" constitutes important political work. In navigating "these forms of marginalization" (Ghose and Pettigrove 2014), gardeners are involved in creating their own spatial and political cultures of organization and decision-making that begins the process of normalizing grassroots-led forms of urban regeneration (Blay-Palmer and Donald 2006; Travaline and Hunold 2010). Rather than try to be "incorporated" into the inhospitable or even hostile political structures of the mainstream political process (Ghose and Pettigrove 2014), gardeners are self-defining what is political, and what is citizenship.

Before discussing neoliberal citizenship and our notion of DIY Citizenship in more detail, we want to stress that we accept aspects of the critique of community gardens: there are tensions. There is some evidence from our analysis of Glasgow's community gardens that supports the tenor of some of these criticisms. As Nathan McClintock (2014:157) suggests, community gardening "can be radical and neoliberal at once". Community gardens can promote a type of "private activity in the public realm" (Rosol 2011:249) or, more appropriately, dilute normative notions of public space by facilitating the particular interests of a group. However, dilution, understood in these terms, is specific to those community gardens that occupy well-used public spaces. Rosol's work in Berlin, for example, is centred upon community gardens located in existing public parks. In Glasgow, most gardens occupy privately owned derelict or vacant spaces or underused (often physically enclosed) derelict or vacant public spaces and, therefore, can be seen to be promoting a type of public activity in what may otherwise be a private realm. In this sense, community gardens can progress public and community relations into previously commodified spaces. Thinking about other forces at work in community gardening we argue that Ghose and Pettigrove's (2014) use of a particular discourse of class struggle to describe community garden volunteering is a partial reading, which undermines politically progressive motivations for this type of volunteering, particularly the potential for creating more autonomous and self-valorizing work practices (Holloway 2005). In our work in Glasgow, motivations ranged from a collective wish to reappropriate enclosed and derelict land for community use to reconnect the self with community and environment. Far from being an experience that alienates people from their labour and the products of their labour, as Ghose and Pettigrove (2014) suggest, community garden volunteering can work towards reconstituting a relationship – long fragmented by the impositions of capitalism – between one another, our environment, and the products of that relationship. We do not doubt Pudup's (2008) suggestion that non-state and quasi-state actors "parachute" into "broken communities" with "green solutions" designed to effect behavioural change in the most "problematic" groups – the young, the unemployed, and repeat offenders, for example. However, as we will argue, there are socially and politically aware state and third sector actors involved in progressive work in Glasgow's emerging community garden network.

On the frictional presence of progressively radical and neoliberal reformist practices at work in community gardens, McClintock (2014:157) argues there has to be both. Writing about urban agriculture more generally he contends: "it would not arise as a viable social movement without elements of both, insofar as contradictory processes of capitalism both create opportunities for urban agriculture and impose obstacles to its expansion". Our contribution to the knowledge of community gardening is to consider what possibilities exist for moving beyond the imposed obstacles of neoliberalism so that we might realize an urban environment where progressively transformative interventions in its everyday spaces are not uncommon. To do so we apply our notion of DIY Citizenship to the work of community gardeners in Glasgow. Here we see a form of citizenship that is generative of collaborative social relations and new urban places, while also being disruptive, in unsettling neoliberalism's penchant for atomized individuals and reversing its frequently wasteful spatial practices.

From neoliberal citizenship to DIY citizenship

Neoliberal citizenship

Nikolas Rose and Peter Miller (2010:298) describe neoliberal citizenship as "performed in accordance with the entrepreneurial 'spirit', as active agents seeking to maximize their own advantage . . . go freely about their business, making their own decisions and controlling their own destinies". Neoliberal citizenship is, thus, defined as one in which atomized individuals are created who are defined by market relations and their ability to act in their own self-interest, independent of any broader social responsibility or embeddedness. Given the ubiquity of the market, citizenship is conceived in contractual terms. Under these conditions the government becomes a marketized but also a repressive entity tasked both with enshrining the shift from a market economy to a market society (Sandel 2012; Wrenn 2014) and with it the disciplining of the citizen as an individualized consumer.

The flipside of this form of the citizenship contract is that government owes less to its citizens. For example, Aihwa Ong (2006:501) describes the UK government under Tony Blair as "no longer interested in taking care of every citizen [preferring] him/her to act as a free subject who self-actualizes and relies on autonomous action to confront global insecurities". Those citizens unable to fulfil their role as consumers receive disciplining through workfare, benefit reduction, and increasingly punitive sanctions. But, as Andrew Gordon and Trevor Stack (2007:130) argue, "neoliberal states have failed to produce the 'free subject who self-actualizes' precisely because they have continued to act as states by reserving their rights on citizenship". Thomas Simon (2013) expands this notion of state manipulation of citizenship in more combative tones by referring to citizenship "as a weapon" used by the state against insiders and outsiders. Look to the Calais "Jungle Camps", which hold thousands of economic and war migrants, to get a vivid example of the "outsider". For examples of the subjugated "insider", see women and the working classes. In effect, both groups cede much of their collective power to be recognized as individual citizens (Gulülp 2013; Pateman 1991; Phillips 1992). What we see in these insider/outsider examples is an unequal distribution of neoliberal citizenship rights. Citizenship is supposed to be inextricably tied to democracy but the kind of citizen emerging under neoliberalism has limited democratic capacity and increasingly does not enjoy real freedom, despite the libertarian rhetoric.

Struggling to find a place among the neoliberal citizenry

The everyday spatial reality for many Glaswegians struggling to find their place among the neoliberal citizenry is one of dereliction, precarity, and impotency (in the sense of having little or no influence over key spatial decisions concerning their neighbourhoods). Yet, as John Holloway (2010) argues, there are cracks in this reality: community gardening is especially evident in old industrial cities where the loss of manufacturing industry has resulted in significant areas of unused space. Glasgow is a particularly pertinent case with 1,300 ha of vacant and derelict land, representing 4% of its total land area and comprising 925 individual sites. As a result, over 60% of Glasgow's population lives within 500m of a derelict site (Scottish Vacant and Derelict Land Survey 2013). Most of this vacant and derelict land is in the more deprived areas of the city, thus disproportionately affecting the poorest citizens. These communities suffer from diet-related ill health, relatively high levels of unemployment and under-employment, relatively low incomes, and in some instances, severe poverty, as evidenced in the increasing reliance upon, and use of, food banks.[3]

Researchers working in the urban environment argue that urban dwellers experience a range of adverse effects from living in close proximity to derelict sites. Andrew Wallace talks about the "policy precarity" (2015:519) of neighbourhood restructuring in the UK that results in "partially constructed neighbourhoods" whose tenants are treated as a "lumpen problem as the vicissitudes of capital and vagaries of regeneration politics shape-shift to embrace abandonment" (2015:536). This moves our understanding of precarity beyond a feature of contemporary working life to the very contours of the urban environment. This work compliments Loïc Wacquant's theory of "territorial stigmatization" and the "dissolution of place" (2007:69), in which a rich narrative of place, with its "shared emotions, joint meanings, supported by practices and institutions of mutuality" (2007:70) is replaced with the emptiness we associate with "space". For Dennis Smith (1987:297) "spaces are potential voids . . . possible threats . . . areas that have to be feared, secured, or fled". Now as problem spaces, the idea that "something has to be done about this" becomes de rigueur. In Glasgow, as in many other post-industrial cities, territorial stigmatization bolsters arguments for state-led market interventions to fix the "problem".

There has been official acknowledgement of the failure of top-down regeneration and business-led initiatives in addressing Glasgow's underlying structural problems (Gray and Porter 2014), and sustainability is now receiving greater attention in urban renewal agendas. In recognition of this, the Scottish Government and Glasgow City Council (GCC) are exploring a number of policy proposals designed to facilitate bottom-up approaches to the urban inequalities discussed here (e.g. Scottish Government 2012). As discussed earlier, such government proposals are frequently treated with suspicion in that they may be consistent with a wider neoliberal urban agenda. While we do not dismiss these claims outright, we question the implication that citizen participation of the "grassroots" type and citizen collaboration with other institutions in urban renewal projects can unproblematically be couched as part of the neoliberal toolbox.

Our discussion of the precariousness of top-down neighbourhood restructuring and the dissolution of place highlights a pressing need – from progressive actors of all institutional backgrounds – for creative social, political, and economic ideas that put communities at the heart of problem solving and planning, countering successive UK and Scottish governments' tendency for technocratic and market-led solutions. The organizational qualities of many of Glasgow's community gardens, and the socio-political sensibilities generated through these organizational practices, we believe, begin to address this need. Before discussing these qualities and sensibilities within the context of our empirical work, we want to further elucidate our notion of DIY Citizenship. Using this conception to frame our analysis, we believe, emphasizes existing and potential benefits of community gardening activities for individuals, groups, and the city more broadly.

DIY *citizenship*

Membership of a polity, based on a system of rights and obligations, is important because individuals and vulnerable groups need protection from powerful forces that would (and do) exploit and oppress them. We argue that this system of protection should be constructed from the bottom-up. We believe that a more progressive and collective form of citizenship formation is evident in the practices of community gardening. Community gardeners in Glasgow, as we will demonstrate, are engaging in a form of political participation. Through a process of learning by being in the presence of difference – different ideas, cultures, social classes, etc. – community gardeners have the potential to sculpt their own identity and their environment and, as such, their understanding of what citizenship entails. Synonymous with our notion of DIY Citizenship, this form of political participation constitutes an interdependent set of relations between people, organizational processes, institutions, and intentional place-making.

In his foundational study of television watching, John Hartley (1999:178) describes DIY Citizenship as:

> The practice of putting together an identity from the available choices, patterns and opportunities . . . no longer simply a matter of social contract between state and subject, no longer even a matter of acculturation to the heritage of a given community, DIY Citizenship is a choice people can make for themselves.

In terms of thinking beyond dominant notions of citizenship, Hartley's concept is useful as a starting point. It separates the state from the subject and in doing so foregrounds the importance of autonomous thought in the process of citizenship formation. Various authors, however, highlight that autonomous thought and action cannot be fully separated from social structures, of both the past and present (Giddens 1984; Holloway 2005; Klein and Kleinman 2002; Latour and Weibel 2005). The implication here is that Hartley's DIY Citizen, although useful, remains an atomized subject. Mike Ananny (2014:362) recognizes this flaw. Problematizing the "Y" in "DIY", but remaining supportive of the concept, he writes:

> It is not only about pursuing self-interests – learning what you want to know – but also about acknowledging the social and institutional contexts of those

interests, environments and conditions in which public goods circulate and from which it is impossible to extract yourself, ignore, or not care about.

DIY Citizenship here is about doing things differently. It progresses Hartley's original concept because it emphasizes this as collective work, being socially aware and progressive in the sense of being prefigurative. That is, work that tries to produce a better future in the present, often in conflict with the nostrums of dominant political and economic actors. However, Kate Derickson (2014), critiquing a recent volume on DIY Citizenship edited by Matt Ratto and Megan Boler (2014), argues that while the insurgent sensibilities of a contemporary politics of DIY are evident, there is little engagement here with the redistributive possibilities promised in the idea of citizenship. Providing a glimpse of people "doing things differently" is useful, but "a far cry from massively disrupting the social order" (Derickson 2014:5). Ratto and Bowler's volume moves DIY Citizenship beyond Hartley's individualizing tendencies to focus on its disruptive qualities but, as Derickson suggests, this new incarnation is a partially collective endeavour: struggling to expand beyond the confines of its immediate environment and, as such, lives a precarious existence.

Our notion of DIY Citizenship is both an extension and critique of the ideas discussed above. We retain "DIY" because, like Hartley, we recognize the importance of individual decision-making in the formation of a new form of citizenship, but we also acknowledge the role played by social structures and institutions (including the local state) in informing those decisions. We are also drawn to the disruptive qualities of DIY Citizenship noted in recent works. Having the collective know-how and confidence to do things differently, particularly when the doing challenges dominant practices, is no small thing. Our extension of the concept centres upon a reworking of the collective form that citizenship might take. Nascent in Glasgow's community gardens is the development of new relations between urbanites on the ground, the spaces they inhabit and a range of institutions, including the state, which cannot be unproblematically categorized as yet another manifestation of neoliberal governmentality.

Creating alternative narratives of democracy and citizenship in Glasgow's community gardens

In the following sections we look more closely at the work carried out by Glasgow's community gardeners, detailing why we understand it as progressive political activity that counters the politically disempowering and socially damaging practices of neoliberal citizenship. First, informed by the ancient Greek condition of paideia, we show how the gardens themselves promote a form of civic education that emphasizes the interdependence of individual and collective life. Second, we focus on the types of social relations we see emerging in community gardens. Here we evidence a "transformative politics of encounter" (Askins 2015:473) that brings together different publics, who might not otherwise have substantive contact with one another. Finally, returning to Ananny's (2014) concerns about the "Y" in "DIY" (see the section "DIY Citizenship" above) we emphasize the supportive role of multiple urban agencies in creating a community garden network in Glasgow.

Our empirical study took place over a six-month period between February and July 2014. Methods employed were participant observation, in the form of site visits to 16 of the city's gardens, and semi-structured interviews with garden volunteers and staff. The gardens were heterogeneous both socially and spatially: from deprived neighbourhoods in the east, north, and south, to more affluent neighbourhoods in the city's west end. Four of the gardens are local community-led projects with nominal input from outside organizations. The other 12 are collaborative projects involving local resident groups and a range of local government and third sector organizations. Twenty-five interviews were conducted mainly with volunteers, but also with local government and third sector workers involved in managing the gardens. Pseudonyms are used.

Community gardens as places of collective learning and social empowerment

The type of interaction between people and place that is evident in Glasgow's community gardens is generative of counter-hegemonic political ideas and practices. Importantly, it is not simply people who are generating such ideas and practices, but people in communion with space. It is in the doing of the work that counter hegemonies emerge. People are placing themselves at the heart of urban problem solving and planning; enabling a heuristic, hands-on form of learning in the urban environment. This poses fundamental questions about the need for a sovereign power to define citizenship and manage citizenship practices. Alex Prichard (2010:9) similarly questions this need:

> The political discourse of citizenship is the contemporary means through which our moral obligations to one another are framed. While there is debate as to where these obligations lie, there is general consensus that this debate should be framed through the language of rights and responsibilities. The challenge is how to have this debate in the absence of a clearly determinate political centre: in the absence of a sovereign.

As a noun, "sovereign" means ruler, head of state, overlord, and such like. As an adjective, "sovereign" means absolute, unrestricted, and total control. As an adjective it can also mean "autonomous, self-determining, independent and free" (New Oxford American Dictionary 2010). There is a distinction between these two adjectives. Unlike the unrestricted sovereign, the self-determining sovereign promotes the idea that an individual or polity's freedom should never be conceived of as absolute. This is summed up beautifully in John Quail's comment: "until all of us are free then no one is free" (quoted in Franks 2007:129). This latter definition presents sovereign subject formation as a collective process involving a dynamic relationship between multiple overlapping centres of power – individuals and communities, however a community may be conceived.

In this sense community is a prerequisite for individuality (Prichard 2010). Bearing these insights in mind, we turn to the ancient Greek notion of paideia as a means to counter the absolute power of a sovereign. Paideia, we argue, strengthens a polycentric understanding of sovereignty and can be seen in more recent contributions, ranging from the works of John Dewey (1859–1952) to Murray Bookchin (1921–2006).

The Greek citizen ideal differed significantly from the modern. Bookchin (1992:59) tells us that citizenship "was not simply some species myth of shared heredity that united citizens of the polis with each other but a profoundly cultural conception of personal development". Translated into English, paideia means education, but this offers a limited explanation of the term. Paideia emphasizes the interdependence of individual and social life. It emphatically promotes within the individual a sense of responsibility to the social world: "Paideia, in effect, was a form of civic schooling as well as personal training. It rooted civic commitment in independence of mind, philia and a deep sense of individual responsibility" (Bookchin 1992:59). The ideal classical citizen differed from the modern "subject" because the former ruled and was ruled, "which meant . . . that he was a participant in determining the laws by which he[4] was to be bound" (Pocock 1995:29).

A similar form of civic education is evident in community garden practices in Glasgow. The community gardens we visited in our research offer a range of learning activities from cookery workshops, to film nights, to up-cycle craft workshops, and place-based cultural heritage workshops. Participation at these learning events has practical implications for the gardeners. People learn about gardening but they also acquire other knowledge and skills connected to their work as community garden volunteers. This can have profound effects on individuals:

> We formed a committee. That prospect was daunting for a lot of us that just wanted to dig holes in the ground. . . . We need four members for this and secretary for that. . . . What's all that about? But you end up learning new skills. Myself I took on the role of secretary for the group and I got sent on a minute taking course and other stuff like that so I've gained qualifications and new skills . . . I wouldn't have known how to take minutes or how to type up minutes or how to put them in order. It wouldn't have crossed my mind.
> (Alistair, community garden volunteer, March 2014)

Skills and education here are linked to organizing creative work practices that build individual and community confidence and autonomy rather than being reduced to a neoliberal employability agenda. More than this, the work generates a collective set of social practices and relations in the city. Another community gardener from the east of the city alludes to ideas touched upon above regarding the importance of active involvement in collective decision-making practices:

> We sort out ourselves. We have had three growing seasons and this will be our fourth. We've tried different models in terms of who is doing what. The

one that worked last year we are going to go through with this year. We have seven raised beds so four of them are team beds. We have a perennial bed, a potato bed and a squash bed so they are communal beds. So you choose your team and agree with the team that you will also grow something communally in your team bed, usually something leafy because that is what people want a lot of . . . any decisions that affect everybody we meet as a group and discuss it and come to some sort of conclusion on it.

(Lucy, community garden volunteer, May 2014)

In these quotes we can see a collective sense of citizenship at play, which evokes paideia. Consider these quotes in relation to a range of recent Scottish Government proposals. For example, "[t]he intention of the [Community Empowerment and Renewal] Bill is to strengthen opportunities for communities to take independent action to achieve their own goals and aspirations" (Scottish Government 2012:8). And, the Commission on Strengthening Local Democracy Interim Report argues that "[p]articipation in and with the system is high" where "[c]ommunities can engage actively, can influence decision-making, and hold people to account for decisions" (Commission on Strengthening Local Democracy 2014:20). As discussed above, many commentators view the "community turn" in government policy practice with suspicion. While alert to the malign aspects of "community" in neoliberal discourse, we proceed with the idea that this legislation is a genuine attempt at initiating a discussion about how participatory democratic processes may encourage communities to construct their own understanding of what citizenship should mean and entail.

What these gardeners are articulating is the act of participatory and direct forms of democracy. Such practices we believe move us away from the citizen as spectator – watching their environment develop without any substantive say in that development – towards an active political citizen involved in the collective production and continuous maintenance of their environment. These quotes also suggest that democracy cannot be jettisoned into communities overnight. People cannot be expected to suddenly become proficient collective decision-makers. The neoliberal urban environment – its landscapes and timescapes – tends to inhibit rather than encourage such practices. "Garden-variety" democracy is a heuristic and collective learning process, like paideia, inextricably connected to the emotional and physical environments within which the learning takes place. Under these conditions the unity of the polity is something collectively built, as opposed to being a "species myth of a shared heredity" (Bookchin 1992:59).

It should be noted that the level of participatory decision-making varies across Glasgow's gardens with larger local government or third sector-led gardens more top-down in this regard. That being said, even in these gardens there are opportunities for volunteers to take the lead in particular areas – for example, organizing community film nights, suggesting and/or organizing particular workshops, designing areas of the garden.

Community gardening and the forging of progressively transformative social relations in the city

To equate community gardening with the notion of citizenship may seem at best exaggerated, and at worst misguided and misleading. For some, the value afforded to political practices diminishes the closer those practices get to the ground. Thankfully, not all share this limited notion of "the political". Consider the first state-sanctioned community gardens in the US. Initiated by the US government in the late nineteenth century, community gardens were perceived by state actors as cultural assimilation spaces, where "new immigrants would assume an industrious persona and learn the American way" (Bassett, quoted in Eizenberg 2010:23). Today in Glasgow, asylum seekers and other ethnic minorities find their way to community gardens, often via government agencies. For example:

> I have eight people in my taskforce. Most don't have English as their first language. There is Roma, Czech Republic . . . I also have someone from Ghana, someone from Gambia, someone from Eritrea. . . . When we had young refugees and asylum seekers last week it was fascinating the things they were telling us about wild garlic, and making soup, and how they would use various herbs in their culture.
>
> (Gillian, community garden sessional worker, March 2014)

Whatever the underlying rationale of social services, the above quote suggests that there has been a trend towards positive recognition and celebration of different cultures within gardens in the city. This resonates with a number of the gardens we visited. Efrat Eizenberg (2012:773) supports this argument. In the context of New York City's community gardens she writes: "While the mechanism of a melting pot de facto aims at flattening differences and assimilation into the hegemonic culture, in their current phase community gardens celebrate past experiences and revive cultural practices rather than repressing them".

In developing the theory of cosmopolitism, Dean Garratt and Heather Piper (2010) draw our attention to the relationship between citizenship formation, community building, and face-to-face relations (see also Beck 2007; Bonham 2004; Osler and Starkey 2001). Referring to Ulrich Beck's (2007) theory of "methodological cosmopolitanism . . . an imagining of alternative paths within and between different cultures and modernities", Garratt and Piper contend that face-to-face constructions of citizenship "represent an aspirational ideal of what citizenship can become, beyond and distinct from a sterile fixation on the binary logic that underpins the empirical investigation of globalization" (2010: 50). In this sense, DIY Citizenship holds the potential of dismantling conceptual and geographical boundaries between the local and the global and pre-determined views on what constitutes an outsider.

It is important to point out that in foregrounding citizenship here as a "politics of difference" (Young 1990), we are not simply talking about a coming together of ethno-cultural differences. Consider the following research diary extracts:

> Crownpoint Garden had a broad appeal. As one volunteer told me, "yi git awesorts a characters innis place": homeless people, people with physical and learning disabilities, professionals and children from the local nursery. According to one volunteer it [the garden] has good growing potential and provided a good yield last season. The St Mungos' high school pupils, who have a raised bed on the garden, supported this position, telling me last seasons yield was regularly used by the school's catering service.
>
> (extract from research diary, 14 March 2014)

> As well as a 784 m² (0.192 ac) raised bed site facilitating 20 local community plot holders the 3Hills Garden includes an NHS Mental Health garden with eight raised beds, an orchard with 20 apple, pear and cherry trees, a sensory garden (which also acts as an outdoor story telling space) for nursery children, and two further adventure gardens – one for the nursery and one for the primary school kids.
>
> (extract from research diary, 31 March 2014)

The foregoing gives a sense of the diverse groups that use community gardens. Considering such diversity in close proximity, one might expect a significant degree of conflict emerging. This was not evidenced in our research. When asked where the challenges arise, participants most commonly pointed towards external pressures, that is, accessing funding, securing land tenure, vandalism. In their use of these gardens, a range of groups, who might otherwise have little substantive contact with one another, meet and exchange ideas and stories as they collectively produce new urban spaces. Use value here produces an environment that seems to promote social cohesion as opposed to fragmentation. Furthermore, the values generated are distinct from those of the neoliberal citizen, who views space as a quantifiable and commodifiable object, something to be enclosed and privatized. These activities also serve to greatly empower individuals and communities in their everyday lives in the city by giving them new forms of agency in the spaces of the gardens.

At one of our garden visits a researcher met and worked with a community gardener who is best described as a "survivor". Living with epilepsy, a childhood marked by physical and emotional abuse and adult life struggling with drug and alcohol misuse, this participant told the researcher that working in the gardens had saved their life:

> The stories I was told by Aleck, the time he spent with me as we tended to lots of little jobs – like fixing the protective mesh over a raised bed, harvesting the broccoli beds, picking up litter, and emptying leaves into the compost heap – was, for me, a humbling and inspiring experience. I'm glad we went for a walk around the garden.
>
> (extract from research diary, 10 April 2014)

Before going out into the garden Aleck gave an interview in a small office that acts as the administrative hub and storage space for various tools for this particular garden. It is important to note that Aleck was more at ease with conversation while out in the gardens than in the office. This is not uncommon. Interviews always contain an element of formality and express a degree of division between researcher and participant that one, if not both, are uncomfortable with. In highlighting a change of attitude in Aleck's interaction with the researcher (and vice versa), we want to explore more closely why this change may have taken place. We suggest that as the material nature of the contact between the two changed, so then did the substance and quality of their conversation. This observation in itself is not groundbreaking – the variety of design evident in public and private spaces points towards a widespread and tacit acknowledgement that our environment influences our interactions with one another. However, what we suggest here is that our interactions with one another are profoundly impacted upon when we collectively produce our environment. Following Kye Askins and Rachel Pain (2011:804), we want to draw attention to the "physical nature of encounters in fostering or foreclosing interaction". Referring to the diary extract above, in the physicality of "tending to lots of little jobs", social barriers, preconceived notions of one another, gave way to a more open and reciprocal form of interaction.

Another episode further illuminates our argument. Alison spoke of her time working in a community garden that was established by a city homeless charity to provide both growing space and a safe space for homeless people to come and relax and growing space for local residents. She made an interesting and important observation: in the physical act of gardening, tensions that existed between homeless people and residents eased. Prejudices were challenged and power relations became less fixed – that is, over time both homeless people and residents took the lead in those activities that they were most comfortable with or excelled in; conversations became more varied and no one group dominated the space. For Alison, a person who had worked with homeless people in various settings, watching this transformation in the group was a profound experience. She claimed that it was the "physical quality" of the interaction that "made the difference" (Alison, community garden staff member, 19 August 2014). Community gardeners are often in close proximity to each other. This is important, as it places local residents in direct contact with marginalized groups in society, such as the homeless, who are frequently ostracized in other circumstances. Details are important. Echoing our observations above concerning the actual "doing" of the work, the participant suggested that digging, seeding, harvesting etc., acts as a sort of counterbalance to what would be an otherwise asymmetrical relationship between homeless people and residents. Returning to Garratt and Piper's work on citizenship and face-to-face relations, we might see the role of this counterbalance as providing space and time for people "to overcome fragmentation by developing new forms of social solidarity and cross-cutting identities" (Garratt and Piper 2010:46). Askins (2015:473) contends that meaningful encounters such as this enable community cohesion through what she refers to as a "transformative politics of encounter":

> With regards to community cohesion, a "transformative politics of encounter" incorporates a radical openness to the simultaneity of difference and similarity, to deconstruct dominant discourses that essentialise minorities as only different. This politics crucially must recognise that encounters between different groups can draw upon and reiterate socially constructed difference, but that they also have the potential to shift how we see and how we feel about our others.

It is important to note that what we are describing here are not simply a series of courteous encounters, which Gill Valentine (2008) points out do not inevitably translate into respect for difference or challenge dominant social values. Rather, what we are suggesting is that the transformative quality of these interactions is coterminous with the transformation of the physical environment. The collective and intentional production of place increases the potential for a more inclusive form of citizenship to emerge. These communities are not occupying a pre-determined environment and operating in it according to pre-determined rules and protocols. Rather, they are building a material environment according to their own culture(s), histories, desires, and visions (Eizenberg 2012) and, therefore, a very different sense of urban citizenship to the neoliberal type.

Community gardens and progressive local collaborations

> A high quality of life gives people, whether as individuals, families or groups, the opportunity to fulfil themselves as human beings. For this they need not only an appropriate material standard of life but also appropriate management of their environment in all spheres (social, economic, institutional, cultural, physical) and appropriate administration by government.
>
> (Lichfield 1996:3)

Nathaniel Lichfield and other proponents of Progressive Localism (Featherstone et al. 2012; Hall and McGarrol 2013; Healey 2011; MacKinnon et al. 2010) take on the task of thinking through what constitutes "appropriate" management of our environment and administration by government in contemporary society. In doing so they reimagine local-central governance relations as "mutually-productive and enabling" (MacKinnon et al. 2010:2). Here local authorities alongside a range of other agencies perform a supportive role in their relations with local groups. Using community gardening as an example, the dynamics of this set of relations goes something like this: people shared a vision to change a part of the urban landscape; they enact organizational processes that allow them to better synergize their ideas and establish next steps; crucial to people realizing these ideas are supportive, approachable institutions, which provide the relevant resources, e.g.

knowledge, expertise, finance; this support carries on through the life of the project, but as the community garden becomes embedded in place the level of support needed diminishes. What we sketch out here is a locally led, co-produced urban regeneration, involving local, city-wide, and national organizations. It is at this point our notion of DIY Citizenship departs from previous incarnations (see Hartley 1999; Ratto and Boler 2014) in that we emphasize the social and collective constitution of the gardens, through the role of the state, particularly in its local form, and a range of other agencies in enabling the community garden network in Glasgow. Consider the following example of the G3 Growers.

Formed in 2011, G3 Growers is in its fourth season of planting. The land at the site of their activities is heavily polluted, which has entailed the use of raised beds, one of which is dedicated to growing herbs, the others a variety of produce. The garden also has six fruit trees and three large pots growing flora planted specifically to attract and sustain bees. The Garden's equipment includes: four composters, two of which were manufactured on site; a poly tunnel; a tool shed; and a homemade greenhouse. The wall panels of the latter were made in collaboration with children from a local nursery school. G3 has approximately 40 volunteers contributing in various ways to the ongoing activities of the garden.

This vibrancy is not uncommon in Glasgow's community garden network. It resonates with our discussion about DIY Citizenship as it is predicated on the collective efforts of volunteers in collaboration with local government and other agencies. A G3 volunteer explains:

> Initially we were looking . . . at the roof of an old bus garage and the Annex [local government Area Partnership organisation] paid for surveyors to check this all out and they came back and said it wasn't weight-bearing. The structure wouldn't hold the garden so we all thought . . . uuhhh – a big let down that it wasn't going to happen. . . . So then we spoke to Glasgow West [Housing Association] about the back court at Breeching Street – it was an old car garage so there was a lot of pollutants in the ground and all that had to be dealt with, so there was lot of scientific stuff going on right at the beginning and thank God the Annex were there because it would have just gone right over our heads.
>
> (Julie, G3 volunteer, May 2014)

Here we see that the advice and assistance the G3 Growers received from the Local Government group was invaluable during the initial set up stage of the garden. Advice ranged from helping the group understand complex planning issues relating to the project to navigating the funding landscape, and enabling access. Crucially, this "partnership" between the gardeners and this local government body continues throughout the first years of the garden. Here the state plays a supportive and enabling role as opposed to a controlling one.

Of course, community gardens come in a variety of forms and there exists a diversity of arrangements organizing gardens. In Glasgow, some are relatively small backcourt style gardens, volunteer only, with the catchment area for volunteers stretching no further than the immediate neighbourhood. Others are larger and employ small numbers of staff. These gardens tend to offer a wide range of classes and events, mainly centred upon the production and consumption of food but also covering local heritage, health and well-being, and more. For example, 3Hills Community Garden, situated in almost two acres of land in the low-income neighbourhood of Priesthill on Glasgow's south side, is a collaborative project involving a number of groups including the local nursery and primary school, Glasgow City Council, and NHS Scotland. Designed as long-term holistic intervention strategy to combat relatively high levels of dietary related illness in the area, the site is made up of four connected gardens – residents' community growing garden, primary school adventure garden, nursery kids sensory garden, NHS "Green Prescriptions" garden – and an orchard with approximately 25–30 fruit trees. Although the impact of the garden on levels of dietary related ill health cannot be measured in the short term (the garden is only two years old) these researchers believe that the 3Hills project marks a genuine attempt by practitioners and policy makers, experts and non-experts to come together and exchange knowledge and expertise with a view to creating and sustaining an important community resource.

Recent legislation in the form of the Community Empowerment (Scotland) Act 2015 has the potential to enable and legally protect many more collaborative projects in Scotland like the 3Hills and G3 Growers gardens mentioned above. There are three major elements of this Act, as summarized here by the Scottish Community Development Centre: (1) strengthening of community planning, to give communities more of a say in how public services are provided; (2) new rights enabling communities to identify needs and issues and to request action to be taken on these; (3) extension of community "right to buy", for the purpose of gaining greater control over assets. It is the most recent development in a long line of legislative initiatives concerned with Scottish land reform, stretching back to The Crofters Holdings (Scotland) Act of 1886. The Community Empowerment legislation is important for the future of community gardening in Scotland because first, it promotes a community-centric approach to land reform and, second, it extends pre-existing legislative and financial support (established in 1999, in the form of the Scottish Land Fund, for assisting rural communities to acquire and develop land) into the urban environment. Thus, urban communities have a legislative framework in place and financial support to enable them to have a greater say in the management of urban land and buildings. Implementation of the provisions of the Act is very much in its infancy. How it plays out in the messy realties of urban life remains to be seen. We suggest the following as points of consideration regarding protecting and extending community garden practices in Scotland's towns and cities.

There may be a temptation to centre attention on the "right to buy". This is problematic for four reasons. First, it further entrenches the hegemony of the private property model. For example, if a community group were to raise sufficient capital to buy an underused public building and its lands, the process of sale would effectively *privatize* that resource. Second, outright community ownership leaves the owners vulnerable to the vagaries of the market. This may result in the reconstitution of the traditional private property model if the community group is forced to sell to developers motivated by profit. Third, the right to buy in the city could result in extending the advantages of already privileged urban groups. Those communities with higher levels of social and financial capital are better placed to navigate the legal landscape of acquisition and post-acquisition development. Fourth, from a practical perspective, the relatively high price of land (when compared to median earnings) suggests that local community buy-outs in cities and large towns on a scale witnessed in rural Scotland highly unlikely.[5]

More promising by way of sustaining and extending community gardening in Scotland are a range of measures in the Act that offer the possibility of producing robust partnerships between community groups and other institutions, such as NHS trusts, local authorities, and housing associations. For example, *participation requests* allow a community group to make a request to a public service authority to permit the group to participate in an outcome improvement process. This might take the form of community group delegates sitting in as members of planning boards on a range of matters, from designing new social housing complexes to designating brownfield areas to be ring-fenced for urban agricultural activities.

A potentially fruitful partnership in this regard would involve community garden groups and schools. A key component of Scotland's Curriculum for Excellence (national education strategy) is outdoor learning. Learning and Teaching Scotland write: "Well-constructed and well-planned outdoor learning helps develop the skills of enquiry, critical thinking and reflection necessary for our children and young people to meet the social, economic and environmental challenges of life in the 21st century" (Learning and Teaching Scotland 2010:8). The architects of Curriculum for Excellence recognize the importance of sustainable outdoor learning experiences that are locally based and embedded in the life of the community. This form of outdoor learning differs from a more traditional "adventure education" model, which can be expensive, usually takes place in sites removed from the contexts of the learners' everyday lives and often provides limited learning autonomy for participants (Brookes 2003; Beamus et al. 2009). We see community gardens as ideal partners co-producing a progressive learning experience that is line with the primary aims of Curriculum for Excellence to help young people become "successful learners, confident individuals, responsible citizens and effective contributors" (ibid). Resonating with the concept of *progressive localism*, which reimagines local – central governance relations as "mutually-productive and enabling" (Featherstone et al. 2012:2), this form of partnership holds much potential for extending and protecting Scotland's community gardens for generations to come.

Conclusion

In making our argument, we adopted an attitude of "tentative non-judgment" towards community gardening. Rather than adjudicate any particular project as a neoliberal induced "flanking mechanism" (Jessop 2002) or an actually existing space of "neoliberal governmentality" (Pudup 2008), we preferred to further theorize the radical possibilities nascent within the gardens. We did this by invoking the practice of DIY Citizenship formation. Our notion of DIY Citizenship emphasizes an interdependent set of relations between people, organizational processes, institutions, and intentional place-making. This is both an extension and critique of previous incarnations of the term (see Hartley 1999; Ratto and Boler 2014). What we see in Glasgow's community gardens is evidence of DIY Citizenship formation, where new collaborative and supportive relations are being developed between urbanites on the ground, the spaces they inhabit and a range of institutions, including the state. This is not to deny the continuing dialectic present within the gardens between neoliberal appropriation and more autonomous collective agency (McClintock 2014).

As befitting our increasingly complex and diverse society, DIY Citizens, through meaningful political engagement, are involved in a continuous reworking of the parameters of citizenship. As such, this polity is well suited to accommodate difference. They are not only promoting a more active form of citizenship to that offered by dominant conceptions; they are also attempting to address real inequalities that exist in contemporary citizenship practices. Enabled by an interlocking process of community and spatial production, this form of citizen participation should be seen as more than simply respite from the pressures of contemporary urban life outside of the gardens. This type of citizenship work encourages us to reconsider our relationships with one another, our environment, and what constitutes effective political practice in the city.

The sites of such progressive practices, however, are precarious in that they are vulnerable to the development agenda that still dominates local political agendas. Glasgow is not unique in this. There is a pressure that stems from the standard economic rubric of (a particular type of) growth, which demands the commodification of place: use value is superseded by exchange value. In such an environment, activities such as community gardening will always be undervalued and, hence, sensitive to the vagaries of access rights and the effects of ongoing austerity on funding sources. Yet the future of community gardens may be brighter as a consequence of a change in the legislative environment, which seems to acknowledge use value, even if impediments remain to its realization in some areas. This reorientation, we venture, renders the beneficial impact of community gardening in Glasgow and elsewhere more sustainable.

Notes

1 George DeMartino, personal communication, 15 June 2015.
2 Racial politics are evident in Glasgow's gardens, but probably not to the extent of Harembee. Wider issues resulting from deindustrialization are pertinent to Glasgow.
3 The Trussell Trust (2014) has found that the number of people in the UK reliant upon emergency food rations provided by food banks has risen from 2,814 in 2005/2006 to 913,138 (including over 330,000 children) in 2013/2014.
4 There are profound differences in our notion of paideia and the classical Greek example. Where we move away from classical Greek notions of citizenship and democracy

is in the separation of the public and private spheres. Aristotle, for example, based his definition of citizenship on a strict distinction between the oikos – the private world of beings and things, managed by woman and the polis – the ideal superstructure of "pure" political interaction, managed by men. In our conception of citizenship as a relation between individuals and a polity we suggest that challenging the bifurcation of the private and public spheres, of the material and political worlds will facilitate the production of a more radical urban citizenship. This is not to say the inner workings of one's private affairs should be open to the will of the polity, however it is conceived. Rather, it is to suggest that for citizenship to be a progressively transformative force, its rights and obligations, democratically arrived at through full access to participation by the every member of the polity, should extend beyond the public sphere into our working and domestic lives.

5 For example, Community Land Scotland, an NGO set up to provide a collective voice for community landowners in Scotland has 69 member groups, all rurally based.

References

Alkon, A. H. and Mares, T. (2012) Food sovereignty in the US food movements: Radical visions and neoliberal constraints. *Agriculture and Human Values* 29(3):401–415.

Allen, P. and Guthman, J. (2006) From "old-school" to "farm-to-school": Neoliberalization from the ground up. *Agriculture and Human Values* 23(4):401–415.

Ananny, M. (2014) Critical news making and the paradox of "do-it-yourself news". In Ratto, M. and Boler, M. (eds.) *DIY Citizenship: Critical Making and Social Media* (pp. 359–371). Cambridge: MIT Press.

Askins, K. (2015) Being together: Everyday geographies and the quiet politics of belonging. *ACME* 14(2):470–478.

Askins, K. and Pain, R. (2011) Contact zones: Participation, materiality, and the messiness of interaction. *Environment and Planning D: Society and Space* 29:803–821.

Beamus, S., Atencio, M. and Ross, H. (2009) Taking excellence outdoors. *Scottish Educational Review* 41(2):32–45.

Beck, U. (2007) Beyond class and nation: Reframing social inequalities in a globalizing world. *British Journal of Sociology* 58:679–705.

Blay-Palmer, A. and Donald, B. (2006) A tale of three tomatoes: The new food economy in Toronto, Canada. *Economic Geography* 8(4):383–399.

Bonham, J. (2004) Cosmopolitan republicanism. In Farrelly, C. (ed.) *Contemporary Political Theory: A Reader* (pp. 169–178). London: Sage.

Bookchin, M. (1992) *Urbanization without Cities: The Rise and Decline of Citizenship.* Montreal: Black Rose Press.

Brookes, A. (2003) A critique of neo-hahnian outdoor education theory: Challenges to the concept of "character building". *Journal of Adventure Education and Outdoor Learning* 3(1):49–62.

Commission on Strengthening Local Democracy (2014) *Commission on Strengthening Local Democracy: Interim Report.* Edinburgh: Commission on Strengthening Local Democracy.

Cumbers, A., Helms, G. and Swanson, K. (2010) Class, agency, and resistance in the old industrial city. *Antipode* 42(1):46–73.

Derickson, K. (2014) Book review. In Ratto, M. and Boler, M. (eds.) *DIY Citizenship: Critical Making and Social Media.* AntipodeFoundation.org, November. https://radicalanti pode.files.wordpress.com/2014/11/book-review_derickson-on-ratto-and-boler.pdf (last accessed 10 December 2015).

Eizenberg, E. (2010) Remembering forgotten landscapes: Community gardens in New York City and the reconstruction of cultural diversity. In Yacobi, H. and Fenster, T. (eds.) *Remembering, Forgetting, and City Builders* (pp. 7–26). Burlington: Ashgate.

Eizenberg, E. (2012) Actually existing commons: Three moments of space of community gardens in New York City. *Antipode* 44(3):764–782.

Featherstone, D., Ince, A., MacKinnon, D., Cumbers, A. and Strauss, K. (2012) Progressive localism and the construction of political alternatives. *Transactions of the Institute of British Geographers* 37:177–182.

Franks, B. (2007) Postanarchisms: A critical assessment. *Journal of Political Ideologies* 12:127–145.

Garratt, D. and Piper, H. (2010) Heterotopian cosmopolitan citizenship education? *Education, Citizenship, and Social Justice* 5:43–55.

Ghose, R. and Pettigrove, M. (2014) Urban community gardens as spaces of citizenship. *Antipode* 46(4):1092–1112.

Giddens, A. (1984) *The Constitution of Society*. Cambridge: Polity.

Gordon, A. and Stack, T. (2007) Citizenship beyond the state: Thinking with early modern citizenship in the contemporary world. *Citizenship Studies* 11:117–133.

Gray, N. and Porter, L. (2014) By any means necessary: Urban regeneration and the "state of exception" in Glasgow's Commonwealth Games 2014. *Antipode* 47(2):380–400.

Gulülp, H. (2013) Citizenship and democracy beyond the nation-state? *Cultural Dynamics* 25:29–47.

Hall, E. and McGarrol, S. (2013) Progressive localism for an ethics of care: Local area co-ordination with people with learning difficulties. *Social and Cultural Geography* 14(6): 689–706.

Harris, E. (2009) Neoliberal subjectivities or a politics of the possible? Reading for difference in alternative food networks. *Area* 41:55–63.

Hartley, J. (1999) *The Uses of Television*. London: Routledge.

Healey, P. (2011) "Civic Capacity, Progressive Localism, and the Role of Planning." Royal Town Planning Institute Nathaniel Lichfield Annual Lecture, 6 October. www.rtpi.org.uk/events/rtpi-nathaniel-lichfield-lecture/rtpi-nathaniel-lichfield-lecture-2011/ (last accessed 10 December 2015).

Helms, G. and Cumbers, A. (2006) Regulating the new urban poor: Local labour market control in an old industrial city. *Space and Polity* 10:67–86.

Holloway, J. (2005) *Changing the World Without Taking Power: The Meaning of Revolution Today*. London: Pluto.

Holloway, J. (2010) *Crack Capitalism*. London: Pluto.

Holt-Gimenez, E. and Wang, Y. (2011) Reform or transformation? The pivotal role of food justice in the US food movement. *Race/Ethnicity* 5(1):83–102.

Jessop, B. (2002) Liberalism, neoliberalism, and urban governance: A state-theoretical perspective. *Antipode* 34(3):452–472.

Klein, H. K. and Kleinman, H. L. (2002) The social construction of technology: Structural considerations. *Science, Technology, and Human Values* 27(1):28–52.

Larner, W. (2003) Neoliberalism? *Environment and Planning D: Society and Space* 21: 509–512.

Latour, B. and Weibel, P. (2005) *Making Things Public: Atmospheres of Democracy*. Cambridge: MIT Press.

Learning and Teaching Scotland (2010) Curriculum for Excellence Through Outdoor Learning, Discussion Paper. https://education.gov.scot/Documents/cfe-through-outdoor-learning.pdf (accessed 16 October 2017).

Lichfield, N. (1996) *Community Impact Evaluation*. London: UCL Press.

MacKinnon, D., Featherstone, D., Cumbers, A. and Strauss, K. (2010) "Rethinking Central Local Relations: Progressive Localism, Decentralisation, and Place." Paper presented to the Inaugural Conference of the Sheffield Political Economy Research Institute, University of Sheffield, 16–18 July. http://speri.dept.shef.ac.uk/wp-content/uploads/2012/07/Danny-MacKinnon-David-Featherstone-Andrew-Cumbers-Kendra-Strauss-Rethinking-Local-Central-Relations-Progressive-localism-decentralisation-and-place.pdf (last accessed 10 December 2015).

MacLeod, G. (2002) From urban entrepreneurialism to a "revanchist city"? On the spatial in-justices of Glasgow's rennaissance. *Antipode* 34(3):602–624.

McClintock, N. (2014) Radical, reformist, and garden-variety neoliberal: Coming to terms with urban agriculture's contradictions. *Local Environment* 19(2):147–171.

New Oxford American Dictionary (2010) (3rd ed.). Oxford: Oxford University Press.

Ong, A. (2006) Mutations in citizenship. *Theory, Culture, and Society* 23(2/3):499–505.

Osler, A. and Starkey, H. (2001) Citizenship, human rights, and cultural diversity. In Osler, A. (ed.) *Citizenship and Democracy in Schools: Diversity, Identity, Equality* (pp. 13–18). Stoke: Trentham.

Pateman, C. (1991) "A New Democratic Theory? Political Science, the Public, and the Private." Paper presented to the International Political Science Association World Congress, Buenos Aires.

Peck, J. and Tickell, A. (2002) Neoliberalizing space. *Antipode* 34(3):380–404.

Phillips, A. (1992) Must feminists give up on liberal democracy? *Political Studies* 40:68–82.

Pocock, J. G. A. (1995) The ideal of citizenship since classical times. In Beiner, R. (ed.) *Theorizing Citizenship* (pp. 29–52). Albany: SUNY Press.

Prichard, A. (2010) David Held is an anarchist: Discuss. *Global Discourse* 1. https://globaldiscourse.files.wordpress.com/2010/10/prichard2.pdf (last accessed 9 December 2015).

Pudup, M. B. (2008) It takes a garden: Cultivating citizen-subjects in organized garden projects. *Geoforum* 39(3):1228–1240.

Ratto, M. and Boler, M. (eds.) (2014) *DIY Citizenship: Critical Making and Social Media*. Cambridge: MIT Press.

Rose, N. and Miller, P. (2010) Political power beyond the state: Problematics of government. *British Journal of Sociology* 61:271–303.

Rosol, M. (2011) Community volunteering as neoliberal strategy? Green space production in Berlin. *Antipode* 44(1):239–257.

Sandel, M. J. (2012) What isn't for sale? *The Atlantic*, April. www.theatlantic.com/magazine/archive/2012/04/what-isnt-for-sale/308902/ (last accessed 10 December 2015).

Scottish Government (2012) *Consultation on the Proposed Community Empowerment and Renewal Bill: An Analysis of Responses*. Edinburgh: Scottish Government.

Scottish Vacant and Derelict Land Survey (2013) www.gov.scot/Publications/2014/ 02/ 7170/0 (last accessed 10 November 2015).

Simon, T. (2013) Citizenship as a weapon. *Citizenship Studies* 17:505–524.

Smith, D. (1987) Knowing your place: Class, politics, and ethnicity in Chicago and Birmingham, 1890–1983. In Thrift, N. and Williams, P. (eds.) *Class and Space: The Making of Urban Society* (pp. 276–305). London: Routledge.

Travaline, K. and Hunold, C. (2010) Urban agriculture and ecological citizenship in Philadelphia. *Local Environment* 15(6):581–590.

The Trussell Trust (2014) Latest foodbank figures top 900,000: Life has got worse not better for poorest in 2013/14, and this is just the tip of the iceberg. Press release, 16 April. www.trusselltrust.org/foodbank-figures-top-900000 (last accessed 10 December 2015).

Valentine, G. (2008) Living with difference: Reflections on geographies of encounter. *Progress in Human Geography* 32(3):323–327.

Wacquant, L. (2007) Territorial stigmatization in the age of advanced marginality. *Thesis Eleven* 91:66–77.

Wallace, A. (2015) Gentrification interrupted in Salford, UK: From new deal to "limbo land" in a contemporary urban periphery. *Antipode* 47(2):517–538.

Wrenn, M. V. (2014) The social ontology of fear and neoliberalism. *Review of Social Economy* 72:337–353.

Young, I. M. (1990) *Justice and the Politics of Difference.* Princeton: Princeton University Press.

12 Political gardening, equity, and justice

A research agenda

Chiara Tornaghi and Chiara Certomà

1. Introduction

This book comes at a time when discussions around urban gardening, urban agriculture, and urban food production have found their way into policy and planning arenas. The food and green agenda have promoted policy programmes, mobilized funding agencies, established business incubators, and helped to multiply the ways through which gardening and food production are almost ubiquitous in the urban experience.[1] They are often promoted as must-have tools for building the so called "sustainable city". The institutional interest for gardening is built upon an enthusiastic uptake of gardening practices by citizens and community groups, to the point that matching green agendas and grassroots initiatives seems a no-brainer, a win-win situation.

However, reality is always more complex than it is possible to appreciate at a first glance. In order to understand the multifaceted relationship between institutions and grassroots gardening initiatives, it is useful to recall the post-political theory already introduced in Chapter 1. As Mike Raco and others have pointed out, widespread post-political and austerity agendas have systematically used the sustainability planning rhetoric "to divert attention from the highly political, structural changes taking place within the state" (Raco, 2014, p. 27), and to equate sustainability with new technocratic, "private-led, state efficiency and managerialism" (ibid.). In doing so, post-political agendas are establishing "new modes of inequality as the political subjectivity of modern citizens" (ibid). The need to affirm the social dimension of sustainability (Agyeman, 2005), and to challenge mainstream environmental politics have already been stressed by urban political ecologists (Leonard and Kedzior, 2014). These works showed how the quest for equity and justice, and other quintessential political dimensions of urban gardening, have had a relatively minimal public profile. We believe this reflects both the popularity of largely depoliticized approaches to environmental questions and the pressures of market-oriented funding agencies, together with the avalanche of funding available in the research sector to deliver positivistic and functionalistic "solutions" for the sustainable city of the future.

These trends do not happen without (at least some) resistance and contestation. However, while the academic and non-academic literature has been prolific in capturing the richness of the new green and food agendas, and to some extent instrumental in their establishment, little attention has been paid to the controversial and contentious aspects associated with the phenomenon of urban gardening.

The collection of essays in this book are – albeit in an updated form – some of the earlier contributions (as well as some new ones) in the geographical literature that have taken up the challenge to reflect critically on the ways in which the political dimension has been articulated (or not) through urban gardening in the cities of the Global North.

In this concluding chapter, we reflect on the insights offered by the critical literature on "the political" and the post-political turn developed by post-foundational scholars, and how they can inform a further questioning of political gardening.

In light of increasing social vulnerability and widespread inequality, and the changing constellations of neoliberal governance, post-foundational scholars have interrogated the changing dynamics and roles of politics. "Post-foundational" theory refers to the acknowledgement that the foundations, that is, the ultimate ground upon which political claims and social orders are established – once believed to be derived from a state of nature or a will of God – are necessarily contingent, contested, historically determined, and plural. Any social order will be attempting to gain legitimacy and control based on a certain constellation of views, values, and rights which will always fail to accommodate and represent the diversity of the social and political views.

The acknowledgement of this plurality and contingency enables post-foundational scholars (i.e. Mouffe, Laclau, Nancy, Ranciere, Badiou, Žižek) to distinguish between "politics", corresponding to the more or less conflictual political activities inscribed in the current social order (a sort of day-to-day activity dealing with the governance of the economic, environmental, and other spheres of social life); and "the political", corresponding to political activities aimed at radically changing and re-grounding the social order, looking for more equalitarian arrangements – for example when insurrectionary acts enable the shift from a totalitarian state to a democracy.

In distinguishing between politics and the political, post-foundational scholars open up an horizon, conceptual and material, for egalitarian activism. Their work is not simply analytical, instead it makes visible a gap, a possibility, and even the necessity of giving new life to a certain way of being political, out of the particularistic realms in which it has been confined by institutional politics. This gives us the tools to understand the breadth of political activities, their aims, their degree of co-optation to the dominant narratives, and ultimately to assess their transformational strength.

While the debate is far more complex and heterogeneous than this simplified distinction illustrates, we found it rich with insights which are useful to interrogate the kind of political reach that the initiatives discussed in this book have achieved. We hope this reflective exercise can give a direction to future researchers eager to investigate the radical potential of urban gardening for building alternative worlds.

2. Political gardening or gardening as politics?

While the origins of post-foundational theory date back almost a century ago, the development of a distinctive "philosophy of the political" (Marchart, 2008) and its systematic engagement with the analysis of urban movements is rather recent and dates to the last decade or so.

Given the increased sense of crisis of democratic politics and the systematic absorption of the political by the social (Laclau, 1990, p. 60), post-foundational scholars have pointed out that despite us living in "the historical condition of possibility for an emancipatory politics" (Laclau in Marchart, 2008, p. 157) – such as the awareness of contingency and historicity of being and the precarity of any social order – these conditions have not led to the spreading of emancipatory claims. Indeed we seem to be deeply lost in what Laclau calls "sedimentation" or the routinization and systematic forgetting of our precarious and contestable origins (Marchart, 2008, p. 139). Rancière and Badiou have particularly stressed how in the current post-political times, we see a progressive "rarification" of radical, political events (Swyngedouw, 2009, p. 608), and a general acceptance of uneven and unjust social orders.

It is therefore no surprise that the recent rise of political insurrections and urban movements, in both authoritarian and democratic regimes, such as the Arab Spring, Occupy, or the Indignados, has catalyzed the attention of critical scholars and multiplied the attempts to assess whether they were yet another example of a short-lived, post-political event, or the start of a new emancipatory politics bringing forward a different world.

Despite advancing different perspectives, post-foundational scholars claim that "the political" has a stronger collective and transformational potentiality compared to political initiatives that inscribe themselves within the existing social order. Moreover, in many respects, as suggested by Marchart, their expectations of long-term commitment and collective endeavours is strictly related to the concepts of equality and justice (Marchart, 2008, pp. 122–129). The latter are described by Badiou via "negative" definitions, rather than positive or normative ones. They are defined for what they are not: non-particular/non-partisan arrangements, almost utopian states of things. Political acts, therefore will be those that strive to unsettle particularistic grounds, those that reach out *horizontally* to a multiplicity of struggling actors in uneven, power-ridden terrains (Badiou, 2005); and *vertically*, remaining faithful to a specific mission or event for collective emancipation, in consideration of the fact that "a political organization of militants is nothing but the collective product of a process of fidelity towards an event" (Badiou, 2001).

The politics/political distinction that emerged from post-foundational theory and post-political literature has been criticized for dismissing the value and transformational paths of political movements busy with the transformation of socio-economic arrangements, particularly issues of social reproduction, within the current social order (see for example Larner, 2014).

Swyngedouw, for example, moving away from large part of his own earlier work, has openly dismissed the political adventures of social movements as merely busy with issues of social reproduction (Dikeç and Swyngedouw, 2017), not quite up to the truly political value of egalitarian movements engaged in a sequence of events with the potential to evolve into a radically new order. It is however unclear how a political movement that (presumably) does not engage with issues of social reproduction can ever produce a new social order aimed at any form of equity or justice. Isn't any given social order a value-based way to organize social reproduction? Where do we, when reading a sequence of events, draw a judgemental line between politics and the political (if indeed we should)?

In the context of this ambiguity, we find ourselves reflecting as to whether the fundamental homology with which we have treated the terms "political gardening", and "gardening as politics" in the book so far assumes different connotations.

The approach we adopt here does not dismiss the political value of these gardening endeavours as secondary by default, nor does it aim to celebrate their achievements beyond their effective transformative capacities. Not only because, as editors of this collection, we don't have the full knowledge of the conditions in which these practices have developed in each context, but simply because we believe in the very existence of a continuum along the axis politics–political. In our transversal reflection on the contributions in this book we look at these instances of political gardening as disrupting practices that can work as moments of reactivation of political capacities, as practices that render the contingency of the *status quo* palpable and ultimately, potentially, as leading movements to re-grounding social orders.

3. Searching for justice and equality in political gardening

When reflecting on the gardening as a political praxis we look for a number of indicators that can help us to assess the extent to which these initiatives have been deeply subversive, radical, and tentatively transformative, aiming at re-grounding the social into new constellations of values and practices.

Inspired by our recent delving into post-foundational literature we have developed a list of categories or "clues" to search for, which we hope will be of use to researchers looking to approach the field of political gardening. These include: a) collective subjectification; b) agonistic practices; c) open ended, emancipatory, and egalitarian events.

3.1 Collective subjectification

The first feature typical of political movements and practices is their collective dimension. According to Badiou (2005), a collective is not defined by a certain number of people, but it is established by the relation of the militants to "universality". An event or practice is collective when it is distinctively non-fragmentary, non-individualistic, non-nimbyist.

What is interesting here is not the collectivity in itself, but the processes of political subjectification that this collectivity triggers or pursues. It is a process that often happens through dis-identification, de-classification, by transforming identities into instances of experience of dispute. The "we" of collective subjects emerges through action, through the contestation of a state of facts that has so far shaped space, opportunities, and identities. Subjectification is identity formation, and it involves strategic considerations. In political gardening initiatives this is often mediated by "convergence in space and spatialized practices" (Karaliotas, p. 55).

3.2 Agonistic

The second, typical feature of a political practice is its agonistic dimension, when it does not take forward consensual erasures of differences, it eludes established government practices and institutionalized structures (Dikeç and Swyngedouw, 2017). In Laclau's vision this is as much as "the moment of institution/destitution of the social /society" (Laclau, 1999): it is the dislocation of a given spatial system, the beginning of a political sequence, and the claim of these new positions vocally, in an attempt to enlarge the base and to re-ground society (Marchart, p. 135). The agonistic nature of these events is predicated as autonomous from other domains of the social, such as morality, the economic, and so on. It is a politics directed against the power, which trigger operations of repression by the state. It has, and must be seen as, a provocative function.

3.3 Open ended, emancipatory, and egalitarian events

Political truth only begins on the occasion of rupture and disorder, which is when business as usual breaks down (Marchart, 2008, pp. 121–122). But the essence of politics lies in the emancipation of the collective (Nancy, 1991, p. 54), in the egalitarian staging of being in common (Wilson and Swyngedouw, 2014, p. 174), in the scaling up of equalibertarian life, styles, and forms of social and ecological organization (Dikeç and Swyngedouw, 2017). Political contradictions here are not reduced merely to policy problems to be resolved with consensual management of economic necessity, but rather engage in agonistic situations that are by definition open, never finite, and staged as political encounter, interruption, and experimentation.

In consideration of the above-described clues, we envisage that a future research agenda on political gardening needs to start from the consideration of how these categories and modalities of political praxis relate to political gardening. The theoretical insights outlined in this chapter force us to interrogate the way we have been questioning political gardening, and its relation to food, social reproduction, and social justice.

At the same time we should be wary that these should not push us to make premature conclusions. Looking for agonism, open ended, emancipatory, and even revolutionary events in the gardens might seem a step too far, especially in light of the many current instances of co-optation to neoliberal agendas. However, it is perhaps the way they endure that is the best entry point into these reflections. We might, then, consider the resilience and permanence of political gardening initiatives; whether they maintain, nurture, evolve their radical potential, or turn into forms of institutionalized routines offering few – or no – critical perspectives on the distribution of power, responsibilities, and opportunities in the city space. The reflections on the interlink between the exposition of injustice, the search for equity, and the processes of political subjectification, which can unfold in and through the territories and practices of urban gardening, call for a consideration of what kind of collectivities do gardeners establish and what kind of structures do they aim to transform. Most importantly the post-political perspective warns us of the possibility for gardening initiatives to become domesticated and co-opted into the current *status quo* and urges us to question whether they transcend the materiality of the garden to both take a stance on *and* to advance alternative socio-political-economic models.

Note

1 See for instance the *Sustainable Food Cities Network* in the UK, or nature-based solutions themes in the *Horizon 2020* research funding schemes of the European Union.

References

Agyeman, Julian (2005), *Sustainable Communities and the Challenge of Environmental Justice*, New York: New York University Press.
Badiou, Alan (2001), *Ethics: An Essay on the Understanding of Evil*, London: Verso.
Badiou, Alan (2005), *Metapolitics*, London: Verso.
Dikeç, Mustafa and Swyngedouw, Erik (2017), Theorizing the Politicizing City, in *IJURR*, 41 (1), pp. 1–18, DOI:10.1111/1468-2427.12388
Karaliotas, Lazaros (2017), Staging Equality in Greek Squares: Hybrid Spaces of Political Subjectification, in *IJURR*, 41 (1), pp. 54–69, DOI:10.1111/1468-2427.12385
Laclau, Ernesto (1990), *New Reflections on the Revolution of Our Time*, London: Verso.
Laclau, Ernesto (1999), Hegemony and the future of democracy: Ernesto Laclau's political philosophy, in Lynn Woshma and Gary S. Olson (eds.), *Race, Rhetoric and the Postcolonial*, Albany: SUNY Press, pp. 129–164.
Larner, Wendy (2014), The limits of post-politics: Rethinking radical social enterprise, in J. Wilson and E. Swyngedouw (eds.), *The Post-Political and Its Discontents: Spaces of Depoliticisation, Spectres of Radical Politics*, Edinburgh: Edinburgh University Press.
Leonard, Liam and Kedzior, Sya B. (2014), *Occupy the Earth: Global Environmental Movements*, Bingley: Emerald.
Marchart, Oliver (2008), *Post-Foundational Political thought: Political Difference in Nancy, Lefort, Badiou and Laclau*, Edinburgh: Edinburgh University Press.
Nancy, Jean-Luc (1991), *The Inoperative Community*, Minneapolis: University of Minnesota Press.

Raco, Mike (2014), The post-politics of sustainability planning: Privatization and the demise of democratic government, in J. Wilson and E. Swyngedouw (eds.), *The Post-Political and Its Discontents: Spaces of Depoliticisation, Spectres of Radical Politics*, Edinburgh: Edinburgh University Press.

Swyngedouw, Erik (2009), The Antinomies of the Postpolitical City: In Search of a Democratic Politics of Environmental Production, in *International Journal of Urban and Regional Research*, 33 (3), pp. 601–620.

Wilson, Japhy and Swyngedouw, Erik (eds.) (2014), *The Post-Political and Its Discontents: Spaces of Depoliticisation, Spectres of Radical Politics*, Edinburgh: Edinburgh University Press.

Index

Note: Page numbers in italics indicate figures and in bold indicate tables on the corresponding pages.

Actor-Network Theory 36
actually existing neoliberalism 67–70
Afri-Can Food Basket 89, 97–100
agency, political 187–189
agnostic dimension to political practice 213
agonism 214
Alkon, A. H. 90
Allemende-Kontor 83n9, 174–176
allotments 111–112, 117–120; access, sociality, and social levelling on sites of 135–140; moving beyond ethno-national divisions in 140–144; see also Plymouth, food activities in
alterity, making of 40
alternative food networks (AFNs) 110–111
Ananny, Mike 192, 193–194
Annenberg Foundation 58
Askins, Kye 199–200
Attoh, K. A. 82
autogestion 47–52, 60, 62; spatial 50–51, 56

backspaces 24, 26
backyards, shared 100–103
Badiou, Alan 212–213
Barraclough, L. 58
Barron, Jennifer 67–68
Beck, Ulrich 197
Belfast, Northern Ireland see Dublin (Ireland) and Belfast (Northern Ireland)
Beunderman, J. 133
Biggs, C. 152
Black Creek Community Farm 99–100
Blair, Tony 190
Blake, A. 101
Blomley, Nicholas 91–93
Boler, Megan 193
Bookchin, Murray 195

Bourdieu, P. 113–114
Brenner, N. 81
Burningham, K. 13

Canada see Toronto
capital 113–114
capitalism 49, 150
Chambers, R. 113
Chatterton, Paul 69
City Seed Farms 100
Civil Rights Act of 1964 47
Classens, Michael 95
Cloutier-Fisher, D. 101
collaborative economy 94–95
collective learning and social empowerment, community gardens as places of 194–196
collective subjectification 212–213
Cologne, Germany see NeuLand
Community Capitals Framework (CCF) 114
community gardens: as actually existing commons in the neoliberal city 67–70; Allemende-Kontor 83n9, 174–176; beginnings of 21–22; claiming the right to the city through actually existing urban commons a 79–81; cultivating a renewal of political life 59–62; cultivating urban space and 52–53; developing new agendas for research on 26–28; in Dublin and Belfast (see Dublin (Ireland) and Belfast (Northern Ireland)); and forging of progressively transformative social relations in the city 197–200; in Germany (see NeuLand); in Glasgow, Scotland (see neoliberal urbanism in Glasgow); growing new spaces of justice through 17–18; local

environments of injustice and 12–17; manifesto of 173; in New York 53–56; as places of collective learning and social empowerment 194–196; progressive local collaborations and 200–203; sharing of 94–95; socio-environmental (in)justices and 24–26; in South Central Los Angeles 56–59; spatialities in 22–24; sustainability and 144–145, 209; in Toronto 95–96; two cases of urban, in the Global North 52–59; in the United Kingdom (*see* United Kingdom, the); visions of projects in 18–20
confused public spaces 23–24
Conway, G. 113
Crane, A. 150–151
Crouch, D. 16, 114
cultivating a renewal of political life through urban gardens 59–62

Death of Environmentalism, The 40
Derickson, Kate 193
DETR (Department of Environment, Transport and Regional Affairs) 122
Dewey, John 195
disadvantaged urban neighborhoods, local environments of (in)justice in 12–17
diverse food economies (DFEs) 110
diverse food networks (DFNs) 113–115, *114*; conclusion on 123–126; contingent factors and outcomes of 120–123; in Plymouth 115–120
Do-It-Yourself (DIY) Citizenship 186, 188–189, 204; from neoliberal citizenship to 190–193; Progressive Localism and 200–203
Dublin (Ireland) and Belfast (Northern Ireland): access, sociality, and social levelling on allotment sites and 135–140; conclusion on 145–146; introduction to 132; moving beyond ethno-national divisions in 140–144; researching urban gardening in Dublin and Belfast and 133–135; toward a shared 133; urban gardening and sustainability in 144–145

Eder, K. 40
Edwards-Jones, G. 110–111
egalitarian events in political gardening 213–214
Eizenberg, Efrat 70, 76, 197
emancipatory events in political gardening 213–214
ethics of care 110

ethnography 152
ethno-national divisions 140–144

FarmStart 100
Federation of City Farms and Community Gardens (FCFCG) 16–17, 24, 108
Ferguson, Sara 53
Flores, C. H. 162
food cultivation, urban 46–47, 62n7–8; *see also* community gardening
food initiatives: allotments 111–112; conceptualising diverse food networks and 113–115, *114*; conclusions on 123–126; introduction to 108; research methods on 115; unpacking (peri-) urban food initiatives **109**, 109–111; *see also* diverse food networks (DFNs)
food production, urban: (re)negotiating property and access to land in 92–95; politics of land and 90–92; redesigning suburban yards for community-based 97–103; reflections on 103–104; sharing private lands for 96–97; in Toronto 95–96
Foust, C. 57
Francis, M. 14
F Troop *see* guerrilla gardening

G3 Growers 201–202
Garratt, Dean 197
genetically engineered (GE) potatoes 169–170
Genève City Council 32
Geoghegan, H. 119
Germany, Allemende-Kontor 83n9, 174–176; *see also* NeuLand
Ghose, Rina 68, 187–189
Giardinieri Sovversivi Romani 38, *38*
Gibson-Graham, J. K. 5, 90, 97, 113
Giuliani, Rudolph 54, 55, 91, 149
Glasgow, Scotland *see* neoliberal urbanism in Glasgow
Global North 1–2, 3, 6, 28; guerrilla gardening in 149–150; politics of land in 90–92; public lands in 89; two cases of urban gardens in 52–59
Global South 28, 62
Goodman, D. 110
Gordon, Andrew 190
Graham, Nicole 93
grassroots gardening practices 1, 3–4
green anarchism 39
green consumerism 39
Green Guerillas 53
Green Thumb programme 54

guerrilla gardening 19, 39; attempts to study 150–152; conclusion on 163–164; defining 148–150; emergence of a "guerrilla trap" in 162–163; evaluating guerrilla practice in 161–162; on the ground with 155, 155–157; introduction to 148; perceptions of three sites of 158–161; public views on 157–162, **158**; study of gardeners engaged in 153, *154*
Guitart, D. 28

Hardman, Michael 155
Hardt, Michael 68
Hartley, John 192
Harvey, David 69, 76, 78
Hester, R. T. 14
Heynen, N. 12
Hinchliffe, S. 36
Hobson, K. 12, 13, 25
Hodgkinson, T. 14
Hoffman, J. 57
Holland, L. 153
Holloway, John 190
Horowitz, Ralph 57–59
Hou, J. 15, 162

instituting of the common 68

Johnson, L. 104
(in)justice: beginnings of community gardening movement to address 21–22; community gardening and socio-environmental 24–26; developing new agendas for community gardening research and 26–28; and growing new spaces of justice in UK cities 17–18; local environments of 12–17; searching for equality and, in political gardening 212–214; spatialities in 22–24; visions of projects addressing 18–20
"just sustainabilities" 15

Kinderbaurnhof Mauerplatz Kreuzberg garden 34
King, Rodney 56
Kölner NeuLand see NeuLand
Kurtz, H. 55

Laclau, Ernesto 211, 213
land and property access: introduction to 89–90; (re)negotiating, in urban food production 92–95; politics of land and 90–92; sharing of 96–97
Lefebvre, Henri 13, 15, 27, 47–50, 59–62, 62n2–3, 67, 82

Lefebvrian theory 5
Lemieux, Erica 100–101
Leopold, Aldo 93
Lichfield, Nathaniel 200
local collaborations and community gardens 200–203
Local Environment: The International Journal of Justice and Sustainability 1–2, 33
local food networks (LFNs) 110
Lololi, Anan 98, 98, 98–100
Los Angeles, community gardens in 56–59
Los Angeles City Energy Recovery Project (LANCER) 56
Los Angeles Regional Food Bank 56
Lownsbrough, H. 133

Madden, D. 133
Marx, Karl 47, 48–49, 50, 62n4
Marxism 47, 48, 186
material politics, political gardening as form of 35–38, *37*
McCarthy, J. 15
McClintock, Nathan 68, 90, 189
McKay, G. 149, 150, 162
McKnight, M. 134, 146
McVeen Farm 100
Metcalf, S. S. 150
Milbourne, P. 150–151, 153
Miller, Peter 190
Morgan, K. 113
Moulaert, F. 144
multiple geographies of affiliation 136

Nature en Ville project 32
(re)negotiating property and access to land in urban food production 92–95
Negri, Antonio 68
neoliberalism: actually existing 67–70; community forestry in 15–16; community gardening, political agency, and 187–189; community gardens representing hybrids in terms of 27; politics of land in 90; property ownership in 92–93; reporting and funding system 176; urban gardening framed within urban 34
neoliberal subjectivities 67–68
neoliberal urbanism in Glasgow: community gardening, neoliberalism, and political agency in 187–189; conclusion on 203–204; creating alternative narratives of democracy and citizenship in 193–203; introduction to 186–187; from neoliberal citizenship to DIY citizenship in 190–193
NeuLand: conclusions on 81–83; as enclosure 78–79; genesis of 73–75;

history of *72, 72–73, 74*; initial motives and motivations of 75; introduction to 66–67; as open and inclusive urban common 76–77; transformation of, 2012–2017 75–79; urban gardening in Germany and 70–72
Newman, Michael 183
New York City Community Garden Coalition (NYCCGC) 53–56
NIMBY-syndrome 81
Nordhaus, T. 40

O'Dowd, L. 134, 146
Ong, Aihwa 190
"On the Jewish Question" 47, 48–49, 62n2
open ended, emancipatory, and egalitarian events in political gardening 213–214
Orti di Via della Consolata 34
Ostrom, Elinor 69, 78

Pain, Rachel 199
Parco delle Energie 36–37, *37*
Parco di via delle Palme 35
Parra, C. 144
participatory process 81
Peluso, N. L. 93
performative politics 37
Petit, C. 57
Pettigrove, Margaret 68, 187–189
Pietropaolo, Vincenzo 95
Piper, Heather 197
place, politics of: access, sociality, and social levelling on allotment sites and 135–140; conclusion on 145–146; introduction to 132; moving beyond ethno-national divisions in 140–144; researching urban gardening in Dublin and Belfast and 133–135; toward a shared 133; urban gardening and sustainability in 144–145
Plymouth, food activities in: conclusion on 123–126; contingent factors and outcomes DFN 120–123; diverse urban 115–120; research methods on 115
policy precarity 191
political gardening: as form of material politics 35–38, *37*; introduction to 1–2, 209–211; multiple political meanings of 4–6, 33–35; or gardening as politics 211–212; *politics* in 33–35; as post-environmentalism 38, 38–41; in a post-political age 2–4; from recognition to exploration 32–33; searching for justice and equality in 212–214; synopsis on book coverage of 6–9; urban gardening manifesto and 173

politics 33–35; citizenship and 204–205n4; community gardening, neoliberalism and 187–189; gardening as 211–212; of land 90–92; performative 37; of place 132–146; political gardening as form of material 35–38, *37*; of urban space 2
Post-Environmentalism 39–40
post-environmentalism, political gardening as 38, 38–41
Post-Marxist theory 5
post-political age, gardening in 2–4
Prichard, Alex 194
Prinzessinnengarten 71
private property 89–90, 92–93
Progressive Localism 200–203
Pudup, Mary Beth 15–16, 26, 27, 67, 121, 153, 187–189
Pulido, Laura 182
Purcell, M. 163

Qroe Farm Preservation 103
Quail, John 194

Raco, Mike 209
Radywyl, N. 152
Ramallah *see* strategizing platform, urban food movement
Raposo, Manuel 96–97
Ratto, Matt 193
"remaindered" spaces 15
resistance 4
Reynolds, Richard 148, 149, 151, 153, 155, 162, 164
Ribot, J. C. 93
right of the city 91
right to buy 202–203
right to the city 91; autogestion and 47–52; claimed through actually existing urban commons 79–81; Henri Lefebvre and 47–49; introduction to 46–47; political gardening and 34; revolution and 49–50; *see also NeuLand*
Right to the City, The 47
Rockstrom, J. 123
roll-out neoliberalism 187
Rose, Nikolas 190
Rosenthal, C. 58
Rosol, Marit 187–188
Royal Horticultural Society (RHS) 16–17

Sax, Joseph 93
Schellenberger, M. 40
Sennett, R. 137, 146
shared backyards 100–103
shared politics of place *see* place, politics of

shared space 94
sharing economy 94–95
sharing of private lands for urban food production 96–97
Shepard, B. 61
Simon, Thomas 190
Smith, C. 55
Smith, Dennis 191
soft squatting 97
Soja, Edward 3, 69
South Central Farmers Feeding Families (SCFFF) 56–59
sovereign, concept of the 194–195
spaces of potential 133, 143–144
spatial autogestion 50–51
squatting 94; soft 97
Stack, Trevor 190
Staeheli, L. A. 55, 58
Stiglitz-Sen-Fitoussi Commission 144
Stop Community Food Centre 101
strategizing platform, urban food movement 167–173; Allmende-Kontor 174–176; contexts 177–183; reporting and funding system 176; urban gardening manifesto 173; values and justice 176–177
Sturgis, J. 149
subjectification, collective 212–213
sustainability and urban gardening 144–145, 209
Swyngedouw, E. 2–3, 212

Teaching Defiance 183
Teixera, Carlos 96–97
tentative non-judgment 203–204
Thirdspace 3
Thompson, E. 149
Thrush, D. 13
't Landhuis 34
Tornaghi, C. 133, 150
Toronto 95–96; redesigning suburban yards for community-based food production in 97–103; reflections on urban food production in 103–104; shared backyards in 100–103; sharing private lands for urban food production in 96–97
Tracey, D. 39, 148, 151, 162
tragedy of the commons 69
transformational sharing 94–95
transformative politics of encounter 193, 200

transformative social relations through community gardening 197–200
Tregear, A. 111

Ujama Farmers Collective 99–100
United Kingdom, the: allotments in 111–112, 117–120; beginnings of community gardening in 21–22; developing new agendas for research on community gardening in 26–28; growing new spaces of justice through community gardening in 17–18; local environments of injustice and community gardening in 12–17; socio-environmental (in) justices and community gardening in 24–26; visions of community gardening projects in 18–20; *see also* Plymouth, food activities in
unperfected commons in-the-making 82–83
urban commons: claiming right to the city through actually existing 79–81; in-the-making 79
urban food movement strategizing platform *see* strategizing platform, urban food movement
urban gardens *see* community gardens

Valentine, Gill 200
values and justice in urban food movement 176–177
Van Wagner, E. 93
Via delle Gardenie 38

Wacquant, Loïc 191
Wallace, Andrew 191
Ward, C. 16, 114
Warpole, K. 13
Wekerle, Gerda R. 95
Whatmore, S. 36
Whitehead, M. 13, 15, 25
Widener, M. J. 150
Williams, R. 13
Wiltshire, R. 119

Young, J. 39–40

Zanetti, O. 151
Ziglio, E. 113

Printed in the United States
by Baker & Taylor Publisher Services